Unequal Worlds of Care

Unequal Worlds of Care

THE POLITICS OF GLOBAL HEALTH IN MALAWI

Amy Zhou

UNIVERSITY OF CALIFORNIA PRESS

University of California Press
Oakland, California

Library of Congress Cataloging-in-Publication Data

Names: Zhou, Amy author
Title: Unequal worlds of care : the politics of global health in Malawi / Amy Zhou.
Description: Oakland, California : University of California Press, [2026] | Includes bibliographical references and index.
Identifiers: LCCN 2025042764 (print) | LCCN 2025042765 (ebook) | ISBN 9780520409187 cloth | ISBN 9780520409194 paperback | ISBN 9780520409200 epub
Subjects: LCSH: AIDS (Disease)—Social aspects—Malawi | Economic assistance—Political aspects—Malawi | Public health—Malawi
Classification: LCC RA643.86.M3 Z46 2026 (print) | LCC RA643.86.M3 (ebook)
LC record available at https://lccn.loc.gov/2025042764
LC ebook record available at https://lccn.loc.gov/2025042765

GPSR Authorized Representative: Easy Access System Europe, Mustamäe tee 50, 10621 Tallinn, Estonia, gpsr.requests@easproject.com

35 34 33 32 31 30 29 28 27 26
10 9 8 7 6 5 4 3 2 1

Contents

Illustrations

Abbreviations

AIDS	Acquired Immunodeficiency Syndrome
ANC	Antenatal care
ART	Antiretroviral therapy
ARVs	Antiretrovirals (medications)
AZT	Azidothymidine, also known as zidovudine
CBO	Community-based organization
CD4	Cluster of differentiation 4 (immune cells targeted by HIV)
CDC	Centers for Disease Control and Prevention
CHAI	Clinton Health Access Initiative
CHAM	Christian Health Association of Malawi
CHW	Community health worker
CMST	Central Medical Stores Trust (Malawi)
DFID	Department for International Development (UK, now part of FCDO)
EGPAF	Elizabeth Glaser Pediatric AIDS Foundation
HIV	Human immunodeficiency virus

HSA	Health surveillance assistant
HTC	HIV testing and counseling
ICAP	formerly, International Center for AIDS Care and Treatment Programs
IMF	International Monetary Fund
Jhpiego	Johns Hopkins Program for International Education in Gynecology and Obstetrics
M2M	Mothers2Mothers
MoH	Ministry of Health
MSF	Médecins Sans Frontières (Doctors Without Borders)
MSH	Management Sciences for Health
NAC	National AIDS Commission (Malawi)
NGO	Nongovernmental organization
NVP	Nevirapine
PEPFAR	President's Emergency Plan for AIDS Relief
PITC	Provider-initiated testing and counseling
PMTCT	Prevention of mother-to-child transmission
PrEP	Pre-exposure prophylaxis
TasP	Treatment-as-prevention
UN	United Nations
UNAIDS	Joint United Nations Program on HIV/AIDS
UNDP	United Nations Development Programme
UNICEF	United Nations International Children's Emergency Fund
USAID	United States Agency for International Development
VCT	Voluntary counseling and testing
WHO	World Health Organization
WTO	World Trade Organization

Preface

This book is about how people in Malawi navigate a healthcare landscape transformed by foreign aid. In the first few months of 2025, that landscape transformed again.

On January 20, 2025, President Trump of the United States (US) signed an executive order for a ninety-day freeze on all US foreign aid, including funding for the United States Agency for International Development (USAID) and the President's Emergency Plan for AIDS Relief (PEPFAR). At the end of the month, the administration began dissolving USAID, terminating thousands of awards. By the end of February, roughly ten thousand contracts—representing 90 percent of USAID's contracts—had been terminated.[1] While some contracts were reinstated, the cuts remained devastating. On March 10, Secretary of State Marco Rubio announced that the administration cancelled roughly 83 percent of USAID programs.[2] These cuts included US financial support to Gavi, an international organization that provides vaccines to impoverished nations, of which the United States was the third largest donor.[3] Later that month, on March 25, PEPFAR's congressional reauthorization expired.[4] While Congress appropriated funding through the end of September 2025, the expiration raises deep uncertainties about the future of PEPFAR programs and PEPFAR's contributions to the Global Fund to Fight AIDS, Tuberculosis, and Malaria, a major multilateral organization supporting global health initiatives. The cuts to US foreign aid were sudden and swift. Of the remaining USAID programs, only $8.3 billion in unobligated funds remain available for disbursement—a sharp decline from the agency's $44.4 billion budget for fiscal year 2024–2025.[5] PEPFAR's loss would amount to about $6.5 billion in annual funding, including $4.8 billion in bilateral aid—funds that had gone directly to countries affected by the HIV epidemic.[6] The effects of funding cuts were felt immediately and profoundly. Cuts to USAID impacted 103 countries.[7] As of April 15, 19,003 jobs had been lost in the United States, and 171,818 globally.[8]

My research examined the impact of global health programs in Malawi, particularly those addressing HIV/AIDS. Cuts to foreign aid hit the world's poorest countries the hardest. Malawi ranks 172 out of 193 countries on the Human Development Index, and has about 70 percent of the population living below the global poverty line of $2.15 per day.[9] US funding, roughly $350 million annually, represented more than 13 percent of Malawi's 2024–2025 national budget.[10] In the health sector, about 81 percent of funding comes from donors, with even greater reliance for HIV and other major disease programs.[11] As of 2019, more than 90 percent of Malawi's HIV response was funded by PEPFAR and the Global Fund.[12] While countries like South Africa and India, which finance over 80 percent of their own HIV programs, are affected by US funding cuts, their stronger economies make them better able to absorb the shortfall, whereas countries like Malawi face more severe consequences.[13] As I detail in this book, global health programs have far-reaching impacts. While patients who use donor-funded medications and services will be directly affected by these cuts, so too will healthcare providers building careers in donor-funded nongovernmental organizations (NGOs) and policymakers now navigating a drastically altered funding landscape.

The reduction in US funding is especially striking in the HIV field, which had historically been a priority. HIV-related aid accounted for 14.7 percent of all US foreign aid, and the United States was the single largest contributor to global HIV programs.[14] From 2009 to 2014, US funding made up 55.3 percent of all foreign aid for HIV programs, which does not include US support for multilateral institutions like the Global Fund, which itself is the second largest donor, providing around 16.8 percent of global HIV funding.[15] These resources have been critical to the success of HIV programs. As more patients have access to antiretroviral therapy (ART), drug treatment for HIV, a once-fatal disease has been transformed into a manageable chronic condition. By 2023, AIDS mortality declined by 69 percent from its peak of 2.1 million deaths in 2004.[16] The success of HIV programs should absolutely be celebrated. But as I argue in this book, because HIV funding largely flowed through parallel systems and NGOs, it has brought little lasting improvement to public healthcare systems. As a result, patients with health conditions not prioritized by donors have often struggled to access care. In a moment of aid volatility, these public systems remain especially vulnerable, as they are unable to consistently provide adequate services—even for those who were once at the center of donor attention.

Although the US government has issued waivers to maintain certain HIV programs, the long-term consequences of the disruptions to aid as well as the future reliability of such support remain uncertain.[17] If funding does not continue, the outlook is alarming. Modeled estimates suggest that if foreign aid is not restored by the end of 2025, more than 176,000 additional adults and children worldwide could die from HIV, and at least 62,000 more could die from tuberculosis, a common coinfection.[18] UNAIDS estimated that we could see 2,000 new HIV infections a day, and in the next four years, an additional 6.3 million infections. As Winnie Byanyima, the UNAIDS executive director, stated: "We'll see it [HIV] come back, and we'll see people die the way we saw them in the '90s and in the 2000s."[19] Funding cuts carry a profound human cost across a range of issues. Dr. Grace Mwale, a physician in Lilongwe, Malawi, explained: "These aren't just numbers in a report—these are mothers who can't get prenatal care, HIV patients turned away from clinics, and children going hungry . . . .We're watching years of progress unravel before our eyes."[20]

In addition to affecting patients, cuts to foreign aid disrupt the work of numerous organizations and individuals dedicated to development and global health. In the HIV field, donor funding has supported what Swidler and Watkins call the "AIDS enterprise," a sprawling industry of international and national NGOs, research institutes, clinics, and community-based organizations.[21] These organizations work in interconnected ways.

While some, like Médecins Sans Frontières (MSF), are not directly reliant on US federal funding, their work can still be disrupted when partner programs, medication sources, or community access points are shut down.[22] Donor-funded organizations have also broadly contributed to local economies. They hire workers to manage programs, implement interventions, conduct research, and more. As I describe in the book, in Malawi, NGOs were a valuable addition to the labor market. Although formal job opportunities exist for those with college degrees, only about 2 percent of Malawians are enrolled in higher education.[23] Donor-funded NGOs provided opportunities for secondary school graduates who had limited job prospects and often survived through piecework—that is, short-term, informal jobs. Those who managed to secure ongoing positions were able to make meaningful changes in their lives. Some of my respondents who were employed by HIV-care NGOs became primary breadwinners for their families and were able to save enough to return to school and further their education. However, NGO work was inherently unstable; it depended on short-term contracts and varying rates of remuneration. The recent US funding cuts are a stark reminder of the fragility of this sector. These cuts not only endanger patient health outcomes but also disrupt the socioeconomic and educational gains that workers were making, thrusting them back into poverty and precarious livelihoods. Beyond healthcare, US funding also supported economic initiatives for economic growth, education, and agricultural productivity. If funding is not restored in the next year, an estimated 5.7 million more Africans would fall below the global poverty line.[24]

The data collected for this book reflects a vastly different foreign aid context than the one unfolding today. I described being in the "late stage" of the HIV epidemic. HIV experts talked about the "end of AIDS": HIV transmission and AIDS-related mortality had declined to such an extent that the elimination of HIV seemed possible. Up until very recently, funding for HIV was strong and steady. Many of my respondents, including national policymakers and healthcare providers, recognized the instability inherent in working within a donor-dependent field, but the instability felt abstract when funding was stable. Discussing Malawi's Option B+ policy, which expanded access to ART to pregnant and breastfeeding women, one policymaker expressed confidence that once donors accelerated the scale-up of

ART, it would be unrealistic for them to reverse course. NGO workers held insecure contract-based positions, yet they felt a sense of career stability due to the abundance of HIV-care NGOs they could potentially join. Even I, as a scholar and author, have written about the possibility of shifting donor interests but implicitly assumed that funding for HIV care would persist. What we experienced in the "late stage" of the HIV epidemic was indeed a *provisional* stability. Now, instead of the end of an epidemic, we may return to an earlier era, marked again by silence and death.

With the sudden changes in US foreign aid, the findings in this book need to be read in historical context—as reflective of a period of provisional stability. But the larger lessons still hold. One of the central arguments of this book is that donors approached health in fragmented ways, concerning themselves with discrete diseases that they thought were best addressed by non-state agencies. The spread of the HIV epidemic in the 1980s and '90s intersected with the spread of neoliberal ideology, which generally promotes shifting power from governments to markets.[25] Framed as a global emergency, HIV attracted an exceptional amount of foreign aid, but much of that aid flowed through parallel supply chains and NGOs. On the ground, this gave rise to a separate world of care: HIV-care programs operated with distinct funding streams, supply chains, NGO providers, and target populations. Meanwhile, public health-care systems were often left behind, struggling with severe shortages of healthcare providers, essential medicines, and basic infrastructure. However, in leaving behind fundamental aspects of healthcare, global health programs were constrained in their potential to improve healthcare and people's lives. For instance, women living with HIV had access to ART, which significantly reduced their risk of AIDS-related mortality and enabled them to resume "normal" life trajectories, including marriage and childbearing.[26] But, while they were *living with* HIV, they were still *dying from* maternal mortality and the many illnesses and injuries that were not donor priorities. By creating separate worlds of care, global health programs addressed health issues piecemeal. The recent cuts to USAID also reflect the fragmented nature of foreign aid. While HIV funding has seen about a 20 percent reduction, more than 90 percent of maternal and child health, family planning, and reproductive health programs have been eliminated.[27]

The uncertainty ahead underscores the limits of a neoliberal approach to healthcare. As donors withdraw funding, the care they supported disappears with them. The parallel structures they created were never meant to be incorporated into a larger public healthcare system. For instance, the parallel supply chain for HIV commodities functioned in isolation and did little to strengthen Malawi's Central Medical Stores Trust, which manages health commodities for the country. The NGOs implementing HIV-care programs focused on their target populations, while individuals with conditions outside of donor priorities were left to a public healthcare system, which chronically understaffed and underresourced, could only provide limited care. Warnings from public health experts about a potential resurgence of HIV highlight not only the severe impact of the withdrawal of US aid but also point to a deeper issue: Despite decades of "exceptional" HIV funding, few lasting structures were established to sustain care in the long term. As vast as the AIDS enterprise is, it is inherently fragile. Maintaining a separate world of care relies on consistent donor interest and funding. Economic development is undoubtedly complex, and I do not mean to suggest that Malawi or other low-income countries could have easily taken themselves off donor support. However, by channeling foreign aid through parallel structures and NGOs, there were years of missed opportunities to strengthen public healthcare systems—opportunities that could have laid the foundation for more resilient care in the face of shifting global politics.

This tumultuous moment highlights not only the critical importance of aid but also the need to reimagine how it is delivered. Emerging reports of child hunger, job loss, and disease resurgence in the wake of US funding withdrawal show just how important sustained aid is.[28] But as essential as aid may be, it has never been without flaws. Social scientists have long raised critiques of global health programs. They have highlighted that US foreign aid has reinforced imperial interests rather than fostering resilient health systems;[29] that global health programs impose Western cultural norms;[30] and that programs frequently operate in ways that are disconnected from local contexts and needs, leading to unintended consequences.[31] I am critical as well. I argue that a neoliberal approach to healthcare—focused on disease-specific interventions and reliance on NGOs—fails to recognize how disease, patients, and health workers are embedded in public healthcare systems and social structures. While donors often overlook these broader structural conditions, they matter significantly for actors on the ground. For example, before Malawi adopted their own policy for preventing mother-to-child HIV transmission, they followed the World Health Organization's (WHO) recommended policies and experienced devastating rates of maternal HIV transmission—about one-third of children contracted the virus, which is about the rate as there would be without any intervention.[32] WHO policies failed not because they were medically unsound but because they could not be implemented in the local healthcare system. In a resource-constrained setting, overworked providers could not remember WHO policies, and CD4 machines used to determine patients' eligibility for treatment were often broken or did not have the correct reagents.

Although this book offers a critique of global health programs, its intent is not to advocate for the withdrawal of aid, but rather to call for a more expansive vision of what aid can be. Aid needs to move beyond a narrow disease focus and address the broader conditions of public healthcare systems, which are in urgent need of support. Healthcare workers, essential medicines and supplies, laboratory services, and basic infrastructure like clinic buildings, electricity, and water, are fundamental for delivering quality care for all patients. In what scholars have called a "diagonal" approach, foreign aid could be used to address major disease threats, like HIV and COVID-19, while at the same time, strengthening public healthcare systems.[33] It does not need to be an either-or question—both goals can and should be pursued together. Global health programs must also become more responsive and accountable to local needs. This requires meaningful engagement with community members and decision-making by donors that is transparent and guided by local leadership.[34] Existing research offers "empirical lanterns" that illuminate the lives of everyday people and their social practices, providing valuable insight into how to engage more effectively with local actors.[35] For instance, this includes working with village leaders as community representatives or collaborating with "brokers"—that is, local individuals who have experience in development work and can bridge the gap between lived realities and the operations of donors and NGOs.[36]

At this moment, it is unclear how other donors will respond to US cuts in funding. Restoring aid will be crucial for ensuring that lifesaving interventions persist. But, amidst this uncertainty, there is also an opportunity to reimagine how aid can be delivered in more compassionate, collaborative, and sustainable ways.

Amy Zhou
May 2025

Introduction

POLITICS OF LEGIBILITY

Steven Brown has spent a significant portion of his career as an HIV pediatrician in Malawi, a small country in sub-Saharan Africa.[1] An American, he began volunteering during medical school with an AIDS education and care program for the homeless. He felt a calling to work with underserved communities, and first joined mission trips in South America, where he provided voluntary pediatric care. Looking for more volunteer opportunities, he called Presbyterian hospitals and learned that they desperately needed doctors in Malawi. Though he was not entirely sure where Malawi was, he went—and the month-long trip was transformative. After two years of mission trips, in 2011, Steven decided to move to Malawi permanently. He now works at a large HIV clinic and codirects an HIV mentorship program funded by the United States Agency for International Development (USAID) to improve the quality of HIV services in local healthcare facilities. The program trains Malawian doctors and nurses, who then travel to hospitals across the country to mentor other providers on HIV care. A leader in the HIV field, Steven is also a fierce advocate for other causes, including essential medicines, primary healthcare, and Malawi's northern region, a place that donors often avoid, because, as he likes to joke, it is too far away from the sit-down lunches at Bombay Palace and other fine dining restaurants in the capital.

I joined Steven once on a trip to the Nkhoma district hospital a few hours outside of Lilongwe, Malawi's capital city. We had come to Nkhoma for the official purpose of getting an update on the HIV mentorship program. Unofficially, we were also there to see Thoko, a boy with an undiagnosed cough. Thoko was about two years old, chubby, and looked healthy except for a persistent, congested, cough that he had had since birth. His mother was a nurse at the hospital, and through a series of connections, had learned that an American pediatrician would be passing through. The pediatric ward was full, so we saw Thoko on a bench outside. Steven listened carefully to his chest, looked inside his mouth at his palate, and placed a small tube in his throat to check his airway. While he was initially confident, like the other doctors at Nkhoma, he too failed to find the source of the cough. But unlike other doctors, Steven could give Thoko and his mother a referral to see his friend, a specialist in ear, nose, and throat conditions, at Kamuzu Central Hospital, one of the most advanced facilities in the country.

On our drive to and from Nkhoma, Steven implored me to think about "the bigger picture." I had reached out to him to understand his work in HIV care. He acknowledged that Malawi has a high prevalence of HIV, so of course, the issue mattered. But, he said, "90 percent of the population does not have HIV." He asked, "What about healthcare for them? We can't run out of malaria treatment. We can't not have asthma medication, or people dying of strokes or heart attacks." HIV is a serious health concern, and one that has deeply impacted the sub-Saharan African region. As of 2022, Malawi had the ninth highest HIV prevalence in the world, with 7.1 percent of its adult population infected.[2] But patients also suffer and die from numerous preventable or treatable health conditions that have not received much global attention. While HIV remains a leading cause of death in Malawi, with 62.9 deaths per 100,000 population, so too are strokes (50.6), lower respiratory infections (44.6), COVID-19 (41.3), tuberculosis (38.4), malaria (37.3), diarrheal diseases (33.7), ischemic heart disease (28.3), preterm birth complications (27.6), and liver cirrhosis (21.5).[3]

Steven's work took place in a new era of the HIV epidemic. Over the course of forty years, HIV care has become the largest program in the global health field. Between 2010 and 2020, there was roughly $20 billion available every year to provide HIV treatment and support various programs for HIV prevention, education, and training for low-income countries affected by the epidemic.[4] These resources have made lifesaving medications accessible to many patients, transforming a deadly disease into a manageable chronic condition. Donor resources also support many nongovernmental organizations (NGOs), HIV clinics, and research institutes now commonplace in Malawi and other countries receiving aid. The attention and resources given to address HIV/AIDS are exceptional. The United States (US) government, which is the largest donor in global health, allocated about 44 percent of its $12.4 billion global health budget to HIV/AIDS programs in 2024.[5]

As HIV has dominated the global health consciousness, there are many issues that fall outside the limelight. We do not see celebrities like Bono campaigning for asthma medication, or pictures of boys like Thoko on websites promoting interventions for respiratory diseases, or a proliferation of NGOs working to improve hospital infrastructure. While acute respiratory infections represented more than a quarter of disease burden in low-income countries, programs addressing respiratory illnesses received less than 3 percent of direct donor funding.[6] The tension that Steven described between HIV care and "the bigger picture" is felt by healthcare providers, including those in Malawi that address HIV. They have seen patients suffer or die from HIV, malaria, sepsis, respiratory infections, and more. They work in public healthcare facilities that struggle with shortages of healthcare providers and essential medicines, crowded spaces, and intermittent electricity and water supplies. This is not to say that HIV does not matter. But it is to say that the struggles of providers and patients extend beyond the disease campaigns that donors prioritize.

Legibility—being recognized as legitimate and worthy of resources—is a core issue in the global health field. What is legible to donors matters significantly for Malawi and other low-income countries that rely on foreign aid. Donor decisions about resource allocation, at their core, determine who lives or dies, who is treated and who suffers. Their implications are deeply felt and affect national healthcare institutions, the providers working within them, and the patients who seek care. In Malawi, where this study took place, HIV-care programs have transformed the healthcare landscape. This is where donor-funded HIV-care NGOs and clinics have proliferated; where foreign doctors, consultants, researchers, and volunteers have come to work; and where citizens become the targets of various HIV interventions. For HIV patients, the illness can be a crucial form of currency that gives them access to HIV medications, specialized clinics, and social welfare programs inaccessible to others. For people like Thoko who suffer from more mundane illnesses, the best they can hope for is a chance encounter with a generous physician who might connect them to the specialized care they need.

How do patients and those working in healthcare respond to global health programs that target certain issues but not others? To what extent have such programs improved people's health and the way healthcare is provided? I find that after decades of global health intervention, care is carved into different worlds. The world of HIV care has immense donor resources and the support of NGOs, whose responsibilities range from consulting policymakers, managing HIV commodities, promoting HIV education and prevention, and providing services to HIV patients. But HIV care sits uncomfortably alongside other healthcare issues that struggle for attention, including a public healthcare system with a severe shortage of providers, essential medicines, and infrastructure. These worlds do not simply reflect donor priorities; they are also the result of a neoliberal vision that sees health as a matter of discrete diseases best addressed by nonstate agencies. Policymakers, providers, and patients move between these unequal worlds of care. While Malawi's public healthcare system and broader social conditions are illegible to donors, these conditions strongly impact local actors. Policymakers must implement HIV policies in Malawi's healthcare system; providers consider both NGOs and the public sector for their careers; and patients have a range of health concerns, including but not limited to HIV, for which they require care.

Being situated between legible and illegible worlds produces what I call a *politics of legibility*, in which actors contend with global health programs that recognize only parts of their social conditions and experiences. These politics can manifest in various ways: for example, as direct political resistance, as when Malawi's policymakers went against World Health Organization (WHO) recommendations and developed their own policy to prevent mother-to-child HIV transmission; through embodied practices, as when women living with HIV refuse or stop treatment; or through struggles to find comprehensive care or good work opportunities in a healthcare field divided between NGOs and the public sector. The partial recognition of health issues—as diseases separate from healthcare systems and social conditions—also produced partial, uneven, and contested forms of recovery. While years of HIV programs have created important opportunities, by leaving behind fundamental aspects of healthcare, these programs were ultimately constrained in their potential to improve healthcare and people's lives.

NEW ERA OF HIV

The history of HIV care and treatment is a striking case of how changes in legibility can transform not only the course of an epidemic but also society at large. HIV first shook the world in the 1980s as a novel and deadly virus. In this first decade, HIV was a crisis. Scientists and physicians were still trying to understand the virus, and there were no effective treatments to save those who were infected. The period was also marked by silence. Early cases in the global North had affected stigmatized communities like the gay community and injection drug users. It took radical mobilization to challenge prejudices, to push governments to address the epidemic, to gain access to scientific knowledge, and to develop treatments.[7]

The second decade of the HIV epidemic was marked by a new form of silence. In 1995, the first successful HIV treatment—highly active antiretroviral therapy (HAART)—was developed, leading to greater optimism and the start of the epidemic's decline in the United States and Europe. But, while patients in wealthier countries could access these lifesaving medications, those in poorer countries often could not. By the early 2000s, it became clear that HIV was mostly affecting countries in the global South. In sub-Saharan Africa, where the epidemic hit hardest, there were an estimated 25.3 million adults and children infected with HIV, comprising roughly 70 percent of global cases.[8] At the time, governments of wealthy countries were against providing foreign aid for treatment, often revealing their stereotypes of Africa and Africans in the process.[9] In 2001, USAID director, Andrew Natsios, infamously argued that the United States should not fund antiretroviral treatment to African patients because they "don't know what Western time is" and would not be able to take the drugs according to schedule—thus wasting US resources.[10] Moreover, academics and journalists portrayed Africans as apathetic to HIV risk, when on the contrary, many were engaged in community-based strategies to try to protect themselves from infection.[11]

In Africa in the 1980s and 90s, the HIV epidemic led to immense suffering and death—first, because treatments were not yet developed and then once developed, because treatments were prohibitively expensive and out of reach to many patients. In 1999, the WHO announced that AIDS was the number one killer in Africa,[12] with deaths reaching 2.4 million.[13] Didier Fassin used the term "political anesthesia" to characterize the indifference in the global North toward HIV in Africa during this time. The indifference "simply suggests that we do not feel we need to know any more than we already know."[14] Wealthy governments acknowledged the devastating effects of HIV in Africa but refused to provide aid. Suffering was seen but ignored. Without access to medications, HIV infection ultimately ends in death.[15] Fassin described one of his last visits with an HIV patient in South Africa, Alexandra, who knew she did not have much time left. He recalled:

> She has made her "memory box" she will leave for her son: a tape on which she has recorded her story in a few dense sentences, a diary containing autobiographical paragraphs, a picture of herself, some clothes, a shoe, and a plaster impression of her palms. She has gone to see the priest to tell him what she would like him to say at her funeral and has chosen the music she wants played on that occasion . . . Everything is thus ready for her scheduled end.[16]

Four decades into the epidemic, responses to HIV look dramatically different. There is a large industry devoted to addressing the illness. In 2001, United Nations (UN) director Kofi Annan called for the creation of a fund to increase spending on HIV, malaria, and tuberculosis. The Global Fund to Fight AIDS, Tuberculosis and Malaria, which was established a year later, pools resources from governments, foundations, and the private sector and invests in programs that address those diseases. In the twenty-two years since its founding in 2002, the organization has invested about $26.6 billion in HIV programs and $5.5 billion in HIV/TB programs.[17] A year after the Global Fund was established, US President George W. Bush announced the creation of the President's Emergency Plan for AIDS Relief (PEPFAR), which would provide $15 billion for a five-year plan to combat HIV in countries most affected by the epidemic. As of 2021, the US government had invested over $100 billion in the global HIV/AIDS response.[18]

This shift in attitudes toward supporting HIV care in the global South did not come easily. Governments of countries affected by HIV and activists around the world pushed to make treatment accessible. Many countries, including South Africa, Thailand, Uruguay, Colombia, and Kenya, challenged pharmaceutical patent laws, arguing that they qualified for legal flexibilities to produce generic versions of antiretroviral therapy (ART).[19] AIDS activists added to the pressure and organized demonstrations in cities around the world.[20] For instance, in South Africa, Treatment Action Campaign (TAC) and the Congress of South African Trade Unions (COSATU) staged protests outside of a court building and the US embassy. In the United States, ACT UP and other AIDS organizations criticized US sanctions against countries challenging pharmaceutical patents held by large multinational companies. Healthcare professionals also worked to counter narratives against providing ART. Organizations, like Partners in Health and ICAP, conducted research at their clinic sites to show that providing ART to patients in Africa was indeed feasible and improved health outcomes.[21] Formal changes were eventually made. In 2001, the Doha Declaration by the World Trade Organization (WTO) allowed countries to circumvent patents and produce generic versions of HIV treatments. The cost of treatment plummeted, from about $10,000 per patient per year to $67.[22] Global collective action brought attention to inequalities in access to HIV care, and it broke down the insidious logic that wealthy countries could treat their own patients but ignore others.[23]

Now, the resources devoted to HIV programs have meant that stories of patients like Alexandra, preparing for death, are far less common. Treatment has become increasingly accessible.[24] While ART coverage globally was under 7 percent in 2005, it rose to 62 percent in 2018, and was up to 76 percent in 2022.[25] The availability of ART has transformed HIV from a death sentence to a chronic condition that one manages with their prescription.[26] In Malawi, public attitudes towards HIV changed from fatalism to optimism. As HIV patients started ART, community members witnessed the decline of HIV-related deaths and patients' return to "normal" lives with respect to sex, marriage, and childbearing.[27] With increased access to treatment, global health organizations are now claiming that the "end of AIDS" may be in sight.[28] Some scholars say that we have entered a pharmaceutical era of HIV care, where donors see ART as a the magic bullet that will treat infected patients and prevent the further spread of HIV.[29]

Donor resources also supported the development of an industry devoted to implementing HIV prevention, treatment, and care programs. There are a myriad donor-funded NGOs working in African countries in roles that range from consulting governments, creating HIV prevention campaigns, training healthcare workers, and providing treatment support for patients.[30] In Malawi, as the field of HIV prevention started to grow in the 1990s, more and more development NGOs turned their focus to HIV.[31] The changes brought by large scale donor investments in HIV prevention and treatment are visible when one lands in Lilongwe. In the city center, modern buildings house the headquarters for donors and international organizations like USAID, the Clinton Health Access Initiative (CHAI), the Centers for Disease Control and Prevention (CDC), and the WHO. Donor-funded HIV clinics, like Lighthouse, Partners in Hope, and Baylor Foundation Malawi, stand alongside Malawi's public hospitals. An array of cultural objects bears HIV messages, including theater productions, radio messages, songs, pamphlets, billboards, and clothing.[32] On the roads, large 4x4 vehicles with NGO logos carry staff across the country, passing signs for World Vision, the United Nations International Children's Emergency Fund (UNICEF), the Johns Hopkins Program for International Education in Gynecology and Obstetrics (Jhpiego), and other NGOs as they go. Throughout the country, foreigners work in hospitals and clinics, some like Steven, for many years, but most for short-term contracts or week-long volunteer trips.[33]

HIV has often been called an "exceptional" illness, and this has come to mean many things: it has been exceptional as an emergent disease, as a global emergency, and more recently, with respect to how much funding is devoted to addressing it.[34] Contemporary debates over global health financing focus not on whether to fund HIV programs but rather on whether HIV programs receive *too much* funding and attention. While some scholars emphasize that attention to HIV care has helped increase overall global health funding,[35] others are more critical. In a commentary to the *BMJ* titled "Are we spending too much on HIV?", Roger England's answer was "yes."[36] England and others have argued that funding for HIV care displaces or takes away resources from other health issues.[37] Numerous other conditions affect patients in poor countries, including parasitic diseases, respiratory infections, diabetes, and injuries. Meanwhile, national healthcare systems remain impoverished, and foreign aid inadequately addresses these issues.[38]

My fieldwork took place in this new era of HIV, when HIV care has become the largest program in the global health field. But how HIV programs work and what they mean in people's lives is inevitably more complex than what is officially laid out in intervention plans or in monitoring and evaluation documents. HIV programs focus on a specific disease and increasingly rely on pharmaceutical interventions, but illness is never experienced in isolation from broader health systems and social structures. HIV patients, for instance, have an illness, but they are also mothers, spouses, family members, and business owners. Their relationship with their partners and the economic necessity of supporting their families are important considerations in their decision to take their medications. The work of healthcare providers includes HIV care but, of course, extends beyond to the many concerns that patients have. While NGOs can support HIV-care services, there is little equivalent for the other tasks providers need to accomplish, which creates discrepancies in care. Policymakers in the Ministry of Health are expected to adopt WHO-recommended policies because they are based on technical expertise, but they must also consider whether those policies would be effective in their own healthcare system. Such complexities often go unseen by the institutions that fund and design global health programs, but they are the lived experiences of local actors. In the following section, I advance a concept—*politics of legibility*—to make sense of these tensions.

POLITICS OF LEGIBILITY

Broadly speaking, legibility refers to the way that institutions "see" or recognize issues, populations, or groups. In James C. Scott's theory of statecraft, he describes the concept of legibility using the image of an abridged map.[39] Legibility entails an abstraction or simplification. The modern state took social practices, which are very complex and illegible, and created standardizations and metrics so that its population and land could be recorded and monitored. The state does not have the capacity or the interest in describing an entire social reality. So, it isolates the aspects of society that it wants to measure from the larger whole. In the example of scientific forestry, the state was interested in a single item—the revenue of timber—and was blind to the complexity of the flora and fauna in a forest, as the complex whole provided no use value for the state.[40] These abstractions are consequential because they come with the force of law. For instance, the state cleared underbrush and planted trees in neat rows so that the forest could be managed and understood by a centralized office. However, state legibility projects often failed in the end. The complexities of the natural world or those of social relations and practices were illegible to the state and led to unintended consequences. With scientific forestry, ignoring the complex relationship between soil, plants, fungi, and animals stressed the ecosystem, which eventually led to a loss in timber production. People were also not easily controlled. Local actors, for instance, resisted state taxation by revolt or quiet forms of resistance, like evasion.

I draw on the concept of legibility for a few reasons. The core tensions explored in this book stem from a process of abstraction. While global health researchers have shown that donor funding priorities do not align with the highest burden diseases, the challenge goes beyond misaligned priorities.[41] The issue lies in how disease priorities become detached from the broader social conditions and relationships that shape health outcomes. I argue that it is the failure to recognize how disease, patients, and health workers are embedded in healthcare systems and social structures that limits the extent to which global health programs improve healthcare and people's lives. In addition, the concept of legibility captures something that moves and changes. Actors see and experience social reality from different positionalities. The vantage point of donors differs from that of national policymakers, which differs in turn from local healthcare providers and patients. For example, donors abstract disease from healthcare systems, whereas for national policymakers, healthcare systems are a salient consideration. But like donors, policymakers also see their population in abstracted ways—as numbers of people on ART or as rates of HIV transmission. By contrast, patients do not experience health through population metrics; they have embodied experiences of prescriptions and care. Healthcare providers see themselves not only as implementers of health policies and programs but also as breadwinners and entrepreneurs working to improve their own lives. Legibility, as something that shifts across social locations, lends itself to an actor-centered account of how different groups perceive and experience global health programs.

Theoretically, I advance the concept of the *politics of legibility* to capture how local actors struggle with and respond to global health programs that only partially recognize their social conditions and experiences. Donors and international organizations have the power to enact their vision through resource allocation and policy prescriptions. What is legible or illegible becomes codified through funding, policies, programs, human and material resources, and infrastructure. Their partial visions remake healthcare in partial ways. In this case, a neoliberal approach to HIV care created a world of care largely outside of the public sector. On the ground, actors navigate a healthcare landscape where only certain elements of healthcare and illness experience are formally recognized and addressed through foreign aid. But the other elements that are not formally recognized are nonetheless important in their everyday experiences. The outcome is a politics—a contentious struggle—with global health institutions over what is legitimate and worthy of aid.

How these politics manifest depends on social location. In some instances, actors resisted global health institutions. For example, Malawi's policymakers went against the WHO and created their own policy for preventing mother-to-child transmission of HIV—called Option B+, it gave pregnant and breastfeeding women access to ART as soon as they tested positive. They argued that WHO policies would not work in their resource-constrained healthcare system and that, therefore, they needed to do something different for the mothers and children of their country. Other times, resistance was indirect. Though policymakers recognized the larger healthcare system, like donors, they saw HIV through population metrics. Rendered illegible were the illness experiences of women living with HIV. While women had access to lifelong treatment, side effects, economic pressures to work, and marital concerns could make it difficult to take their medications. Their decisions to take, refuse, or stop ART were an embodied politics—though not necessarily conscious or articulated, they pushed back against policies that saw their disease status but not the social and economic realities of their lives. Finally, actors struggled in a healthcare field divided between NGOs and the public sector. Women struggled to receive comprehensive care. While their HIV status granted them access to ART and NGO programs, their pregnancy and other health concerns fell to the state, which with constrained resources, could provide only cursory care. Healthcare workers struggled to improve their life circumstances. They faced a difficult trade-off: NGO positions offered potential for career growth but were precarious, while public sector work provided stability but had low wages and limited advancement opportunities.

Legibility and Power

In the global health field, legibility works in a unique way. There is no single institution, like the state, that determines what is worthy of aid; instead there is an assemblage of institutions that work together. There are numerous donors that contribute foreign aid. They range from donor organizations that provide billions of dollars each year to small scale altruists, like church groups funding volunteers.[42] The largest donors include governments of wealthy countries, such as USAID (US), Department for International Development (DFID, UK), Norwegian Agency for Development Cooperation (NORAD, Norway), German Corporation for International Cooperation (GIZ, Germany), and Japan International Cooperation Agency (JICA, Japan), as well as major foundations like the Bill and Melinda Gates Foundation. These donors either directly fund global health programs or pool their resources with multilateral organizations, like the Global Fund, which then allocates resources. Resources often flow in a top-down manner. Donors fund governments or large international NGOs, who then subcontract to organizations regionally, nationally, and locally until programs are implemented with citizens.[43]

With humanitarian aid, donors enact power by granting *certain* groups the right to live. As Fassin argues, unlike the state, donors do not use direct force to control populations. Instead, they enact "biolegitimacy": their funding decisions construct meaning and assign differential value to life.[44] Depending on donor interests, certain issues like HIV, malaria, or tuberculosis may receive significant funding, while other issues receive far less, regardless of disease morbidity and mortality.[45] HIV patients can access lifesaving treatment and support programs through donor-funded NGOs, while other patients are left to an underresourced public healthcare system.[46] Donors can also add conditions to aid. To receive funding, countries may need to change organizational structures—for example, they may need to establish free-standing HIV-care organizations or country coordinating mechanisms that allow for nonstate stakeholder involvement.[47] Countries may also face restrictions on how funds are used. For example, US foreign aid cannot be used for abortion services—only for postabortion care, which treats complications from abortions.[48]

International organizations are also authoritative but in a different way. They do not have the financial power of donors but instead derive authority from a global consensus around their leadership.[49] Organizations like the WHO, the Joint United Nations Program on HIV/AIDS (UNAIDS), and UNICEF can call attention to issues and set overarching goals, such as reducing maternal mortality, ending preventable newborn deaths, or ending AIDS by 2030. Even if specific targets are not met (they often are not), they shape global norms around healthcare. They are also considered experts.[50] The WHO is charged with guiding responses to global public health issues, and their policy recommendations are seen as the gold standard. Governments receiving foreign aid are often expected to follow expert guidance and adopt WHO policy recommendations for various treatment or prevention programs and, more broadly, to show that they share the same healthcare goals as international organizations like UNAIDS.

In this context, the state is no longer the central institution that dictates policies and manages population health.[51] While governments in aid-receiving countries engage in legibility projects in the sense that they need to measure and monitor their population, how they do so is tied to a broader context of foreign aid. Governments may require local healthcare providers and researchers to collect data that donors are interested in. The metrics that this data produces, like maternal mortality ratios (MMR), often obscure a messier reality. For instance, behind an MMR statistic, researchers may have used estimates when data was not available, or providers may have kept records for data collection but at the expense of their time spent in clinical practice.[52] Metrics hold value for both governments and donors: they demonstrate that a country is a worthy recipient of aid, is making measurable progress, and that money is well spent.[53] Foreign aid also shifts the relationship between the state and its citizens. Because governments are increasingly accountable to foreign agencies, there is a democratic deficit. Citizens can lose trust in the ability of their government to act on behalf of their needs.[54] While issues that receive the most donor resources, like HIV, matter to citizens, there are a range of other concerns like clean water, agriculture, education, and healthcare in general that are important to them but are not well addressed through foreign aid.[55] But unlike with their government, citizens cannot vote on leaders of donor organizations or their initiatives, and there are few mechanisms for them to express their needs or to hold foreign agencies accountable.

The structure of the global health field shapes how legibility works within it. There are larger patterns in how resources are allocated, which produce tangible effects on the ground. But because the field consists of an assemblage of institutions, there is a degree of variation and messiness. Visions of healthcare are not always uniform. For instance, some donors, like PEPFAR, strongly prefer funding NGOs to implement programs, while other donors contribute both to NGOs and to funds jointly managed by ministries of health.[56] Donors themselves differ in influence. In the HIV-care field, the United States plays an outsized role. Between 2009 and 2014, funding from the US government comprised more than 50 percent of all foreign aid for HIV care.[57] On the ground, this means that programs that the United States promotes, like the "ABCs"—abstinence, be faithful, and use condoms—have a prominent presence in local health facilities.[58]

Implementing policies is also messy. Donor funds travel through a long series of contracts and subcontracts at the international, regional, national, and local levels before reaching intended beneficiaries.[59] Along the way, the message of health campaigns can fracture into alternative practices or be disregarded by the time they reach their target populations.[60] Providers, for their part, often adapt programs according to their social norms.[61] In Malawi, HIV counselors occasionally disclosed confidential test results to caregivers because they believed it was in the best interest of the patient.[62] Women in Uganda found female condoms difficult to negotiate in their relationships and instead found economic value in them: They refurbished and sold them as colorful bracelets.[63] Additionally, as powerful as global institutions are, the messy assemblage creates opportunities for negotiation from below. One of the reasons that Malawi was able to successfully promote Option B+ was because several of the key actors involved had unique positionalities as both policymakers embedded in local healthcare systems and as global HIV experts that participate in academic conferences and WHO panels. They were able to navigate donor contracts while promoting Malawi's policy to a broader global health audience. While this book examines the broader impact of foreign aid from donors collectively, the variation within this field is significant, as it creates distinct challenges and opportunities for those working on the ground.

Neoliberal Visions of Healthcare

What is legible to donors is informed by underlying ideologies. While legibility involves abstraction, the contours of that abstraction—what stands out and what does not—are guided by ideological frameworks that change over time. Neoliberalism has been an influential ideology in the global health field. Broadly defined, neoliberalism "stresses the necessity and desirability of transferring economic power and control from governments to private markets."[64] Starting in the 1970s, proponents emphasized the free market, with minimal involvement from the government and other political institutions. They believed that market competition not only would improve economic outcomes but also would be the most effective and efficient way of allocating social resources like healthcare and education.[65] Neoliberalism has had wide-ranging impacts; its ideas have shaped economic policies across the world, and other domains as well, like humanitarian aid, governance, knowledge production, and individual identities.[66]

In the global health field, the rise of neoliberalism produced new norms around how to approach public health. Just prior to the neoliberal turn, in 1978, the WHO's Alma-Ata conference convened 134 countries and sixty-seven international organizations to affirm a commitment to primary healthcare for all, as well as supportive public health measures like promoting safe water and food supply.[67] The WHO argued that social inequality was a health problem, and that such inequalities within and across countries must be addressed.[68] This moment represented a consensus, albeit a short-lived one, around a rights-based and multidimensional approach to health and socioeconomic development. However, the global debt crisis and the conservative turn in the United States and United Kingdom during the 1980s paved the way for the spread of neoliberal ideas. Donors shifted away from broadly defined goals to more targeted ones. Rather than primary healthcare for all, they pursued "selective" primary healthcare, which focused on low-cost technical interventions for specific issues—namely, growth monitoring, oral rehydration techniques, breastfeeding, and early-childhood immunization (GOBI).[69] These targeted interventions were seen as the most likely to maximize returns on donor investments.

Neoliberalism also diminished the role of governments in providing healthcare. This "de-stating" effect occurred both directly through imposed policies and indirectly through increased resources for nongovernmental organizations.[70] In the 1980s and '90s, in response to a global debt crisis, the World Bank and International Monetary Fund (IMF) attached conditions to their loans known as structural adjustment policies, which required governments to take certain actions, like devalue currency, eliminate subsidies, and reduce overall spending, to "stabilize economies." To meet these conditions, governments often cut spending in social sectors like healthcare, exacerbating existing resource constraints.[71] By the 2000s, it became clear that structural adjustment policies failed to improve economies, but financial institutions continued to limit state capacity. For instance, the IMF's debt relief program limited government spending for civil service hiring, recurrent budget items, and investment in training institutions.[72] At the same time, critics of development aid saw governments as inefficient and sometimes corrupt.[73] NGOs came to the forefront as part of a paradigm shift from government-led to private-led development.[74] While in 1980 the UN recognized just over nine thousand NGOs, by 2006 there were nearly twenty-eight thousand.[75] NGOs have become deeply incorporated into the global health and development fields. By 2018, nearly 90 percent of World Bank projects involved an NGO, compared to just 21 percent in 1990.[76]

Neoliberalism enables and constrains certain courses of action in global public health. While there are several possible ways to address health problems, creating targeted programs and relying on NGOs has become the norm. Reflecting this trend, NGOs seeking donor funding will sometimes narrow their goals—for example, from "maternal health" to "drug treatments for postpartum hemorrhage"—because the economic value of the latter is more easily calculated, thus making a program easier to "sell."[77] Cost-effectiveness analysis is also commonly included in grants to demonstrate maximum returns on investment.[78] Recently, scholars have argued that the global health field has taken a biomedical turn, with donors emphasizing pharmaceutical and technological solutions for specific diseases.[79] For instance, donors might advocate achieving Guinea worm eradication by introducing straws that filter larvae, rather than by developing clean water projects.[80] They might also expand ART programs to both treat and prevent HIV infection, rather than support community-based or health-systems interventions.[81]

Other approaches to global health fall into what Keshavjee calls "neoliberal realms of programmatic blindness."[82] Problems that public healthcare systems face with their workforce, supply chains, data collection, transportation, and brick-and-mortar health facilities and laboratories become a "normal emergency" or one of the mundane problems associated with poverty, rather than a target for foreign aid.[83] While calls to strengthen health systems have increased since the mid-2000s, the impact of such calls is unclear. Total funding for health systems has increased, but its relative proportion in the field has decreased over time as donors have invested significantly in major disease programs, like HIV, malaria, and tuberculosis.[84] In addition, some donors, like the Gates Foundation, have historically resisted health-system interventions, while other donors support health system investments but only within the framework of disease intervention, such as providing refrigerators to remove bottlenecks for vaccine distribution or training healthcare workers for HIV programs.[85] Systemic improvements may occur but in silos.

The rise of the HIV-care field intersected with neoliberalism. Donors saw the global HIV emergency through a neoliberal lens, addressing the disease separately from the broader structure of healthcare. The exceptional resources devoted to the HIV epidemic largely flowed outside of the state. When donors started to scale up funding for ART in the mid-2000s, they set up parallel systems, arguing that it was necessary to work around the government in order to accelerate HIV-care provision.[86] In Malawi, a government nurse may prescribe ART to a patient, but the bottle of medication was procured by UNICEF, stored in private warehouses, and delivered by private trucking companies. Donor funding has also contributed to a proliferation of HIV-care NGOs. While they work alongside or within government facilities, they are an enclave with their own funding, human and material resources, and accountability structure.[87] As Pfeiffer argues, HIV-care programs are awkwardly grafted onto public healthcare systems. Though they may operate within public facilities, their separate structures do little to improve overall conditions in the health sector. In Pfeiffer's case, despite significant PEPFAR funding for HIV care in Mozambique, the health worker shortage remained amongst the worst in the world.[88] And the same is true in Malawi.

Neoliberalism abstracts health in a particular way. Donors tend to treat global public health in a piecemeal manner, broken into isolated diseases or issues that can then be addressed by NGOs through targeted, and increasingly biotechnical, programs. This book describes the implications of a neoliberal approach to health. In Malawi, this approach has been codified through parallel supply chains, NGOs, and targeted interventions for HIV care such that HIV care exists in a world separate from the rest of the public healthcare system. The *politics of legibility* that I describe in this book are a politics that emerge specifically from a neoliberal context. While donors may approach diseases in isolation, policymakers, providers, and patients experience them as part of broader healthcare systems and social conditions. Policymakers need HIV-care policies to work in local healthcare systems; providers, even those in HIV-care NGOs, do not see patients as suffering or at risk of a single disease; and patients' experiences of HIV are shaped by the social, cultural, and economic conditions in which they live. Ultimately, addressing disease in isolation is limiting. While patients may be spared from AIDS-related mortality, they continue to face risks of illness and death from other health conditions as the broader healthcare system supporting providers and patients remains largely unchanged.

Social Consequences of Legibility

Legibility is imbued with inequality. Being legible to donors grants *certain* individuals and organizations access to scarce resources. Nguyen's concept of "therapeutic citizenship" captures how individuals with certain illnesses are privileged by the state.[89] In West Africa, HIV patients received healthcare as well as social services, including food aid and school fees, through the HIV treatment system that others could not access. Similarly, in post-Soviet Ukraine, citizens valued "illness" because the state provided social benefits like pension, healthcare, and education for children of people affected by Chernobyl radiation, whereas being "healthy" meant being illegible to the state.[90] In today's global health context, a similar dynamic occurs, but through donors and NGOs instead of the state. Rather than being therapeutic citizens, patients are "therapeutic clients" of the NGOs that donors fund.[91] Healthcare is not a right for all citizens but a service given by (patron) donor-funded organizations to those who are eligible and in the know.[92]

Because legibility is tied to resources, individuals and organizations often shape their actions to reflect donor priorities. But legibility can be a double-edged sword. On the one hand, being a therapeutic client entails unique access to NGO services. An individual's relationship with an NGO resembles a patron-client relationship: in exchange for services, one is expected to give something in return—for example, participate in counseling, adhere to medication prescriptions, or perform narratives for program evaluators.[93] For instance, Benton describes the process of *becoming* HIV positive.[94] To be HIV positive in a way that NGOs recognize, patients in Sierra Leone had to publicly disclose their status and talk about "positive living"—practices that are rooted in coming out processes in LGBTQ+ communities in the United States. However, to patients, disclosure meant something different. In Sierra Leone, it carried social risks, including physical and emotional abuse, abandonment, and the disruption of familial and other social relationships. Being legible to donors can therefore give individuals access to valuable resources, but it can also pressure those who are suffering or marginalized to reveal a stigmatized status or perform their experiences in ways that are not genuine.

Organizations face similar pressures to conform to donor interests. For instance, with the global scale-up of HIV testing, NGOs focused on meeting performance metrics for the number of tests conducted with populations deemed at risk.[95] While providers may recognize that their clients need services beyond an HIV test, they often have little time or resources to explore other prevention and care possibilities, without risking their funding. In addition, like patients, providers learn global health discourses. In Malawi, providers working in the HIV-care field speak with buzzwords like "fighting stigma," "vulnerable women and children," or "harmful cultural practices," even if they do not agree with the meaning.[96] For instance, in Malawi, providers sometimes tell visitors that villagers believe sex with a virgin cures AIDS because they think the story speaks to Western imaginaries of Africa not because they think it is true.[97] Performing in order to be legible to outsiders can create layers of mistrust. Community members may question whether NGOs are genuinely committed to their well-being or are merely seeking donor funds.[98] Providers, in turn, see individuals as both in need and as potentially scheming, aware that patients often adopt strategies to appear legible to programs, such as performing certain narratives or hiding assets to seem more vulnerable.[99]

Building on previous scholarship, this book centers a different kind of contentious struggle. The focus is less on how individuals try to make themselves legible to donors and more on how they navigate a broader healthcare setting in which donors recognize only select aspects of their healthcare experiences. The concepts of therapeutic citizenship and clientship capture the inequalities that arise when state or nonstate institutions recognize certain groups, but these concepts frame belonging in terms of individual citizens or clients. Whereas I argue that in a neoliberal context, populations are seen in more fine-grained ways—through disease status. The actors in this book are simultaneously legible and illegible to donors. For instance, women living with HIV were clients of NGOs, but they only belonged for their HIV care and only during the duration of their pregnancy and breastfeeding, while the rest of their care fell to the resource-constrained state. More broadly, patients in the global South seek care through various institutions with different levels of resources. As a result, health is often addressed in piecemeal and unequal ways.[100] Moreover, even in the domain of care supported by donors and NGOs, treatment was not a panacea. The larger life challenges women living with HIV faced—poverty, food insecurity, relationship tensions—could hinder their ability to stay on ART, thus limiting the benefits tied to being visible to donors.

In addition, I consider the structural changes that have resulted from a neoliberal vision of healthcare. As I show in this book, foreign aid for

HIV care largely flowed outside the state and produced a structural divide in healthcare. Changes in the structure of healthcare affect multiple groups and processes. It is not only patients as therapeutic citizens or clients that are impacted by donor decisions about resource allocation. Just as patients navigate a fragmented healthcare system to seek care, providers must make career trade-offs in a landscape divided between NGOs and the public sector. Policymaking has also undergone changes. At donors' behest, policymaking includes nongovernmental stakeholders in discussions, often in order for donor interests to be integrated—although, as I show in chapter 2, this process is also an opportunity for local actors to introduce new ideas and to promote them globally. Thinking with the concept of *politics of legibility* opens new avenues of analysis. I consider how various groups, who are simultaneously legible and illegible to donors, respond to a healthcare landscape unevenly transformed by foreign aid.

SETTING: MALAWI

I conducted my research in Malawi—a small country in sub-Saharan Africa, neighboring Zambia, Tanzania, and Mozambique, with a population of roughly twenty million people (see map 1).[101] Malawi has been severely affected by the HIV epidemic. In 2003, just before the rollout of its national ART program, adult HIV prevalence in Malawi was 14.4 percent overall, with rates reaching 23 percent in urban areas.[102] Although HIV prevalence had dropped to 7.1 percent by 2022, an important achievement, the country still has the ninth highest rate in the world.[103] Malawi's epidemic is similar to that of its neighbors. Sub-Saharan Africa has been disproportionately affected by HIV and remains home to the majority of people living with HIV/AIDS. The region has about 68 percent of global cases and approximately 38 million patients.[104]

Malawi is considered a "donor darling" for foreign aid to address the HIV epidemic. The country has received an outpouring of donor funds, with roughly $200 million available annually between 2010 and 2020.[105] Foreign aid has a particularly strong influence in Malawi. According to a 2015 CHAI estimate, 81 percent of Malawi's health expenditure and 99 percent of its HIV care expenditure come from donors.[106] In the 1990s

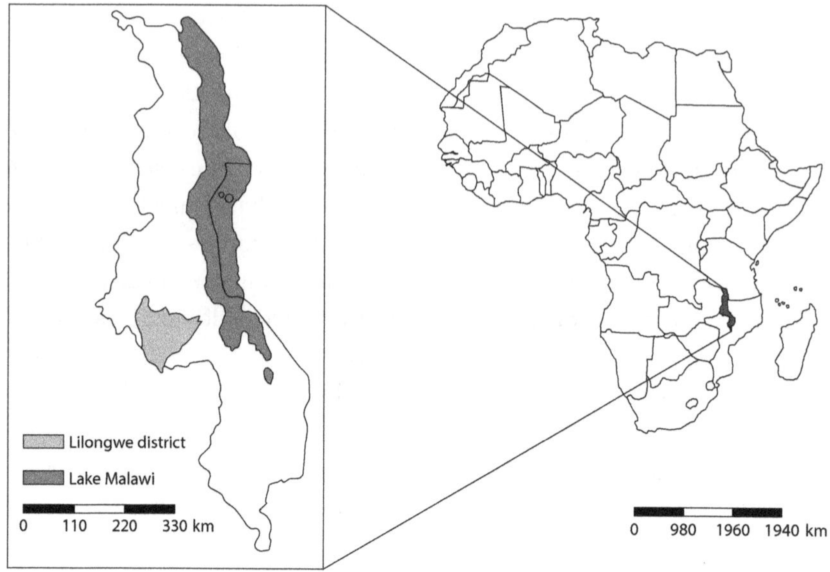

Map 1. Map of Malawi and location of Lilongwe district. SOURCE: Chisomo Mussa and Judith F. Kamoto, "Groundwater Quality Assessment in Urban Areas of Malawi: A Case of Area 25 in Lilongwe," *Journal of Environmental and Public Health*, no. 1 (January 30, 2023), 6974966.

and 2000s, the HIV-care field grew into the leading industry within development programs in Malawi. HIV-care NGOs overtook work in other development sectors, such as agriculture and other health needs, rising from 9 percent of development jobs in the period from 1990 to 1995 to 48 percent of jobs in 2001–2005.[107] The HIV-care field has continued to grow into what Swidler and Watkins call the "AIDS enterprise"—a sprawling industry consisting of donors, development contractors, international and national NGOs, research institutes, HIV-care clinics, and community-based organizations (CBOs).[108] In this sense, Malawi is a prime example of what some have called "HIV exceptionalism": There has been an overwhelming response to HIV which is exceptional relative to other health and development issues.[109]

Much of my research centers around policies to prevent mother-to-child transmission of HIV (PMTCT). In 2011, Malawi implemented a new policy called Option B+, which gave pregnant and breastfeeding women access to ART as soon as they tested positive. Malawi's policy departed from the WHO recommendation that HIV patients start ART after their disease progresses to a certain degree of severity, marked by clinical symptoms or a CD4 test (which measures immune function). While this book speaks to the societal implications of global health programs more broadly, the Option B+ policy is distinct in several ways. First, Malawi's development of the policy was surprising since it went against the WHO's recommendations. Countries with less power and resources rarely challenge international organizations and innovate new global policies and norms. In chapter 2, I discuss why Malawi developed Option B+ and how policymakers made the policy legible to a global audience. Second, Option B+ followed a test-and-treat logic, which called for women to be tested for HIV and, if positive, receive their first bottle of medication at the prenatal clinic. Although policies for preventing mother-to-child transmission existed for many years, Option B+ further integrated HIV care with prenatal services. As I show in chapter 4, this creates striking contrasts in care within the same prenatal clinics. Third, PMTCT policies and programs target pregnant and breastfeeding women to protect children from acquiring HIV. These interventions are often intertwined with gendered discourses on motherhood and responsibility.[110]

The exceptional attention and resources devoted to HIV care takes place in a country struggling with poverty and uncertainty. On the Human Development Index, Malawi ranks 172 out of 193 countries, with about 70 percent of the population living below the global poverty line of $2.15/day.[111] Uncertainty is pervasive in everyday life. In rural regions, many families depend on farming for food and cash. Livelihoods and food security can change suddenly due to natural conditions (e.g., too much or too little rain)—an uncertainty exacerbated by climate change—or due to job loss, divorce, illness, or a death in the family.[112] Educational opportunities are limited; in 2018, only 2 percent of men and 1 percent of women were enrolled in tertiary education.[113] With a small formal labor market, many workers struggle to find stable jobs and instead do piecework (i.e., various short-term jobs) or rely on small side businesses for income.[114] Meanwhile, Malawi's health sector has struggled to develop and continues to deal with resource shortages, with many facilities lacking sufficient staff, medicine, supplies, and space. One study showed that across the country, the availability of essential medicines was only 47 percent.[115] When President Bingu wa Mutharika died of a heart attack in 2012, rumors circulated among locals that it was because Kamuzu Central Hospital had run out of the drug needed for cardiac resuscitation.[116] In 2022, Malawi's health-worker shortage was among the worst in the world, with 0.5 physicians and 5.1 nurses and midwives per ten thousand people, while the WHO recommends a minimum of forty-nine doctors, nurses, and midwives per ten thousand people.[117] In chapter 1, I show that these challenges stem from a long history of missed opportunities to develop the healthcare system. The tensions described in this book between what is legible or illegible to donors are relevant to many aid-receiving countries, but they look particularly striking in Malawi where resources are especially constrained.

GLOBAL HEALTH FROM DIFFERENT VANTAGE POINTS

This book centers the experiences of actors in Malawi and follows them as they confront a healthcare landscape transformed by foreign aid. I conducted fieldwork in Malawi's health centers and interviews with different people involved in healthcare. I included patients affected by HIV-care policies, providers working in Malawi's health centers, and policymakers designing the country's HIV-care policies. The perspectives of these groups represent key vantage points in the global health field. Writing about globalization, Michael Burawoy explains that the process "looks different from different nodes in the chain—from the international agency, from the NGO, from within the nation-state, and from the urban or rural community."[118] In the global health field, policymaking, healthcare careers, clinical practices, and patient experiences are key nodes, and each domain offers an important vantage point for seeing how interventions are produced, enacted, and experienced by different groups of actors.[119]

My data comes from twelve months of fieldwork in Lilongwe, Malawi's capital city, and its surrounding region. I conducted over 150 interviews with policymakers, NGO staff, government healthcare providers, and women living with HIV. Lilongwe is a good site for studying the implications of HIV-care programs. This is where HIV-care policies are made, where many donor and NGO headquarters are located, and where several hospitals and clinics conduct HIV-care programs. Because of this concentration, working in Lilongwe provides an opportunity to observe HIV-care programs and how different actors interact with them. I do not claim, however, that my findings are representative of the country as a whole. Much of the country is rural. HIV-care programs are also prevalent in Malawi's rural regions, though they are less concentrated than in urban areas.[120] My findings about the contrasts between donor-funded HIV-care programs and Malawi's public healthcare system are relevant for rural areas, but the contrasts are particularly striking in cities like Lilongwe.

I conducted my fieldwork primarily in three health centers in Lilongwe. Health centers are local clinics and often the first place that patients go; patients with more advanced conditions are referred to district hospitals or central (tertiary) hospitals. In the health centers, I observed everyday clinical activities, especially those related to HIV and prenatal care. The health centers also provided a way to meet potential interview respondents. I interviewed government and NGO providers about their work at the health centers as well as their career trajectories and aspirations. I worked closely with the Baylor College of Medicine Foundation—Malawi's "Tingathe" program, an NGO program dedicated to PMTCT and keeping HIV positive women in care.[121] For my interviews with women living with HIV, I included participants with a range of experiences taking HIV medications. NGO staff introduced me to their HIV positive clients, some of whom were coming to the clinic and taking medication regularly and others who had refused or stopped medication for some period of time. I recruited policymakers both through networks I developed during fieldwork and through direct outreach, including numerous emails and phone calls. I was interested in speaking with those involved in Malawi's PMTCT policy, Option B+, to understand the motivations for developing a policy that differed from the WHO recommendation. Over years of HIV programming, international actors have taken a more active role in national policy discussions. So, the policymakers I interviewed include members of the Malawi Ministry of Health and those working for international organizations and NGOs.

Fieldwork and interviews were conducted a few months each year, between 2014 and 2017. My interviews with each group took place during specific times, while my fieldwork at health centers and other sites in the region took place throughout. Interviews with women living with HIV were conducted from June through September 2014 (N=65). Interviews with providers regarding their practices were conducted May through September 2014 and June through September 2015 (N=37). A second round of interviews focusing on providers' careers and future plans took place between June and August 2017 (N=44). Interviews with policymakers spanned the course of three years, with most taking place June–September 2016 (N=30). My relationship with Baylor's Tingathe program started as a research collaboration to understand patients' use of ART; from there, I continued building relationships with the program's community health workers for my research.[122] At the clinic, I mostly observed the providers' work and participated minimally by helping with clerical (nonmedical) tasks.

As a graduate student from an American institution, my positionality affected what I was able to do and how others responded to me. For instance, when I mentioned my research to people, many were initially eager to give me well-rehearsed narratives about HIV in Malawi. This happened less as I developed my relationships, but as one of many researchers studying HIV-care in Malawi, it took time to move beyond the narratives and buzzwords that people thought I wanted to hear. At the clinics, my limited ability to understand Chichewa meant that I relied heavily on my research assistant or providers at the clinic to translate or explain events to me. As such, the details of everyday interactions, like what patients say to one another while waiting or providers' lunchtime conversations, were often lost on me.[123] Nonetheless, I believe my observations were useful in capturing activities at the clinic and in building rapport with providers, who were also interview respondents.[124] My positionality also shaped my lens in sampling. When I designed the project, I was interested in understanding the (unintended) consequences of HIV-care programs. I sampled accordingly, focusing on HIV-care policymakers, providers implementing HIV-care programs, and women living with HIV. Though I was critical of the global health field, I also saw my respondents according to disease categories, mirroring the ways they were legible to donors and international organizations. Themes of legibility and illegibility emerged through my data analysis as my respondents spoke about other issues at the clinic or other life concerns. While I believe my findings illustrate these themes, they also point to the need for further research on the experiences of those who have fallen into the shadows of global health.

OUTLINE OF THE BOOK

The book is organized into chapters that describe the experiences of policymakers, providers, and patients in Malawi. By examining these groups, I show how a *politics of legibility* manifest at different levels of society.

Chapter 1 provides historical background and describes how Malawi's unequal worlds of care came to be. Just as the spotlight on HIV was made from multiple institutional decisions to change policies, provide funding, and build facilities, the surrounding shadows were also the result of decisions—but of decisions to limit or neglect. Colonial administrators prioritized healthcare for Europeans but not Africans; national political leaders and the economic policies of international organizations limited healthcare spending at the dawn of independence; and despite growth in the global health field, donors have not invested significantly in the broader health sector. The exceptional world of HIV care emerged from a still nascent global health field. For the first two decades of the epidemic, HIV care in Malawi mirrored its broader healthcare system, until, through immense global activism, donors increased their investment. But, as these investments went largely through parallel structures and NGOs, HIV care diverged from the rest of Malawi's healthcare system, forming a separate world that operated with its own set of resources, structures, and discourses. These unequal worlds of care set the context for the rest of this book.

Chapter 2 focuses on the experiences of policymakers. Malawi's implementation of Option B+ in 2011 deviated in important ways from the global norm. While the WHO was initially resistant, Malawi's policymakers stood by their choice, challenging long-standing assumptions about the WHO's authority to influence national policy decisions. This chapter tells the story of how and why Malawi developed Option B+ and highlights the politics between international organizations and national policymakers over how to address health problems. The creation of Option B+ was motivated by the failure of past WHO policies to control maternal HIV transmission. While the WHO recommended effective treatments to prevent transmission, the conditions of the healthcare systems in which policies would be implemented were illegible. But to Malawi's policymakers, the conditions that were illegible to the WHO were a central concern—they needed the policies to work in their healthcare system. The test-and-treat design of Option B+ reflected tensions in legibility. Policymakers leveraged the ample donor resources for HIV testing and treatment, while making implementation far simpler for their staff, who worked in resource-constrained conditions in the public sector, which received little donor assistance. A few years later, Malawi's Option B+ would become a new global norm. Though policymakers relied on donors for funding, they took advantage of their close ties to NGOs, knowledge of the field, and professional networks in and outside the country to promote their policy globally.

Like Malawi's policymakers, healthcare providers work in a space between global health institutions and the Malawian healthcare system. Chapter 3 examines how providers think about their work and career trajectories. NGOs offered *precarious opportunities*—insecure jobs with a tenuous path to upward mobility—whereas public sector work offered *stagnant stability*, stable jobs with, however, limited opportunities to progress professionally or in terms of socioeconomic status. Neither sector offered an ideal path to improving one's life circumstances. For a younger generation of providers, NGO work was often appealing because it spoke to their aspirations for upward mobility. However, the short-term nature of NGO contracts made it difficult to maintain steady progress toward this goal. Meanwhile, public sector work felt incompatible with aspirations. With low wages and few training and educational opportunities, providers did not see any path toward upward mobility. While the structure of healthcare has changed in significant ways, economic conditions for workers have remained relatively the same, with Malawian workers continuing to struggle with poverty and economic uncertainty.

The divide in the healthcare profession also manifested in clinical routines. Chapter 4 takes readers into Malawi's prenatal clinics, which have become a key site for HIV interventions to prevent mother-to-child transmission. Legibility and illegibility have material consequences, creating distinct conditions for care, healthcare practices, and in the end, outcomes for patients. Within the same prenatal clinics, healthcare practices diverged. NGOs took on almost all aspects of HIV care, from managing the supply chain, HIV testing and counseling, and tracking adherence to treatment. With donor support, NGOs had the staff and resources to identify HIV-positive women and intensively monitor their adherence to treatment. Government providers were responsible for prenatal care for all women, but with minimal donor support, they struggled with shortages of staff and medicine and, as a result, rationed time and services for each patient. Prenatal care was a cursory process, and women's concerns about their health and pregnancy often went unaddressed. Donors saw women through the lens of their HIV status, yet women's health extends beyond a single disease. While NGOs provided high-quality care, they targeted specific populations and addressed only specific issues. Consequently, women's health was managed in a piecemeal way; there was immense focus on preventing maternal HIV transmission, but women were left at risk for other problems that might occur before, during, or after childbirth.

Chapter 5 dives further into the impact of global health programs on women's lives. I interviewed women living with HIV, some of whom were taking their medications and others who had refused or stopped. While women's HIV status was legible to global institutions, other aspects of their lives—their social, economic, and cultural conditions—often were not. Yet these illegible conditions were crucial for their illness experience and decisions about taking ART. Women understood their prescription and wanted to protect their child from infection, but treatment could disrupt essential aspects of their everyday lives. Side effects, which often were exacerbated by food insecurity, made some women feel worse and incapable of work. An HIV diagnosis and treatment could also strain the micropolitics of trust between couples and potentially threaten marriages. The challenges women on ART faced reflected their legibility as HIV subjects. Seeing HIV as a disease that can be treated and prevented through biomedical intervention alone represents a partial vision of health. This partial vision sidelines patient experiences of illness and their social and economic conditions, all of which shape how they take (or do not take) their medications.

As I was writing this book, another pandemic shook the world: COVID-19. In the conclusion, I reflect on the implications of my findings for global health programs as well as emergent disease threats. In a neoliberal context, global health institutions have sought recovery through targeted biomedical interventions that operate largely outside the state. But these efforts abstract disease from healthcare systems and social conditions, which ultimately limits the extent to which patients can recover. In the maternal healthcare setting, women were *living with* HIV, but still *dying from* maternal mortality and the range of illnesses and injuries that could occur in their lifetime. COVID-19 was a new pandemic, but it revealed familiar patterns. Long-standing problems in the public sector, such as shortages of essential medicines—including oxygen and ventilators—and infrastructural problems like limited space and inconsistent water supply, were not only resource constraints but risk factors in the context of COVID-19. Just as the illegibility of public healthcare limits the potential of global health programs to improve people's health and lives, it also limits countries' ability to prepare for and manage new disease threats.

1 Constructing Unequal Worlds of Care

HIV is often described as exceptional. Peter Piot, director of UNAIDS, stated: "This pandemic is exceptional because there is no plateau in sight, exceptional because of the severity and longevity of its impact, and exceptional because of the special challenges it poses to effective public action."[1] As an exceptional condition, HIV warranted an exceptional response. It has become the largest disease program in the global health field, with roughly $20 billion available annually between 2010 and 2020.[2] In Malawi, these resources have produced noticeable changes. Specialized health facilities, research offices, and nongovernmental organizations (NGOs) working on HIV care mark the physical landscape; messages about HIV have spread widely through posters, radio, health education talks, and community conversations; and people are now *living with* HIV rather than dying from it. HIV programs are part of a distinct world, with their own donor support, human and material resources, and spaces within or outside of government facilities. The emergence of this world, however, was not without controversy. In 2007, the Malawian newspaper *The Nation* printed the headline: "So, AIDS is money?"[3] As HIV shifted from a crisis to a more manageable condition, the article scrutinized donor efforts for overlooking other important health issues and potential corruption within HIV programs.[4] While donor funding fueled community-based organizations (CBOs) focused on HIV, it treated other diseases as secondary "by-the-way" issues. One respondent for *The Nation* article stated: "People would like to know why there are more CBOs talking about HIV and AIDS and not TB [tuberculosis], which has been there for a long time and is killing millions of people."

In a 2022 article titled "Bring your own syringe," reporters for *The Guardian* wrote that Malawi's shortage of medical supplies had become a crisis.[5] The labor ward at Bwaila District Hospital in Malawi's capital city of Lilongwe was facing temporary closure. As a notice posted on a wall stated, "We don't have equipment/supplies to work with." Across the country, in the Mulanje district, women who came for family planning implants were told to buy their own syringes. In the previous year, nearly half of Malawi's district hospitals had to close their surgical centers because they lacked anesthetics. The Association of Malawian Midwives and the National Organization of Nurses expressed their frustration, stating:

> Nurses, midwives and other health professionals are unable to resuscitate patients needing oxygen therapy, put up intravenous infusions that provide a lifeline in acutely sick patients, young and old, due to poor lighting, professionally conduct deliveries in labour wards, suture tears and episiotomies, remove umbilical cords around babies' necks, do manual removal of placentae, perform vacuum extractions.

Malawi's public healthcare system constitutes another world. It is a world that is not considered exceptional and has long operated with limited resources, but it is responsible for the numerous "by-the-way" issues left behind by international donors and aid organizations. Scholars have described the stark contrasts between HIV programs and the rest of healthcare as a spotlight against the shadows of global health, abundance next to scarcity, or an island in a sea of underprovision.[6]

While HIV has been framed as an exceptional emergency, the frustrations of citizens exposed to other health risks and Malawian nurses working with limited resources are often taken for granted. To many working in global health, the story in *The Guardian* about medical supply shortages is devastating but not surprising. Malawi is one of the poorest countries in the world, ranking 172 out of 193 countries on the Human Development

Index.[7] Shortages of medical supplies, health workers, and basic infrastructure, like water and electricity, along with greater exposure to disease and risk, can seem to be a natural consequence of poverty. But it is not that simple. Care has long been carved into worlds that have limited the development of Malawi's national health sector.

In this chapter, I describe how Malawi's unequal worlds of care came to be. Just as the spotlight on HIV was made from multiple institutional decisions to change policies, provide funding, and build facilities, the shadows are also the result of decisions—decisions to limit or neglect. The ways that healthcare failed to develop in Malawi were produced over time. Colonial administrators in the late nineteenth and early twentieth century prioritized healthcare for Europeans over Africans; national political leaders, along with the economic policies of international organizations, limited healthcare spending at the dawn of independence in 1964; and despite growth in the global health field in the 2000s, donors have not invested significantly in broader healthcare systems. The exceptional world of HIV care emerged from here. For the first two decades of the epidemic in the 1980s and '90s, HIV care in Malawi took place within the broader healthcare system. While donors funded prevention programs, these programs did not provide treatment despite the development of effective therapies in 1995. This changed through immense activist efforts. But as donors increased investments in HIV, they did so largely through parallel structures and nongovernmental organizations. As a result, HIV care began to diverge from the rest of Malawi's healthcare system, operating with its own set of resources, structures, and discourses. These unequal worlds of care and how patients, providers, and policymakers navigate between them is the subject of this book. The tensions between these unequal worlds shape action in various ways. They can be a driving force, as when policymakers created Option B+, a foil with which to compare one's career and future, or an inescapable part of clinical work and everyday life.

EXCEPTIONAL AND SLOW EMERGENCIES

Emergencies are not always obvious. In the fourth decade of the HIV epidemic, it seems obvious that HIV *is* a global emergency, one that warrants an exceptional response. This discourse is powerful. International donors were initially indifferent to the suffering of HIV patients in the global South.[8] Through activism, attitudes changed, which galvanized donors to provide aid to address an emergency.[9] The framing of HIV exceptionalism is often used to justify a massive deployment of resources and to explain why responses to the epidemic must differ from other public health interventions.[10] Today, it is difficult to imagine a world where ART is not available to patients or where organizations like the Global Fund do not manage billions of dollars for HIV programs. By contrast, Malawi's public healthcare system is in another kind of emergency—a "slow emergency." Slow emergencies are "unspectacular, distanced from the policies that instigated them, and reified through constant inattention."[11] Though conditions in the health sector deeply impact patients and those working in healthcare, they do not galvanize the kind of dramatic response that we have seen for HIV. These two types of emergencies have different temporalities, meanings, and implications for political action. What kinds of emergencies are rendered legible or illegible to global health institutions as worthy of action and aid shapes the structure of healthcare on the ground, producing unequal worlds of care.

Emergencies imply eventfulness. They have a quality of unpredictable and rapid change, in which time-sensitive action needs to be taken to forestall an undesired future.[12] Emergencies also grant exceptions, in which the practices of everyday life can be governed in different ways. The dramatic growth of the HIV field was an exception to previous norms. In 1990, development assistance for health totaled $5.6 billion, whereas in 2007, $5.1 billion was available for HIV care alone.[13] More specifically, HIV was an emergency under neoliberalism, which produced particular exceptions. HIV was an exception that was thought to require verticality—that is, separate funding, programs, and personnel siloed from the state.[14] As Nguyen has described, HIV-care programs represented a "government-by-exception." As resources and technologies went to vertical programs, questions of characterizing and managing populations—what the state normally does—were now in the hands of global institutions and NGOs.[15] Exception also meant granting a particular group access to resources and care that others could not receive.[16] The construction of HIV exceptionalism was never about meeting basic resource needs; it was about providing a sociotechnical solution to one subgroup "in emergency."[17] As such, exception entails different valuations of life, where only some are considered worth saving.[18] Finally, emergencies invite a future-oriented temporality that motivates action. In the HIV field, targets of 3x5 (treating 3 million by 2005), or of 90-90-90 (by 2020, 90% of people living with HIV know their status, 90% of people with HIV receive sustained ART, and 90% of people on ART are virally suppressed), or of an "AIDS-free future" signal that change *can* be made.

While HIV is considered an exceptional emergency, hospitals closing because they have run out of supplies has a different meaning and temporality. It is a "slow emergency"—or put differently, it is "slow violence" or "crisis ordinariness."[19] Unlike the eventfulness of an emergency, slow emergencies are not exceptional, urgent, or actionable. They are instead characterized by attritional lethality, imperceptibility, and foreclosed action.[20] While closed hospitals, missing medications and supplies, and overworked providers do produce tangible harms, they are harms that unfold gradually. These harms become ordinary in that they are not a state of exception but are interwoven into everyday life.[21] And because they are produced over time, it can be difficult to pin down their causes. For instance, by the time the buildup of toxic waste produces tangible environmental and public health outcomes, the original causes are distant from present-day reality.[22]

The ordinary conditions that attend slow emergencies also make them easier to ignore or naturalize. Political actors often describe slow emergencies as unfortunate conditions, without addressing how those conditions were produced or proposing tangible solutions to address them.[23] For instance, with COVID-19, political leaders in the United States acknowledged the effects of structural racism in producing unequal health outcomes, while simultaneously claiming that there was nothing to be done about it.[24] Health disparities were framed as an intransigent historical truth rather than a problem caused by policies that could be countered.[25] In a similar vein, in global health, weak healthcare systems are often acknowledged to be a key challenge, but the discourse about "health systems strengthening" rarely translates into sustained action.[26] Donors often address systemic issues, like supply chain management, in a piecemeal fashion—primarily when those issues create obstacles for specific disease programs.[27] Moreover, given the longue durée of slow emergencies, it is difficult to galvanize action because the political causes feel distant and are obfuscated. As a result, political inaction embeds sacrificial logics.[28] In this sense, slow emergencies are a form of necropolitics—by *not* acting and providing necessary social supports, states and other institutions let certain communities die.[29] While patients with HIV are seen as a group that the international community must act to save, patients with other conditions that could be treated or managed are allowed to suffer or die.

While slow emergencies may not be recognized by institutions, they are palpable to those most affected by them. For instance, to Black communities in the United States, COVID-19 was an emergency, as was the structural racism that manifested in their everyday lives, which now included their heightened risk of infection.[30] These emergencies are not experienced separately but are entangled.[31] Likewise, in my case, women living with HIV were not only grappling with their HIV infection, but also pregnancy, marital conflict, and housing and food insecurity. Multiple emergencies also compound one another. The HIV virus interacts with and worsens other conditions like tuberculosis, malaria, and bacterial infections, and the resulting illnesses and deaths have weakened economies and exacerbated already precarious livelihoods.[32] It is a privilege to be able to distinguish emergency from normality. As feminist, critical race, and postcolonial scholars have long described, for the oppressed, emergency is a regular state of being, in which there is no stable normality to be returned to.[33] Even though HIV patients with access to ART can resume their life trajectories with less fear of AIDS mortality, their everyday lives remain characterized by a "predictable precarity," in which unexpected economic downfalls, agricultural problems, sickness and death are to be expected.[34] For healthcare providers, donor funding for HIV care has only partially transformed their healthcare landscape; their work still takes place within a national health sector that has long struggled with resource shortages. While patients and healthcare workers experience diseases, healthcare systems, and the predictable precarity of everyday life in interconnected ways, treating HIV as an exception detaches it from the broader ongoing crises in which it is situated.

In the following sections, I unpack the construction of Malawi's worlds of care. What global health institutions recognize as an emergency deserving action and aid should not be taken for granted. Approximately two decades passed before the suffering of AIDS patients in Africa was recognized as "exceptional," while long-standing scarcity in the health sector, endured by generations of providers and patients, continues as a slow emergency. The ability to shape temporality is itself an expression of power, determining which issues are made legible as emergencies requiring urgent action and which are rendered illegible—seen as ordinary and unchangeable—leaving communities suspended in a state of waiting for resources.[35] In Malawi's history, power has changed hands from colonial administrators to governmental leaders to donors and international organizations. But throughout the different eras, political decisions to provide or to limit and neglect created inequalities in care, whether between Europeans and Africans or between the groups donors saw as worth saving and those they let die.

HEALING IN SOUTHEAST AFRICA

Healing practices before colonialism in the southeastern region of Africa shared many similarities. Societies were not yet bounded by the borders set by European powers during the late nineteenth-century Scramble for Africa, when European nations competed to claim territories across the continent. In the first half of the nineteenth century, most people in southeast Africa were farmers living in village settlements. The area consisted of groups that had arrived from earlier migrations.[36] While they intermarried and traded, they also retained specific languages and cultural practices.[37] Economic interests created turbulence in the region. Most groups were loosely organized under the Maravi Confederacy, which spanned regions of present-day Malawi, eastern Zambia, and northern Mozambique, and was involved in the slave and ivory trade.[38] After the confederacy's power waned, Yao traders arrived seeking captives and ivory, while Ngoni raiders came seizing land and livestock from local farmers.[39] Together, these incursions displaced thousands, weakened local agricultural economies, and promoted opportunities for foreign commercial and political interests.[40] The slave trade in the region would later become one of the justifications for missionary presence in the mid-nineteenth century.

In the precolonial era, African conceptions of health and healing were broad and collective, a framework that remains today. Medicine and healing were intertwined with religious, political, and community practices. While rulers were not considered divine themselves, they were guardians of the land and had the ability to consult with ancestral spirits.[41] Their authority was based on their ritual power to ensure prosperity for their people—namely, the fertility of the land, good rains, well-being of people and livestock, and protection against natural and supernatural dangers.[42] Community and individual health were also connected. Fractured social relations, for instance, might be expressed in sickness or other misfortunes, like drought, crop failure, and business difficulties.[43] Illness and injuries could be physical in origin or the result of witchcraft.[44] For this reason, healing was not limited to the individual body but, depending on the ailment, might include social and supernatural remedies.[45]

The dichotomy between biomedicine and indigenous healing is largely a Western construction. For patients and providers in Malawi, these two worlds have not been incompatible but intertwined. Healers have been open to outside influences from Islamic medicine, Pentecostalism, biomedicine, and elsewhere.[46] People sought and continue to seek care from a variety of sources, including herbalists, spiritual healers, and diviners, as well as from biomedicine.[47] For instance, during the colonial era, indigenous healing was often used alongside Western biomedicine, especially since access to and quality of care in government hospitals was limited.[48] During the HIV epidemic, patients often took ART while also seeking care from traditional healers.[49] While the focus of this book is not on indigenous healing, it is a salient aspect of local understandings of health and illness.

WORLDS OF CARE FOR EUROPEANS AND AFRICANS

Scottish and British missionaries arrived in southeast Africa in the mid-nineteenth century, about two decades before colonial rule. Providing healthcare was part of the mission to bring civilization, commerce, and Christianity to Africans.[50] In 1891, the British claimed what is now Malawi as their protectorate—Nyasaland. Missionary and colonial medicine were distinct healthcare systems but also intertwined in their roles and practices.[51] While both systems provided Africans with healthcare and medical training, the care provided was limited and came with the ulterior purpose of proselytizing or maintaining social control. Efforts to improve healthcare access and services were repeatedly constrained during the seven decades of British rule. By creating a world of care that was primarily for Europeans and not Africans the country was left without the necessary infrastructure for Malawians to establish their own public healthcare system at the end of colonial rule in 1964.

Medical missions, established prior to colonial rule, continued to play a central role once British administration began. They remained the primary providers of healthcare and medical training for Africans, as the new colonial government was eager to offload their responsibilities for education and healthcare onto them.[52] Throughout the late nineteenth and early twentieth centuries, missions provided primary care, ran vaccination campaigns, and worked with colonial administrators to address epidemic diseases, like smallpox and leprosy.[53] They also ran some of the most ambitious medical training programs in Anglophone Africa.[54] In Nyasaland, the Blantyre Mission Hospital opened in 1896, and by the 1920s, they were exporting medical dressers and hospital assistants to other African cities.[55] The first midwifery school opened at Mlanda Mission in 1920.[56] But, while missions did notable work, their reach had limits. Many Africans could not access medical missions; the facilities were too distant or their fees for healthcare services were unaffordable. In 1940, when the government first reported figures for clinic attendance, they found that less than 4 percent of Africans in Nyasaland visited a mission outpatient clinic over the course of a year.[57] Mission training programs were also limited by rank. Though some Africans received sponsorships to attend medical school abroad, the bulk of missionary training focused on producing "medical middles," or lower-ranked staff, like nurses and midwives, medical dressers, and hospital and laboratory assistants.

When the British named Nyasaland their protectorate in 1891, they were already spread thin across the continent. Nyasaland was not a priority for the British as it was considered an unprofitable territory. Although British presence was minimal, extraction still took place. Africans in Nyasaland worked on plantations for little pay, served as a reserve labor source for Britain's more profitable colonies, and were conscripted into wars, often as carriers transporting supplies on difficult routes.[58] They were also taxed, largely for things that they did not benefit from. For decades, a significant proportion of tax revenue went toward paying for a railway that local African businesses did not use.[59] Colonial policies revolved around prioritizing the health of Europeans, maintaining an African labor force, and reducing government expenditure on social services for Africans, including healthcare.[60]

Healthcare conditions for Africans under colonial rule were bleak. In the first half of the twentieth century, government healthcare was almost entirely for Europeans and was not accessible to African people. The amount the colonial government spent for inpatient care at hospitals for Europeans was more than two times higher than that spent for African ones.[61] In 1925, of the fourteen government hospitals for Africans, only seven had a medical officer; many were overseen by subassistant surgeons, who were only present for two to three months a year.[62] A senior medical officer in Blantyre explained: "The present position of the Native Hospital is unsatisfactory from all points of view. . . . There is only one ward, which has to be used for all classes of cases."[63] While medical officers complained about poor conditions to the British government, they were generally offered little aid. In 1921, Nyasaland's principal medical officer proposed to build a network of rural dispensaries across the country to increase healthcare accessibility to Africans, but he only received enough funding for a handful of dispensaries located in administrative centers.[64] Things were not significantly better in the 1930s. The next principal medical officer reported that "little progress has been made."[65] While European hospitals were considered "adequate for their purposes," conditions in African hospitals were not.[66] There were only 170 beds for a population of 1.4 million. Unless seriously ill, most Africans did not want inpatient care at government hospitals. People continued to rely on indigenous healing practices, seeking care from diviners, herbalists, and prophetic healers for their needs.[67]

The government established their own medical training school for Africans in the 1930s. Like medical missions, they trained lower-level personnel.[68] But the goals of missionary and colonial medicine were not always aligned. Mission-education Africans helped to extend colonial reach to other regions but were also at the forefront of anticolonial movements.[69] As it crushed rebellions, the government also increased surveillance of Nyasaland's educational structures.[70] Each institution, the missions and the colonial government, wanted control over Africans for their respective purposes, thus foreclosing the possibility of collaboration. Historian Markku Hokkanen noted that had the two institutions pooled their resources instead of competed, they could have established a strong medical school.[71] Instead, there was no medical training in Nyasaland; outside of the Africans sponsored by missionaries to attend medical school abroad, most physicians were Europeans trained in Europe. Malawi's College of Medicine would not open until 1991.

Improvements to healthcare were often made as a response to discontent. Throughout British rule, the government provided free healthcare to Africans—but not simply out of benevolence. Promoting Western biomedicine was a way to counter indigenous healing, which officials considered to be a source of resistance.[72] In the 1940s, labor unrest across the West Indies and British Africa led to the creation of the Colonial Development and Welfare Act, which increased funding for social services.[73] In the 1950s, African protests erupted over the establishment of a British Federation joining Nyasaland with Northern and Southern Rhodesia.[74] In response, the British invested in infrastructure, building the new Queen Elizabeth Central Hospital along with roads and railways, though this effort did little to change public opinion. During this time, Africans went to government hospitals in greater numbers, mostly due to the arrival of antibiotics and treatments for tuberculosis, malaria, syphilis, and gonorrhea.[75] While treatments were beneficial, the distribution reflected the divide in care between Europeans and Africans. The same medications that had been available in the 1940s in America and Western Europe were not prescribed to African patients until the 1950s, after prices dropped[76]—a pattern that would play out again in the early 2000s with HIV treatment.[77] Moreover, because of limited funding, hospitals continued to face shortages of medications. In 1956, Nyasaland's medical specialist complained that they had run out of streptomycin, writing that it was "impossible to continue to treat tuberculosis patients in any satisfactory way."[78]

Nationalist movements across Africa in the 1940s and '50s captured the widespread discontent against colonial governments. After several years of civil unrest, the government agreed to elections in Nyasaland. Dr. Hastings Banda, who led the Malawi Congress Party, won the election. The British federation collapsed, and Nyasaland became independent Malawi in 1964. Missionaries and the colonial government brought biomedicine to

Nyasaland but neither developed a healthcare system that could provide adequate care to Africans. Mission hospitals provided primary healthcare but operated separately from the government and only reached a portion of the population. During the seven decades of British rule, opportunities to develop healthcare were repeatedly constrained. Nyasaland's medical officers saw the poor healthcare conditions, but their calls for improving hospitals, building facilities, and providing medicine to Africans were often met with indifference by the British government. And because healthcare training by missionaries and the government was largely limited to subordinate positions, when the British left, so too did many of the doctors in the country. In May 1964, Malawi had no radiologist, no psychiatrist, and no director of the public health laboratory, and the number of government medical officers fell from thirty in 1962 to twelve in 1964.[79] Although the physical structures of medical facilities remained intact, they were stripped of the medicines and healthcare providers required to provide care.

POSTCOLONIAL CHALLENGES

Healthcare in Malawi's new dawn had a rocky start. While the colonial era left little for the new government to work with, national and international decisions further stifled healthcare development. Malawi's first president, Hastings Banda, declared himself president-for-life and stayed in power for thirty years, from 1964 to 1994. Despite being a medical doctor, Banda did not prioritize healthcare.[80] When the economy grew in the late 1960s, he did not invest significantly in the public healthcare system. For example, in response to requests for new health facilities, he asked villagers to volunteer their labor for its construction.[81] Healthcare improvements were often made to resolve political crisis. Banda donated to hospitals after an unpopular user fee policy, which led to resignations in his cabinet, and he built a new maternity ward at Queen Elizabeth Central Hospital after a tour of its dilapidated conditions threatened his image as the protector of the Malawian people.[82] At the same time, healthcare was not a priority for international development agencies either. In the 1970s, agencies focused on population control. Health projects were often not funded because they believed that without controlling the population, there would be no point in addressing disease. Moreover, Banda refused donors' family planning initiatives because they contradicted his rhetoric of "wealth in people": People, not money or mineral resources, were the real value of Malawi.[83]

Like many other countries, Malawi was affected by the global economic crisis in the 1980s. Prices for tobacco, a major export, dropped by 36 percent; rising global fuel costs depleted the country's reserves of foreign exchange; and economic decline in neighboring countries closed off migrant work opportunities.[84] With a troubled economy, Malawi took several loans from the International Monetary Fund, which came with structural adjustment policies.[85] Rooted in neoliberal ideas that emphasized the free market, the policies required governments to promote economic liberalization and privatization, prioritize austerity, and limit expenditure.[86] The polices resulted in cuts in spending in social sectors like healthcare and education. In Malawi, healthcare expenditure dropped from 7 percent of total government expenditure in 1978 to 5.2 percent in 1982.[87] Healthcare workers' salaries were frozen, and patients were often asked to buy their own drugs and supplies, which were no longer available at clinics.[88]

The 1980s also marked the start of the HIV epidemic. Neoliberal policies coupled with a growing epidemic had devastating effects for Malawi's national health sector. As patients flooded healthcare facilities, many were lost in the shuffle. Mistaken diagnoses or poor treatment decisions were easy to make when there were limited medical supplies and when providers were increasingly exhausted and demoralized.[89] Without basic medications, like co-trimoxazole (an antibiotic), acetaminophen, chloroquine, and antiseptic alcohol, all patients, including those with HIV attempting to manage opportunistic infections, suffered from inadequate care.[90] This confluence of events led to rising mistrust in Malawi's political system. In 1993, Banda agreed to a referendum, allowing voters to choose a single-party or multi-party system; voters chose the latter, and a year later, Bakili Muluzi won the election.

THE "POOREST PEACEFUL COUNTRY" IN THE WORLD

President Bakili Muluzi began his term with a struggling economy and health sector. By the 2000s, it was clear that structural adjustment policies did not improve economic conditions.[91] In Malawi, the budget deficit widened to 4.5 percent of GDP; the kwacha had depreciated by almost 40 percent; inflation increased from 6.75 percent in 1996 to 20 percent in 1998 due to a small maize harvest; and GDP growth slowed to 5 percent in 1997.[92] In response to structural adjustment policies, the government had also reduced its state capacities. In 1997, four ministries were cut, principal secretaries were reduced by twelve, and government retrenched 3,194 nonestablished workers (i.e., removed roles that previously existed)—following earlier civil service reforms in 1995 that had already retrenched more than 20,000 workers.[93] Due to earlier privatization efforts, when harvests were weak in the 2000s, there was no grain left in the country's strategic grain reserve; the reserve had been sold to private speculators, who then resold it back to Malawi at exorbitant prices.[94] In 2002, Malawi was deemed the poorest peaceful country in the world. The country had a per capita gross national product (GNP) of $166 and depended significantly on donor funding, with about three-fourths of the budget coming from external sources.[95]

Global health funding increased tremendously in the second half of the 2000s. While this created moments of optimism for Malawi's national health sector, much of the aid targeted HIV care and other diseases of donor interest. Donors had rendered HIV legible as an emergency but addressed it largely through vertical programming, thus dis-embedding it from the public healthcare system. The rise in funding for HIV care changed the trajectory of the epidemic, which I discuss in more detail below. But problems in Malawi's public healthcare system persisted as a slow emergency. At the time, Malawi had one of the worst health-worker shortages in the region, with only 1.1 doctors and 25.5 nurses per one hundred thousand people.[96]A 2003 survey reported that of the 397 health centers in the country, 243 had no operational water source, 204 had no operational electricity, and 244 had no operational communications system (radio or telephone).[97] Health initiatives struggled to succeed in this context.[98] A report from a safe-motherhood program noted that the scale of staff shortages dwarfed their training efforts—the number of births attended by a doctor or nurse remained virtually unchanged.[99]

In 2004, the start of Malawi's HIV treatment program made the larger healthcare system legible, for a moment. Donors recognized that ART scale-up would be difficult without simultaneously addressing health worker shortages.[100] In 2004, the government of Malawi, Global Fund, and DFID funded the six-year, $272 million Emergency Human Resources Program (EHRP). The program would boost salaries by 52 percent for all health workers, expand preservice training, and recruit doctors and nurses from abroad; it also added incentives like rural allowances, housing, and transport to improve retention.[101] The goal was to raise staffing levels in Malawi to equal those of neighboring Tanzania. While still short of the WHO's minimum of 2.5 health workers per one thousand people, it was considered an attainable goal.[102] The EHRP led to some success—the number of health professionals trained rose from four hundred per year in 2004 to over one thousand per year in 2006.[103] And by 2009, health worker to population density had risen 66 percent, from 0.87 per one thousand to 1.44 per one thousand.[104]

Improvements to Malawi's health sector, however, stalled with the 2008 financial crisis. Development assistance slowed from annual increases of 11.2 percent between 2000 and 2010 to 1 percent between 2010 and 2017.[105] The Malawian public made sharp critiques of the retrenchment of aid. In a July 2011 interview, Dorothy Ngoma, executive director of Malawi's National Organization of Nurses and Midwives stated:

> Don't let anyone convince you that [past efforts] have relieved the emergency. While we can see improvements in pockets, we are still in a crisis. Without money on the table, we can't make progress. . . . Where are our partners? . . . Why are there so many people dying for want of basic needs?[106]

Health worker density was still below the WHO recommended minimum. While task shifting—when tasks normally assigned to higher-level staff are shifted to lower-level staff—allowed for more work to be done, it also led to increased workload and burnout.[107] In addition, many healthcare facilities had insufficient stock of essential medicines.[108] For instance, 56 percent of hospitals were stocked out of lidocaine (local anesthetic), 44 percent out of hydralazine (blood pressure medication), and 22 percent out of ORT (oral rehydration tablets). While medication shortages were felt across the board, they were worst in health centers—smaller facilities where most patients receive primary care. Staffing shortages were also widespread. More than half of the country's doctors work in one of the four central hospitals, leaving fewer for district hospitals and often none in health centers.[109]

Dorothy Ngoma's statement captures the slow emergency of Malawi's public healthcare system. For generations, there have been shortages of staff and medicine, providers who feel demoralized because they cannot adequately provide care, and patients who die of treatable conditions. Healthcare has occasionally been legible to governments and international donors, but only in specific and temporary ways, such as to quell anticolonial sentiment, resolve political crises, or address a disease emergency. As a result, the same challenges persist and are reified through routine inattention. The public healthcare system was a "crisis ordinariness"[110]—a crisis that is "'neither a state of exception nor the opposite, mere banality, but a domain where an upsetting scene of living is revealed to be interwoven with ordinary life after all.'"[111] While this crisis has often been illegible to donors, it is seen and felt by people in Malawi. They encounter the challenges in the healthcare system on a routine basis—when providers go to work or when patients seek care—and they feel the consequences acutely. As Wendland argues, what is absent is consequential. The providers, medicines, and technologies *not* present shape care, illness, and death. In Wendland's case, maternal mortality is as much about eclamptic seizures as it is the lack of sterilized equipment, the ambulance without fuel, the missing clinician, and the nurses stretched thin.[112] With the growth in the 2000s of the global health field, which was driven by the rise of HIV care, the political construction of slow emergencies becomes strikingly apparent—one disease, framed as an emergency, garners a vastly different response.

SLOW START TO HIV CARE

The world of HIV care emerged out of the slow emergency of Malawi's national health sector. Initially, though HIV was a novel and deadly virus, care for HIV was not significantly different from other aspects of healthcare. The first case of HIV infection in Malawi was documented in 1985. In the coming years, the epidemic would spread with devastating effects. Today, Malawi's epidemic is generalized, which means that more than

1 percent of the population is infected and that infection is distributed in the general population rather than concentrated in a subpopulation.[113] At its peak in the early 1990s, HIV prevalence was 17.5 percent, with an estimated one hundred thousand new infections annually.[114] Before treatment was available, HIV infection led to death. In 1996, the National AIDS Commission reported that about 70 percent of Malawians knew of someone who had HIV or had died of AIDS.[115] AIDS deaths left many children orphaned: In 2009, the National Statistical Office reported that roughly 12 percent of children under eighteen had lost at least one biological parent.[116] By 2015, AIDS had claimed more than 1.1 million Malawians.[117]

In the early years, the Malawi government was largely silent. President Hastings Banda tightly controlled information on HIV and constrained the response efforts of expatriate healthcare providers.[118] His successor, President Bakili Muluzi, claimed he would tackle HIV during his term but was slow to respond. Since AIDS has a long latency period, Muluzi, like other leaders in the region, did not view the epidemic as an immediate priority requiring significant resource investment.[119] While HIV infection had been documented since the 1980s, the government did not declare it an emergency until 1999. The international community was silent as well. Malawian patients were visible as research subjects to test possible therapeutics, but they did not benefit from the research outcomes.[120] HAART, the first effective HIV treatment, was developed in 1995. While patients in the United States and Europe started to recover, treatment was priced out of reach of most in the global South.[121] Until 2004, when Malawi's public treatment program began, patients had to pay for their own medications.[122] About one million Malawians were infected at the time, but only three thousand were receiving treatment.[123]

Patients with HIV sought care from a variety of sources. They went to hospitals, but because biomedicine had little to offer at the time, they also sought traditional healing, which was more accessible and financially feasible.[124] In this time of uncertainty, patients chased promises of a cure. In 1995, a remedy created by a farmer who claimed that spirits came to him, drew crowds ranging from three hundred thousand to one million to his village.[125] Relatives, mostly women, were the primary caregivers for the sick, along with religious congregations, which offered care and promoted HIV prevention.[126]

Donor-funded HIV prevention programs began in the late 1980s, but their messages did not always resonate. Programs were often framed through a Western lens of heteronormative sexuality.[127] A popular slogan, known as the ABCs—abstinence, be faithful, and use condoms—may have been more effective for early target populations, such as truck drivers and commercial sex workers, but made less sense as HIV spread among married couples, for whom abstinence and condom use were inappropriate.[128] Malawians, however, were not apathetic to HIV infection. They developed their own strategies for prevention.[129] Although there was still much to learn about the virus, it was clear that infection involved sexual relationships. *Mtengano*, meaning dying in two, was often used to describe the fact that spouses shared the same fate.[130] To reduce their risk of HIV, individuals performed "social autopsies"—they used their social networks to assess a potential partner's sexual history along with visual cues of their health status.[131] Past partners were scrutinized for signs of potential HIV infection: whether they were ill, dead, had symptoms like weight loss, diarrhea, or skin disease, or failed to respond to treatments. For married couples, fear of AIDS became a new rationale for divorce. While it had been more common for men than women to divorce an unfaithful spouse, this changed in the context of HIV. Chiefs encouraged women not to put their lives at risk for the sake of marriage.[132]

By the early 2000s, most Malawians knew what HIV was, how it was transmitted, and that it was deadly.[133] At this time, HIV was exceptional in some ways but not others. It was exceptional in its novelty and lethality.[134] Yet it was routine in that care fell to a public healthcare system that had long struggled to develop. Though effective treatments had been developed as early as 1995, patients in the global South were not yet legible as part of a global emergency and were not considered worthy of aid. Thus, for the first two decades of the HIV epidemic, the world of HIV care in Malawi was not so distinct from the rest of healthcare.

A NEW WORLD OF CARE EMERGES

The collective effort of HIV activists, governments, and medical professionals made the deaths of patients with HIV in the global South legible to donors and international organizations. Donor funding for HIV increased sharply in the second half of the 2000s, marking a shift in recognition of HIV as a global health priority. Globally, funding for HIV rose from roughly $5 billion in 2000 to $15 billion in 2010; although austerity measures in 2008 dampened growth, funding remained steadily high with around $20 billion available annually between 2010 and 2020.[135] As the global HIV care field grew, so too did Malawi's world of HIV care. Mirroring global trends, total annual HIV care expenditure by international aid and the government of Malawi rose from $10.5 million in 1996 to around $200 million between 2010 and 2020.[136] Donor resources brought HIV test kits and lifesaving treatment, and it supported a burgeoning industry of HIV organizations and workers. With the rise of neoliberalism, as a global norm, which emphasized a transfer of power from governments to markets, donors often channeled resources outside of government institutions.[137] HIV funding was used to create parallel supply chains and to support a field of NGOs. The world of HIV care began to diverge from the rest of the public healthcare system and grew along its own path.

With donor support, Malawi's HIV treatment program began in 2004. ART became available free of charge; and patients who were eligible according to WHO criteria started lifelong treatment. While the treatment program is technically part of the Malawi Ministry of Health, much of the structure behind it is separate. There was initial discussion around using donor funding to improve national procurement and supply chain management, but the World Bank advised donors against it and recommended a parallel structure instead.[138] Funding for ART comes from the Global Fund. The drugs are procured by UNICEF from India; flown to Copenhagen, where they are individually packed; and then flown to Malawi, where they enter a separate warehouse and distribution system for delivery to health facilities.[139] The Global Fund has rigorous reporting requirements to ensure that the medications they purchase are accounted for. Technical advisors working in the Ministry of Health established a monitoring and evaluation system, according to which every quarter, a supervision team visits ART clinics across the country to audit patient data and check physical stocks of medication.[140] With monitoring, there have been few reported instances of ART stockouts. Donors have continued to use this parallel structure to this day.

Access to HIV treatment has changed the course of the epidemic in Malawi. In one year, the number of patients on ART increased from about three thousand to 38,000 patients.[141] By 2010, more than two hundred thousand patients had started ART, and by 2015, nearly nine hundred thousand.[142] From 2005 to 2010, HIV prevalence dropped from its peak of over 17 percent to 11 percent, and AIDS mortality continued to decline.[143] Attitudes also shifted. While Malawians were initially uncertain about the efficacy of ART, over time, they became more optimistic. It was clear that people living with HIV who were on treatment were healthy and could resume productive lives in terms of work, marriage, and childbearing.[144] Nationally and globally, the HIV field has moved toward greater access to ART. Previous eligibility criteria had meant that only patients who reached a certain stage of disease severity, marked by a laboratory CD4 count or clinical symptoms, could begin lifelong treatment. Now, the field has moved toward universal access. Malawi started this approach in 2011 with their Option B+ policy, according to which pregnant and breastfeeding women could begin lifelong ART as soon as they tested positive. The government made it a universal policy for all patients in 2016. Since then, an estimated 80 percent of the HIV population receives ART, with rates being near perfect, at 95 percent, for pregnant women who attended prenatal care.[145]

In addition to treatment, donor funding has supported the development of an organizational field around HIV. In 2003, the National AIDS Commission (NAC) counted over 300 HIV nonprofit organizations and 582 smaller community-based organizations in 2006.[146] Not only were new HIV organizations established, but existing organizations also shifted their goals to include HIV in their programs.[147] By 2005, about half of all development NGOs in Malawi were addressing HIV. While government agencies continue to receive funding, donors have increasingly gravitated toward NGOs as neoliberalism became a global norm.[148] Today, numerous organizations are involved in what Swidler and Watkins call "the AIDS enterprise." This enterprise consists of various donors, like the Global Fund, USAID, DFID, and the Gates Foundation (see figure 1). Their resources support foreign research institutions, like Baylor College of Medicine and the University of North Carolina (UNC); international NGOs, like UNICEF and Save the Children; development contractors that provide technical assistance, like Management Sciences for Health; national umbrella NGOs like the Malawi Network of AIDS Service Organizations (MANASO) that connect the HIV organizations in the country to one another; national-level NGOs, like World Vision Malawi; local government structures, like district health offices; and smaller community-based organizations.[149]

HIV organizations have the human and material resources to operate in their own world. While public healthcare facilities are often understaffed, the HIV field has numerous people working within it. NGOs employ foreign medical professionals, consultants, and researchers and have also created a range of job opportunities for Malawians. Malawian elites, with college and postcollege education, often lead programs within the country, work in national offices of international organizations, and are doctors and nurses in HIV clinics. There is a much larger group of "interstitial" elites with secondary school education who do the on the ground work of implementing HIV programs.[150] They are community health workers, HIV testing and treatment counselors, prevention educators, research assistants, survey field teams, data-entry personnel, office staff, and volunteers. Malawians working in HIV care not only carry out programs, but they also reproduce a distinct culture around HIV. The HIV field has its own discourses, with buzzwords like "empower women" and categories like OVC (orphans and vulnerable children), and it produces an array of cultural objects, like billboards, radio messages, and pamphlets.[151] The ability to work in HIV NGOs and speak this discourse gives Malawians access to a global HIV field, while also giving donors their imaginary of HIV in Africa.[152]

Organizations involved in the HIV field also set up their own material infrastructure. Some are more embedded in Malawi. Organizations like UNC, Baylor College of Medicine, and Partners in Hope have been working in Malawi since the 1990s, and they have their own clinics, offices, and research facilities. For instance, in 1999, UNC worked with the Ministry of Health to establish a "center of excellence" for HIV research and care within Kamuzu Central Hospital.[153] As its own center, UNC Project and similar organizations operate on multiple fronts. They conduct research, provide HIV testing, counseling, and clinical care; they also train personnel and implement a range of donor-funded programs on HIV treatment support, maternal health, and nutrition. As the name "center

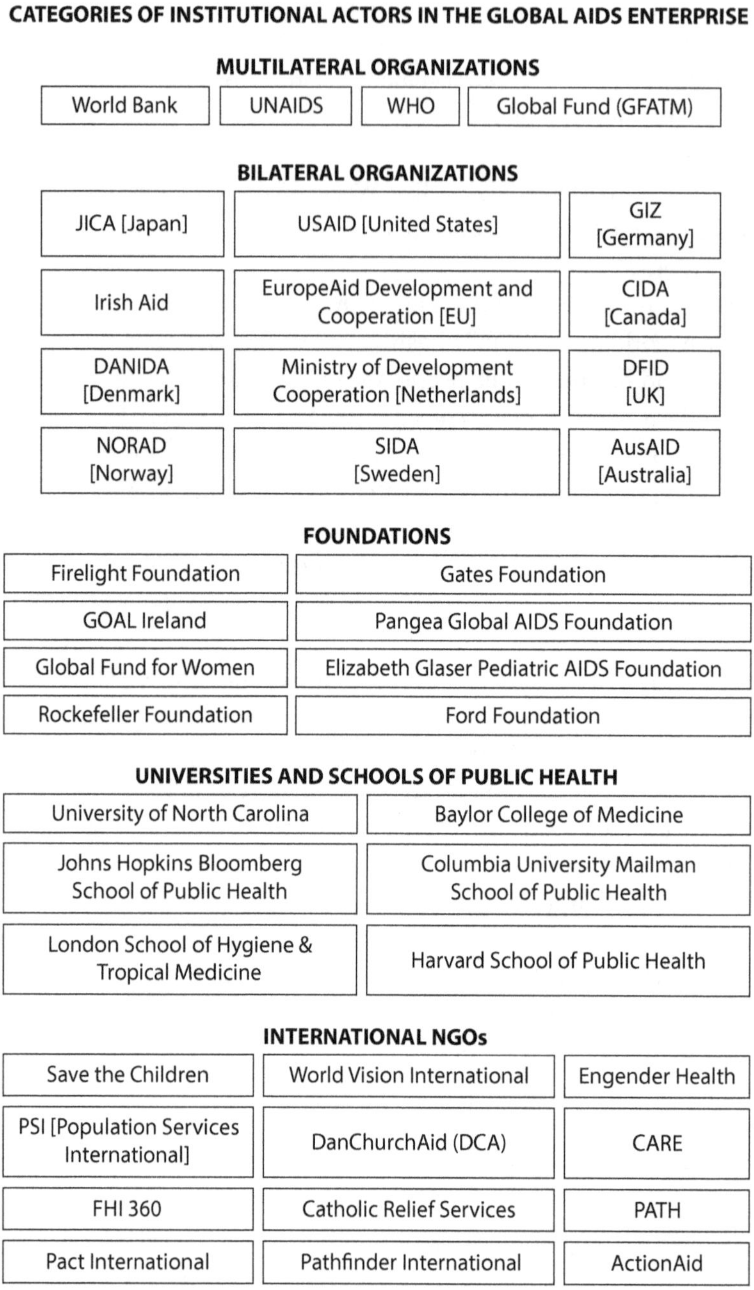

CATEGORIES OF INSTITUTIONAL ACTORS IN THE GLOBAL AIDS ENTERPRISE

MULTILATERAL ORGANIZATIONS

World Bank	UNAIDS	WHO	Global Fund (GFATM)

BILATERAL ORGANIZATIONS

JICA [Japan]	USAID [United States]	GIZ [Germany]
Irish Aid	EuropeAid Development and Cooperation [EU]	CIDA [Canada]
DANIDA [Denmark]	Ministry of Development Cooperation [Netherlands]	DFID [UK]
NORAD [Norway]	SIDA [Sweden]	AusAID [Australia]

FOUNDATIONS

Firelight Foundation	Gates Foundation
GOAL Ireland	Pangea Global AIDS Foundation
Global Fund for Women	Elizabeth Glaser Pediatric AIDS Foundation
Rockefeller Foundation	Ford Foundation

UNIVERSITIES AND SCHOOLS OF PUBLIC HEALTH

University of North Carolina	Baylor College of Medicine
Johns Hopkins Bloomberg School of Public Health	Columbia University Mailman School of Public Health
London School of Hygiene & Tropical Medicine	Harvard School of Public Health

INTERNATIONAL NGOs

Save the Children	World Vision International	Engender Health
PSI [Population Services International]	DanChurchAid (DCA)	CARE
FHI 360	Catholic Relief Services	PATH
Pact International	Pathfinder International	ActionAid

Figure 1. Categories of institutional actors in the global AIDS enterprise. SOURCE: Ann Swidler and Susan Cotts Watkins, *A Fraught Embrace: The Romance and Reality of AIDS Altruism in Africa* (Princeton University Press, 2017).

INTERNATIONAL DEVELOPMENT CONTRACTORS

Chemonics	John Snow Inc. (JSI)	Abt Associates	Management Sciences for Health

NATIONAL GOVERNMENT STRUCTURES (MALAWI)

Ministry of Health	Office of President and Cabinet Department of Nutrition, HIV and AIDS
National AIDS Commission	Other government ministries, e.g. Gender, Child Welfare and Community Services, Rural Development

REGIONAL/NATIONAL UMBRELLA NGOs (MALAWI)

African Council of AIDS Service Organizations	Council for NGOs in Malawi (CONGOMA)	Southern Africa Network of AIDS Service Organization	Malawi Network of AIDS Service Organizations (MANASO)

NATIONAL-LEVEL NGOs (MALAWI)

Catholic Development Commission in Malawi (CADECOM)	Salama Shield Foundation	National Association of People Living with HIV and AIDS (NAPHAM)
Youth Network and Counseling (YONECO)	World Vision Malawi	Society for Women and AIDS in Malawi (SWAM)

LOCAL GOVERNMENT STRUCTURES (THE SAME FORMAL STRUCTURES IN EACH OF 28 DISTRICTS, MALAWI)

Zomba District Health Office	Mchinji District Youth Officer	Nkhatabay District Social Welfare Office
Mangochi District Assembly	Chiradzulu District AIDS Coordinating Committee	Rumphi District Agriculture Office

COMMUNITY-BASED ORGANIZATIONS (MALAWI)

Bondo Youth Club	Limbikani Orphan AIDS Support Group	Phinda Community Home Based Care Organisation
Chimteka Village AIDS & Orphan Care Support	Noor Women Group	Mponela AIDS Information and Counseling Centre

of excellence" suggests, these facilities operate at a different level. They offer more advanced diagnostics and care and conduct globally recognized research that public healthcare facilities are not always equipped to do. Most organizations are less embedded. Donors often fund short-term projects that require temporary infrastructure. For instance, a research survey might require: laptops, extension cords, cameras, scanners, printers, and paper carried from abroad or purchased in Lilongwe; housing for researchers and rented minibuses to carry them around the country; biometric tools, like HIV rapid tests; and a Malawian field team to conduct the surveys across many villages.[154] At the end of the project, this infrastructure will be taken apart or repurposed for a future project.

As HIV became legible as a global emergency, donors poured immense resources into response efforts. HIV care started to develop along its own path, and over time, it has produced tangible changes in health outcomes as well as in Malawi's healthcare landscape. The world of HIV care in Malawi feels well established. HIV NGOs, clinics, centers of excellence, prevention programs, research, and discourses have been active for several decades. But, at its core, this world is temporary and precarious. The human and material infrastructure built for HIV services depends on donor funding and works largely outside of governmental institutions. Having a reliable supply chain, for instance, was crucial for the success of the HIV treatment program, but because it was never incorporated into the larger healthcare system, it only benefited one disease program and will always be reliant on donor aid. Creating a separate world of care for HIV allowed donors to bypass many of the challenges in Malawi's public healthcare system, but in doing so, it also bypassed opportunities to address those challenges. The slow emergency of the public healthcare system continues to be present. As distinct as the world of HIV care is, it cannot avoid the other world of care it sits beside.

INTERSECTING EMERGENCIES

The exceptional treatment of HIV and the slow emergency of Malawi's national health sector are distinct but intersecting worlds. With its donor funding, parallel systems, and NGO support, HIV care stands in stark contrast to the broader healthcare system. But for patients and those working in healthcare, these worlds are not experienced separately. Policymakers addressing HIV must evaluate how proposed policies would function within their healthcare system. Providers deliver HIV treatment and care in government healthcare facilities; they address overlapping populations and conditions, caring for patients with and without HIV. Patients embody multiple emergencies—HIV risk and infection cannot be easily disentangled from other health concerns or precarious livelihoods. The way that HIV care has become legible as an exceptional emergency obscures not only the larger healthcare system and social structures but also the intersections of these two worlds for local actors.

When designing Malawi's HIV treatment program, national policymakers and international consultants had to account for the constraints within the country's healthcare system. Simplicity and standardization were key components to a "low-resource" approach.[155] The country used fixed-dose tablets and had a single first- and second-line regimen for all patients, instead of having multiple treatment options. Determining eligibility for ART and monitoring patients' outcomes on treatment were often done based on clinical symptoms rather than with laboratory testing. While symptoms do signal disease progression, they are less precise than CD4 tests, which measure a patient's immune function. Amid shortages of medical professionals, HIV patients were no longer required to see a physician. The task of prescribing and refilling ART shifted down to nurses, which allowed for greater ART distribution but not necessarily greater clinical attention.[156] When Malawi's policymakers developed their 2011 Option B+ policy, they faced similar constraints in their healthcare system. The simplicity of the policy's test-and-treat approach was their way of preventing mother-to-child transmission given the longtime challenges with laboratory testing and provider shortages.

At the clinic, providers delivering HIV care also faced constraints. Nurses could prescribe ART, but they could not address the other HIV-related health concerns that patients had. In Rosenthal's study, one nurse stated: "All I can do is give him the [ART] refill and hope for the best."[157] She did not have the necessary medications to treat her patients' chronic sores, which can arise with HIV infection. ART scale-up also translated to additional work. While the Ministry of Health's quarterly supervision of

ART prevented stockouts, it created more record-keeping for providers, which was a time-consuming manual task.[158] During my fieldwork, electronic health records had been adopted, but because computer systems and electricity were unreliable, providers also manually recorded data in paper-based registers. Requirements to count pills to track ART adherence further depleted provider time and limited communication between providers and patients.[159] In the settings I observed, NGOs had a greater role in HIV care, taking on supportive tasks like HIV testing, counseling, home visits, and record keeping. But while NGOs alleviated some of the human resource challenges for HIV care, these challenges remained for providing non–HIV care.

Patients experience both exceptional and slow emergencies. HIV is still a leading cause of death in Malawi, but so too are neonatal conditions, lower respiratory infections, diarrheal diseases, malaria, and tuberculosis, and noninfectious diseases like stroke, heart disease, and liver disease, and injury (see figure 2).[160] While people living with HIV now have access to HIV treatment, they continue to struggle to receive other forms of care. In chapter 4, I discuss how pregnant women who tested positive for HIV gained access to specialized NGO programs and received intensive counseling and treatment support. But their pregnancy fell to the public sector, which with limited staff and medical supplies, could not provide all recommended services. Economic precarity is also pervasive and has long affected children's health. In the early 2000s, almost half of Malawian children under five were chronically malnourished, and one in seven died before their fifth birthday.[161] In 2018, 37 percent of children under five were still suffering from chronic malnutrition.[162] Economic conditions also shape the HIV illness experience. When patients are hungry, ART side effects can worsen, making it difficult to take treatment on a regular basis.[163] And, as I describe in chapter 5, when side effects disrupt one's ability to work, a tension between two vital needs—HIV treatment and financial survival—arises.

These intersecting emergencies are often rendered illegible. To global health institutions, mothers living with HIV are legible for their disease status but not for their pregnancy or the many other struggles they encounter in everyday life. While Malawi's PMTCT program is globally celebrated for lowering rates of maternal HIV transmission, overall maternal

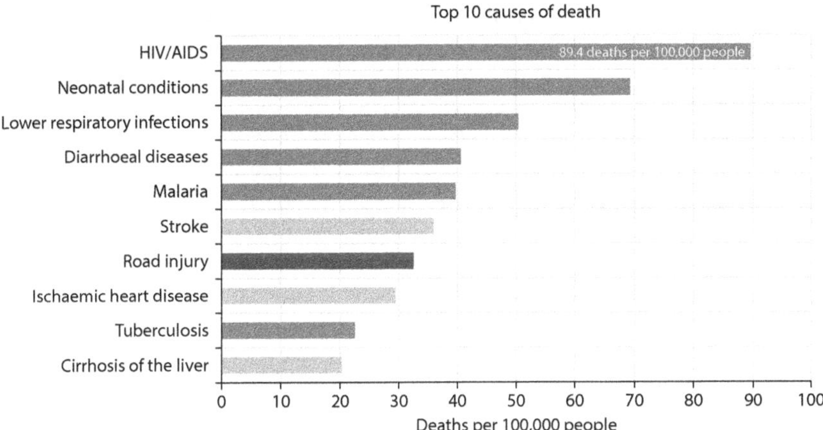

Figure 2. Top ten causes of death in 2015 in Malawi for both sexes and all ages. SOURCE: Adapted from data found in WHO, "Global Health Estimates: Leading Causes of Death," The Global Health Observatory, 2015 (accessed August 25, 2025).

mortality remains among the highest in the world.[164] In addition, the need for simplicity and standardization in HIV care sidelines those who fall outside of the standard. Patients with treatment failure have few alternative regimens to fall back on.[165] Treatment is also geared toward adult patients, leaving care for children born with HIV largely ad hoc.[166] Fixed-dose tablets are not commonly available at smaller dosages, so providers may need to cut adult pills to manage dosing for children.[167] Moreover, children and teens have unique social, emotional, and behavioral needs that providers are often not equipped to address.

Also missing are the men. A 2002 headline from *The New York Times* read: "In Africa, AIDS has the face of a woman."[168] Indeed, gender disparities in HIV prevalence are significant and persistent. In Malawi, as of 2023, despite a decline in overall rates of HIV infection, gender disparities remain: Prevalence among women aged fifteen to forty-nine was 8.4 percent, compared to 4.8 percent among their male counterparts.[169] Worldwide, women are also more likely to be infected with HIV, comprising 53 percent of infections globally.[170] However, in a generalized epidemic, like Malawi's, HIV travels mostly through heterosexual sex, making men an important part of the transmission process as well as a significant population infected with HIV. Moreover, men are more likely to die from AIDS;[171] they are less likely to be tested and tend to start treatment later in their disease progression.[172] While sex between men and women drive the HIV epidemic, it is only women who tend to be targeted for interventions. In an analysis of policy documents from the WHO, UNAIDS, and PEPFAR, women were mentioned over twice as often as men and were often framed as vulnerable and in need of aid.[173] By contrast, in these same documents, men tended to be framed as invulnerable and in power, thus making them an inappropriate target for aid. This framing assumes that "women" and "men" are homogenous categories, which neglects that gender intersects with race, class, and sexual orientation in ways that produce variation in experiences. It also neglects the structural reality of countries in sub-Saharan Africa where economic and social destabilization shape both men and women's sexual behaviors and HIV risk.[174]

As a result, interventions neglect the relational nature of HIV infection. In Malawi, because almost all women have children, provider-initiated testing and counseling for women in prenatal clinics has led to near universal testing of women; and Malawi's 2011 Option B+ policy gave pregnant and breastfeeding women access to ART as soon as they tested positive.[175] In contrast, since the 1980s, few HIV-care programs have targeted heterosexual men, and there has been little innovation beyond providing information and condom-skills-building.[176] While campaigns for "male involvement" in prenatal, maternal, and HIV care recognize men, they primarily frame men's role as a means to improve women's health rather than addressing men's own health needs.[177] By only seeing women as vulnerable, programs limit possible strategies for reducing HIV transmission. For instance, in Malawi, wealthy men are a key vector of HIV transmission, as they tend to have larger sexual networks—but they are rarely the targets of intervention.[178] Moreover, programs place the burden of responsibility for HIV prevention and treatment on women's shoulders alone. In contexts where men have greater structural and interpersonal power, asking women to take matters into their own hands often falls short of desired outcomes.[179] As I describe in chapter 5, while women received ART as part of Option B+, they then went home to difficult conversations with their husbands about their HIV infection and relationship, which could lead to more or less supportive contexts for taking treatment.

CONCLUSION

Exceptional and slow emergencies are constructed. Malawi may never have had a robust national health sector, but its continued underdevelopment was produced through various decisions over time, like prioritizing care for Europeans, limiting funding and medical training, cutting social sector spending, and funding NGOs. As a slow emergency, shortages of medical professionals, medicine, and infrastructure can feel routine and simply an unfortunate consequence of poverty. But unpacking the trajectory of Malawi's unequal worlds of care shows how present conditions in the public healthcare system are the result of decades of underinvestment and missed opportunities. The exceptionality of the global response to HIV is also a construction. Four decades into the epidemic, we take for granted that HIV is a global emergency and that it is worthy of major investment. This was not always the case. In Malawi, the first two decades of the HIV epidemic were marked by silence and invisibility. Without the collective push from activists, governments, and medical professionals, the lives of HIV patients in the Global South were not seen in an "emergency" context as urgent and exceptional.

Over time, Malawi's world of HIV care grew further apart from its public healthcare system. It is a world with its own donor resources, supply chains, research institutions, development contractors, INGOS, NGOs, and smaller CBOs. It has its own discourses and cultural production. It staffs expats and Malawians, builds physical infrastructure for clinics, offices, and centers of excellence, and provides a range of temporary infrastructure for small projects. As Street argues, ruination is not a state, but a process involving both improvement and decline: "From this perspective, ruination does not consist in a linear process of deterioration and destruction but in the dialectic between the ongoing improvement of some spaces and the simultaneous decline and abandonment of others."[180] This dialectic captures the disparate ways health issues have been addressed—in particular, the way treating HIV as an exception has detached it from the broader healthcare system and from other social structures. While HIV became legible as an emergency that must be addressed through humanitarian aid, the slow emergency of the public healthcare system—shaped over generations—remains illegible. This illegibility is particularly striking in the contemporary context, where, through the HIV epidemic, we have seen that large-scale foreign-aid mobilization is possible. The dialectic also captures how patients and healthcare workers in Malawi are situated between unequal worlds of care, experiencing them not as separate domains but as co-existing and intertwined. While donors may focus on developing HIV programs, Malawian policymakers, providers, and patients see and experience both the improvements in certain aspects of healthcare and the stagnation or decline of others. This chapter has described how Malawi's unequal worlds of care formed. In the following chapters, I describe how being situated between these worlds produces a politics—a struggle between what donors and international organizations see as worthy of aid and how healthcare is actually practiced and experienced on the ground.

2 For the Mothers and Children of Our Country

In 2011, Malawi began implementing their national policy for preventing mother-to-child transmission of HIV (PMTCT), called Option B+. Following a simple test-and-treat approach, the policy gave pregnant and breastfeeding women access to lifelong antiretroviral therapy (ART) as soon as they tested positive. Option B+ would later serve as the foundation for what is now the global standard of HIV care—namely, ensuring that every adult who tests positive for HIV receives immediate access to lifelong treatment. But the development of Option B+ was unusual. Malawi, a small country in sub-Saharan Africa, had gone against the World Health Organization (WHO), the UN agency responsible for managing global public health, whose policy recommendations are seen as the international gold standard. The WHO had recommended two different options: Option A, which relied on a combination of other medications to prevent mother-to-child transmission, or Option B, which temporarily placed women on ART while they were pregnant and breastfeeding. After breastfeeding ended, like other adult patients, women would be eligible for lifelong ART when their illness progressed to a certain degree of severity as measured by CD4 count, a laboratory test of immune system function, or based on clinical symptoms. While the difference between the WHO's policies and Malawi's Option B+ may appear minor—a matter of when women start lifelong ART—it is significant given the global power dynamics in which these policy decisions take place.

In an article for *The Lancet*, a leading medical journal, John Donnelly reported: "Malawi's decision marks an unusual stand by a developing country against WHO guidelines for treatment of a disease."[1] Unlike the WHO, Malawi is navigating global politics from a position of far less power and authority. Malawi's decision was also unusual because the country relies on donor funding for their HIV program. Despite this, the Malawi Ministry of Health started Option B+ before donors were fully on board. Thomas Warne of the CDC, for instance, said that the costs were "substantial" and that the "US government, like other donors, is not in a position to advocate either way."[2] In addition, some scientists called Option B+ "premature," arguing that it was not backed by evidence and a full assessment of risks.[3] UNICEF also raised human rights concerns over whether Malawi was giving women a choice in their treatment and what it means to give one group access to ART before others.[4]

But the Malawi Ministry of Health stood by their policy. As Dr. Frank Chimbwandira, the director of the HIV/AIDS Service, said, "This is something we're doing for the mothers and children in our country."[5] Policymakers believed that Option B+ was a policy that would work in their healthcare setting and for their patients. The stakes were high—without proper treatment, about one-third of children born from HIV positive mothers would contract HIV. Policymakers argued that they needed to implement Option B+ right away because it would be unethical to wait two to three years for the results of a pilot study.[6] The risk paid off. A couple of years later, Malawi's policy would become a new gold standard in PMTCT care. In 2013, the WHO listed Option B+ in their policy recommendations for all countries. Why and how did Malawi's policymakers develop Option B+? While they had less power in the global health field, how did they assert their ideas and make their policy legible to a global audience?

This chapter highlights the politics between international organizations and national policymakers over how to address health problems. Option B+ was motivated by the failure of past WHO policies to control maternal HIV transmission. As the global health field moved toward more targeted and pharmaceutical approaches, what was legible to the WHO were policies that relied on evidence-based medication regimens while the conditions of healthcare systems in which policies would be implemented were illegible. But to Malawi's policymakers, this illegible world was a central concern—they needed policies to work in their healthcare system. Option B+ was designed around a unique set of constraints. Donors provided HIV testing and treatment but did little to support healthcare providers, laboratories, or data management. Option B+'s test-and-treat approach leveraged donor commodities while making implementation far simpler for their staff. In this case, Malawi's policymakers successfully pushed back against the demands of international organizations and made their policy legible to a global audience. Though they relied on donors for funding, they took advantage of other resources—close ties to NGOs, their knowledge of the field, and professional networks in and outside the country—to promote their policy and create a new global norm.

CHANGING GLOBAL NORMS AND POLICIES

Malawi's Option B+ policy challenges sociological expectations of where policy innovations come from and how they spread globally. Early work by scholars of world society theory emphasized the top-down diffusion of policies, in which cultural models established at the global level shape actions at national levels. From this perspective, international organizations are important "teachers of norms."[7] While international organizations lack the legal authority to impose policies on countries, they possess rational-voluntaristic authority. Because countries see themselves as part of a larger social contract, they find it rational to comply with models espoused by international organizations.[8] Scholars point to the global convergence of policies in areas such as sexual violence legislation, human rights, education, and security-sector reform to demonstrate that countries respond to cultural models at the global level rather than to domestic interests alone.[9]

In addition to normative influences, coercive pressures also shape policy adoption. This is especially the case for low-income countries that depend on aid, loans, and trade from wealthier countries.[10] Foreign aid often comes with conditional terms.[11] Structural adjustment policies are a notable example—in order to receive loans from the World Bank or International Monetary Fund, countries had to make significant changes to economic policies, such as reduce government spending, open free trade, and devalue currency.[12] In global health, countries may adopt donor-funded initiatives despite what they believe to be the country's health needs.[13] Biesma's review of national health systems showed numerous instances in which funding applications for national priorities, such as health systems strengthening or counseling for abortion, were rejected by donors, who had strict requirements for allocating funding.[14] Such patterns illustrate how, despite varying health needs and healthcare systems, policies across countries may look quite similar due to pressures to conform to donor requirements.

Top-down models of policy diffusion help account for the global convergence of policies. But they offer little insight into uneven policy diffusion or surprising moments like Malawi's Option B+ decision. From the standpoint of world society theory, resistance is limited to the decoupling of formal policy adoption and actual practice.[15] For instance, countries can adopt policies but fail to implement them (policy-practice); they can implement policies but for different goals (means-end); and they can adopt policies but only implement them for segments of the population (differentiated decoupling).[16] However, while decoupling acknowledges flexibility with practices, it generally entails a static and unidirectional view of global norms. The starting point is norms already created by powerful global institutions; what countries can control is the extent to which they follow through on their commitments.

But global norms also change. Halliday and Carruthers conceptualize global norms as recursive, emphasizing the cyclical nature of global policymaking whereby policy agendas are reshaped by local divergences.[17] Conflicts may arise when global and national actors disagree on a problem or solution, or when there are disagreements within international organizations. Such tensions can drive cycles of change. Understanding the diffusion of policies and resistance to them requires a closer look at the actors shaping and promoting these policies the practices through which they are enacted. Chorev's work on pharmaceutical patents for HIV medications shows how developing countries challenged global institutions through a process of "reactive diffusion."[18] Less powerful countries learned how to leverage exceptions and flexibilities in WTO patent laws and then shared that information with one another, and this accumulation of experiences led to transformations in global norms around access to medicines.[19] In Chorev's case, transnational activists and state officials played a key role in spreading information and strategies between countries.

With transnational governance, there is a messy assemblage of organizations and actors coming from multiple international organizations, governments, NGOs, and firms that need to coordinate on issues. What this assemblage of actors does matters for how policies are adopted, changed, or resisted. As Halliday notes, these actors stand between global and local contexts and are "key conduits for the creation and implementation of norms."[20] The transnational nature of global health policy is important. Those working in this field often traverse different networks. They have relationships with other policymakers, NGOs, academic and professional networks, former employers, international organizations where they have consulted, and other professional contacts.[21] How global health professionals navigate their peer and organizational networks may be important for shaping the extent to which they control transnational issues.[22] In addition, professionals do not necessarily represent their profession or the organization they work for. In other words, we cannot assume that someone working for a particular organization—say, UNAIDS, CDC, or PEPFAR—shares the organization's official stance on an issue and always complies with it. Thus, in order to explain policy adoption or resistance, we need to understand the actual practices, interests, and strategies of professionals navigating their field.

This chapter focuses on actors in Malawi who were involved in HIV policymaking and their role in developing Option B+. By following the work of Malawi's policymakers, I also draw attention to the role of professionals in global health. In this field, there are state officials, representatives of international organizations and NGOs, researchers, healthcare providers, and consultants who are involved in health policymaking. Though their work is what ultimately creates policy, their practices are not well understood. Theoretically, unpacking the story of Option B+ helps us understand how and why uneven policy diffusion and resistance to global policies and norms occur. In the following sections, I describe the tensions that emerged with WHO policies and how Malawi's policymakers strategically promoted a new policy in the face of structures meant to impose conformity. The in-between position that some policymakers occupied, as part of both the global HIV field and working in local healthcare institutions, served as a conduit to promote new policy ideas. Their actions made Option B+, and more broadly the conditions of healthcare systems in which policies are implemented, legible to donors and international organizations who have often rendered these conditions illegible.

CHALLENGES WITH PAST WHO POLICIES

Prior to Option B+, Malawi struggled with preventing mother-to-child transmission of HIV. As in many countries, Malawi had followed WHO policy recommendations. Before WHO policy recommendations are published, they go through a rigorous review process. The WHO conducts a systematic literature review that assesses the quality of evidence in studies published on the topic and convenes experts to evaluate various treatment options for safety and efficacy. In the years leading up to Option B+, Malawi had been implementing the 2006 WHO policy for PMTCT. But WHO polices failed to work in Malawi's healthcare system. What was legible to the WHO was the disease and medications that could effectively prevent HIV transmission but not the healthcare systems in which these policies would be enacted. Though illegible, the conditions of healthcare systems critically shaped the outcome of PMTCT policies.

The idea for Option B+ emerged within the HIV/AIDS unit of the Malawi Ministry of Health around 2010. In the HIV/AIDS unit, technical advisors from donor-funded NGOs worked alongside state employees. Since 2003, the International Training and Education Center for Health (I-TECH), a PEPFAR-funded program, has supported Malawi's national HIV response, primarily by seconding experts to the Ministry of Health and other institutions to provide technical assistance. In 2009, there was a team from I-TECH supporting the HIV treatment program. The team's focus had been on routine tasks, such as updating the monitoring and evaluation system. However, they soon realized that something was wrong—WHO policies were not working. Technical advisors updated data collection tools to standardized patient registers based on unique identification numbers to ensure that each patient was counted and only counted once. In doing so, they discovered inaccuracies in past data on PMTCT that led to a false appearance of positive results. As a technical advisor explained:

> It became very obvious that the numbers we had looked at before weren't real. And there were a few factors that we identified as the main culprit. One was the double counting that came from antenatal records. Because we had a visit-based reporting system before, so we couldn't distinguish between women and visits. And so somebody who got nevirapine was counted potentially multiple times on the subsequent visits. It looked as if it was women receiving nevirapine, but it was the same woman counted three times. It was also that there wasn't a standardized primary record at the sites, so it was all improvised hard cover registers.

While donors and international organizations require data to be collected, the quality of that data is variable.[23] Ministry of Health actors were not maliciously trying to "cook" the books. In this case, the Ministry did not have staff with expertise in designing a patient register system or resources to train providers at healthcare facilities on how to collect data. HIV data was legible to global health institutions, but the system for collecting it was not. Moreover, there were incentives for both donors and national programs to show good results—for example, to show that money was well spent and the country was implementing programs well, which as one technical advisor explained, "led to some very optimistic reporting."

The HIV/AIDS unit realized that the 2006 WHO policy did little to slow down rates of maternal HIV transmission. About one-third of children born from HIV-positive mothers contracted the virus, which is roughly the same rate as if there had been no intervention at all.[24] As one technical advisor described: "We had analyzed our PMTCT program, it was struggling. It was a mess, basically. Whenever we looked at transmission rates, they were still hovering above thirty, above thirty, no matter what we do." The 2006 WHO policy relied on a combination of preventative medications. To prevent maternal HIV transmission, mothers who were not yet eligible for lifelong ART for their own health needed to take: zidovudine (AZT) starting at twenty-eight weeks of pregnancy; a combination of single-dose nevirapine, zidovudine, and lamivudine (sd-NVP +AZT+3TC) during labor and delivery; and zidovudine and lamivudine (AZT + 3TC) for seven days postpartum. Their infants needed to take sd-NVP + AZT for seven days. The WHO also recommended that mothers limit breastfeeding to six months.[25] The policy was simpler for mothers already on lifelong ART, who added seven days of AZT for their infant. But as we will see below, determining eligibility for lifelong ART was itself a challenge in Malawi. WHO policies had failed—but not because they were medically unsound. The medications in the 2006 WHO policy could indeed prevent maternal HIV transmission. But getting medications to hospitals, having enough providers to prescribe and explain the regimen to patients, and following their progress over time was a different story. What was illegible to creators of WHO policies was how the policies would work in local healthcare systems. And this was where things fell apart in Malawi.

Malawi faced several challenges. First, there were challenges with the medication supply chain. In an evaluation of Malawi's Central Medical Stores Trust (CMST), Mueller et al. noted several challenges, including cumbersome World Bank procurement procedures, insufficient staff to perform quantification, high staff turnover, poor warehousing and lack of space, poor inventory systems, and lack of funds to procure sufficient drugs in advance.[26] Stockouts of medication were common. The HIV/AIDS unit found that while the preventative medications for the 2006 WHO policy were purchased, they were not necessarily available at healthcare facilities. One of the technical advisors explained: "It was pretty much a black hole. So things were received, UNICEF delivered to the CMST receipt station, and then after that, it became difficult to figure out where things went."

Second, healthcare providers struggled to remember the details of the WHO policy. Malawi had a critical shortage of health workers—defined as fewer than 2.28 doctors, nurses and midwives per one thousand people—with only 0.019 physicians and 0.283 nurses and midwives per one thousand people.[27] At that time, about 50 percent of available posts in the Ministry of Health were filled.[28] Providers working in public healthcare facilities were often stretched thin, with each individual responsible for numerous patients across several departments. Under these conditions, it can be difficult to recall complex medication regimens. A technical advisor described a key moment when they realized the WHO policy was not feasible for providers. He said:

> And we had one amazing observation that when the ANC [antenatal care] and maternity registers were introduced, I conducted the TOT [training of trainers]. We had a room full of eighty or so program coordinators from the districts and the big leading sites, and not one of them at that time was able to recite the policy that was supposed to be used for the combination prophylaxis. It was evidently too complicated for even the program coordinators to recall what was supposed to happen. So, that really just drove home the point that it was an unrealistically complicated and differentiated policy that just couldn't be implemented.

Though WHO policies are meant to be simple and standardized so that they can be widely implemented, with severe health worker shortages, policies that seem simple may actually be challenging in practice.

Third, it was difficult for the HIV/AIDS unit to monitor women's use of treatment over time. Once a woman was diagnosed with HIV, it was on good faith that she took the WHO's combination of preventative medications. Many women come to the prenatal clinic for their first visit and receive HIV testing but do not always complete all of the recommended services for preventing maternal HIV transmission and prenatal care. Studies show that less than 20 percent returned for all subsequent prenatal care, delivery, and postnatal visits.[29] With few follow-up visits, providers did not know how women were doing on the preventative medications—or if they were taking them at all.

New Policy, Same Problems

When the WHO released updated policy recommendations in 2010, the HIV/AIDS unit saw that they would face similar problems. The 2010 WHO policies included two options. Option A was another version of the 2006 policy—it relied on the same combination of preventative medicines but included updates to the regimen for exposed infants and breastfeeding practices.[30] Option B would temporarily place women on ART during pregnancy and breastfeeding.[31] After breastfeeding, like other HIV patients, women would be eligible to start lifelong ART based on the severity of their illness. If her CD4 count was below 350, she would start lifelong

ART; if it was above 350, she would stop ART until her illness progresses to a further stage. According to the WHO, following either option should significantly reduce rates of maternal HIV transmission. They stated that the *elimination* of maternal transmission was "now considered a realistic public health goal."[32]

Malawi's policymakers felt that neither of the two options given by the WHO would work in their context. Option A was dismissed right away. It was too similar to the intricate 2006 policy and would obviously fail. As a technical advisor explained: "So we could embark on Option A and do a very lousy job at it. . . . We're not going to set ourselves on a path of failure." Option B was simpler, but it would also cause problems in Malawi. The country did not have enough working CD4 machines to implement the policy. In a feasibility appraisal for the WHO, the Ministry of Health noted that "in quarter 4, 2010, only 60 out of 417 ART clinics in the country had a CD4 machine of which only 53 produced any results in that 3-month period."[33] Many machines were broken or did not have the correct reagents—the substances used in chemical analysis—to run the tests. After donors purchased CD4 machines, the machines became illegible, with the logistics of their maintenance left to government agencies that had limited resources for fixing machines, buying reagents, or ensuring electricity to power laboratories. A technical advisor explained the problem:

> Some of the machines have broken down, so they have not been functioning for a week, for two weeks, and so on and so forth. They have run out of reagents. They have been given wrong reagents. At that time, we had two types of machines. We had Partec and the BD, Becton Dickinson BD. . . . So, this country had two CD4 testing machines because we had to follow the procurement processes. And the reagents do not cross match. So, there were many cases where you have Partec reagents delivered to a health facility which has BD. BD facilities are receiving Partec reagents. And the one who is receiving the reagents is just receiving really. . . . They just deliver a note, they sign, the delivery vehicle leaves. And then they realize, two to three days later, "Oh, we got the wrong reagents."

These kinds of mishaps are not uncommon in the global health field. There are many donors, and each may have different requirements for how medical commodities are purchased and distributed.

In addition, implementing the WHO's Option B would require an overhaul of how the HIV/AIDS unit tracked drug supplies. The HIV/AIDS unit counted the total number of HIV patients on lifelong ART at each facility, which made it easy to calculate the "opening and closing balance" of drugs at the end of each quarter. This was important because they needed to report drug supplies to donors on a quarterly basis.[34] Because the WHO's Option B asked women whose CD4 count was above 350 to start and stop ART, the HIV/AIDS unit would need to base their data collection system on cohorts of patients rather than total counts. They saw no way to track cohorts on a nationwide scale. Their projections for ART supplies assumed that patients continued taking medication, and it would be logistically challenging to make projections when some patients were discontinuing their allocation. As one technical advisor explained: "We wouldn't know how many are due to start now, and how many are due to stop. You see? Our calculations were based on patients continuing to take drugs. . . . So for the projections, we now had to be capping, discontinuing their allocation and that was going to be a logistical challenge." Technical advisors also felt that starting and stopping treatment would be cumbersome in Malawi's cultural context, where women on average were having five to six children. Women would likely stop treatment only to restart soon after with a subsequent pregnancy.

Ultimately, these challenges have implications for patients. Without working CD4 machines, for instance, women may not know whether they are eligible to start ART and thus delay treatment. One study found that over half of the HIV-positive pregnant women in their sample did not know their CD4 count or had never been clinically staged.[35] Women had learned of their ART eligibility from participating in the study. Delays in treatment have negative implications for women's long-term health and increase the risk that children become infected with HIV. PMTCT programs have high stakes. Without intervention, around 25–35 percent of infected mothers will transmit HIV to their child. In the years prior to Option B+, approximately 50 percent of HIV positive children in Malawi died before age two.[36] One technical advisor explained:

> We saw that pediatric AIDS burden. And to this day, pediatric treatment is a mess. The viral suppression rates amongst kids in Malawi are around 50 percent, 60 percent. But out of 85 percent or 90 percent, they're not doing

> well on ART. And the long term . . . Firstly, most of them still don't get detected early enough to start treatment while they're asymptomatic. They come in sick. If you have a sick infant in Malawi, you're screwed. It's just a disaster. And so it seemed really obvious that we needed to do something drastic. We couldn't just look the other way and say, "That's the PMTCT Program, so we'll just deal with ART." So it seemed really unethical just to continue pushing for something that had, in our eyes, no promise of ever working.

Donors and international organizations had a partial vision of maternal HIV transmission. WHO policies addressed a biological mechanism of disease transmission through medications but not the practical challenges of getting medications to patients. These partial visions have historical roots. Looking back, in the 1970s, the WHO was a major proponent of healthcare as a right and for promoting primary healthcare for all, but as neoliberalism took hold, they had to adapt to the changing climate and focus on cost-effective disease priorities.[37] While the WHO acknowledges healthcare systems, they try to design policies that work *around* those systems. Their goal is to keep policies simple and standardized, rather than tailored to individuals, so that they are feasible given constraints in low-income settings. In the 2010 policy recommendations, the WHO did note potential challenges with implementation, writing that key activities, such as identifying HIV-positive women, screening for ART eligibility, and linking PMTCT with HIV treatment programs, could "burden health systems (including health facilities and healthcare workers) or could fail to be implemented unless simple new health system protocols and practices are tested locally and put in place."[38] But they concluded that the policies should not add greater burdens to existing healthcare systems.

Government workers and technical advisors in the HIV/AIDS unit saw Malawi's healthcare needs from a different position. Though they faced expectations from donors and international organizations to follow WHO policies, they did not want to do so blindly. Knowing the problems with past WHO policies, they were primarily concerned with the practical challenges of implementation in their healthcare system. The work of the I-TECH technical advisors also brings to light ironies in the global health field. Technical advisors worked for donor-funded programs meant to improve Malawi's response to the HIV epidemic. But Malawi's HIV response is itself constrained by the partial way donors see healthcare—the country cannot truly improve its HIV services separately from the rest of its healthcare system. The problems that technical advisors found had little to do with the efficacy of the HIV test kits or medications that donors purchased; instead, they were with the management of supply chains, hospital staffing, data collection tools, and the mismatch between WHO policies and local fertility patterns. Given these issues, the HIV/AIDS unit was motivated to try something new.

MALAWI'S OPTION B+ POLICY

The idea for Option B+ came out of discussions around the 2010 WHO policy recommendations. The HIV/AIDS unit took the WHO's Option B, which placed women temporarily on ART, and changed it to lifelong ART—making the policy Option B *plus*. This change would solve several problems. It eliminated requirements for a CD4 test to determine when HIV-positive women should start lifelong ART. As one technical advisor said plainly, "We can't do it [CD4] anyway." Lifelong ART also made sense based on fertility patterns. A technical advisor explained: "According to our statistics, we could see that a pregnant woman, after she has delivered, it would take only about a year or two before she needs ARVs. . . . So, what are you doing? You're just postponing ARVs for a year or two? It didn't make sense to us." The test-and-treat model of Option B+ would also be easy for healthcare providers. HIV testing was already routine in prenatal clinics, and prescribing ART was simpler than remembering more complex combinations of preventative medicines that often changed each time the WHO updated its recommendations. Keeping women on ART also made it easier for the HIV/AIDS unit to collect data. The HIV/AIDS unit would not need to make major changes to their monitoring and evaluation system. Pregnant women would count the same as any other adult HIV patient on ART; they only needed small modifications to the clinic registers to accommodate an additional reason for starting treatment.

Option B+ threaded the needle between legible and illegible worlds of care. The policy design leveraged the hypervisibility of HIV treatment programs. By placing pregnant women on ART, policymakers turned PMTCT, which at the time was a distinct program, into part of the larger adult HIV treatment program. In doing so, policymakers could rely on an ART supply chain that donors managed attentively. In the early 2000s, donors had created a separate supply chain for ART. At the time, there was discussion around using donor funds for ART to improve the national system for procurement and supply chain management, but this was quickly curtailed when the World Bank advised donors against using Malawi's Central Medical Stores Trust in favor of NGOs.[39] To this day, UNICEF oversees ART supplies in the country. The Global Fund, which purchases most of the ART, also has strict reporting requirements. On a quarterly basis, the HIV/AIDS unit sends out a supervision team to audit patient data and conduct physical checks of drug stock.[40] The result of donors' attention to ART management is that there are few stockouts of this medication. Though it would be politically contentious to increase the amount of ART donors would need to purchase for Option B+, policymakers knew that *if* they could increase their ART stock, there was a system in place that would ensure medication would be available for treatment based on their policy.

At the same time, the extreme simplicity of Option B+ spoke to constraints in the public healthcare system. With little donor support to improve laboratory function, hospital infrastructure, supply chains, and staff shortages, paring a policy down to as few steps as possible was a solution with the potential to work in their setting. Simplicity, though, has its drawbacks. A member of the PMTCT department in the Ministry of Health felt that using ART glossed over the specificities of maternal and child healthcare. The policy would be "almost turning maternal and child health facilities into ART [clinics]." He explained:

> In my comparison with ART, PMTCT is a bit more complex. You are talking about testing of the woman. You are talking about delivering the [baby]. . . . You are talking about following both the mother and the child. You're talking about testing the child. If the child is infected, to be put on treatment. And then to link them. . . . While with ART, you are talking about [testing] positive, start ART.

Later, in chapter 5, we will see that for women living with HIV, Option B+'s test-and-treat approach was not always easy. It meant that they managed a new diagnosis, lifelong prescription, and pregnancy at once while also navigating how their HIV status affected their sense of self, marriage, and work obligations.

To the HIV/AIDS unit, Option B+ followed a public health approach. While this can mean different things, such as reducing population illness by managing risk factors or focusing on preventative measures, in Malawi, a public health approach had a distinct meaning: providing care for the maximum number of people given resource constraints. It could be considered the opposite of personalized or precision medicine, which seeks to tailor treatments to individual characteristics and needs and has become popular in the global North. As a technical advisor described: "It's quite simple. It's the best for the most basically. Being willing to cut a few corners in terms of things that we are unlikely to achieve. It's being very pragmatic, and recognizing the constraints that are unlikely to be overcome." With Option B+, policymakers felt that the simplicity of the policy, and thus the ease with which it could be implemented, would allow them to help more patients. To critics who might argue that the country is providing "second-rate medicine," a technical advisor said:

> If some American university implements a clinic in Uganda, and they can show fabulous outcomes, and it will read in a paper like, "In Uganda we have delivered ART to these people, and everybody's happy, and healthy, and everybody's recovered." And so, that's the opposite of the public health approach because it's almost like a bailout. They can throw twenty American physicians at a two-thousand-strong patient cohort, and surprise, surprise, it looks really good.

To him, these programs are "not representative of what happens to the 99.9 percent of the population that are never going to have access to that kind of level of care." Unlike NGOs who only need to demonstrate the success of their particular project (which is easier to do with donor funding), those working in the Ministry of Health are concerned with improving health outcomes across the entire population of Malawi. By keeping Option B+ simple, they hoped to have a bigger impact on population health.

The design of Option B+ reflects a healthcare landscape in which certain issues are legible to donors but not others. While the change from temporary to lifelong ART may seem like a small twist on WHO's Option B, it is significant given Malawi's place in global power dynamics. By pursuing their own policy, Malawi was challenging the wisdom of the preeminent global public health institution. In addition, Malawi's HIV/AIDS program depends almost entirely on donor funding. Without explicit support from donors to purchase additional supplies of ART, switching to lifelong ART for Option B+ was risky. And yet, from a position of less power and authority, Malawi legitimized their policy and created a new global norm for preventing mother-to-child transmission. In the following sections, I describe how policymakers made Option B+ legible to the global health field and secured the resources necessary for the policy to succeed.

A NEW PROCESS FOR POLICYMAKING

The structure of policymaking in Malawi helped the HIV/AIDS unit promote their idea for Option B+. National HIV policies are made in a unique way. In this area, governance is no longer a matter only for civil servants in government agencies but is instead increasingly shared with nongovernmental organizations and actors. The incorporation of NGOs into government policymaking was part of a broader neoliberal trend in global health, according to which donors moved away from state-led initiatives to relying on NGOs.[41] Brass describes a new hybrid structure that has emerged since the 1990s:

> Often at the behest of donors, who would like governments to coordinate its activities with private actors, NGOs now sit on government policymaking boards, development committees, and stakeholder forums; their strategies and policies are integrated into national planning documents; and their methods of decision making have, over time, become embedded in government's own. NGOs have become institutionalized in the governing processes of public service provision.[42]

In Malawi, the Council for Non-Governmental Organisations in Malawi (CONGOMA) was established in 1992 as an umbrella organization for all NGOs in the country, and with the passage of the 2001 Non-Governmental Organizations Act, CONGOMA was formally tasked with promoting coordination between the NGO sector, the government, the donor community, and the commercial sector in Malawi.[43] In Malawi's first Growth and Development Strategy in 2005 and its subsequent iterations, NGOs were considered a key stakeholder.[44] For HIV care, donor funding comes with expectations to include nongovernmental actors in policymaking processes. In a study by Nitsan Chorev and collaborators, a Global Fund representative stated: "But when we say country-owned, we don't necessarily mean government-owned. Of course, it means beyond that, it means all stakeholders in the country."[45] For countries to apply for a Global Fund grant, they must develop their proposal with stakeholders, which include NGOs, civil society, academic institutions, faith-based organizations, people living with HIV, the private sector, and multilateral and bilateral agencies.[46]

On the one hand, a hybrid structure imposes conformity. Requiring stakeholder involvement means that the interests of donors, international organizations, and NGOs are expressed in national policies. But, on the other hand, it also can create unique opportunities for groups with less power to assert their interests. The HIV/AIDS unit in the Ministry of Health could be considered a "pocket within the state": an exceptional, relatively autonomous agency, with unusual access to donor funding and alliances, that is distinct from other state bureaucracies.[47] In India, Vijayakumar found that the hybrid structure of the National AIDS Control Program created space for activists to demand rights for sexual minorities and sex workers.[48] Though these groups were stigmatized and criminalized in the country, they were accepted by the state as important target populations for HIV-prevention programs, health interventions, and resources.[49] With hybrid structures, we need to rethink who policymakers are and how these structures can enable and constrain opportunities for certain groups.

In the HIV/AIDS unit of the Malawi Ministry of Health, state civil servants work alongside members of donor-funded NGOs. Most state agencies include some NGO representatives, but due to the significant funding allocated to HIV NGOs, the HIV/AIDS unit has a particularly large number of NGOs involved in their policymaking process. The HIV/AIDS unit is also physically set apart from the rest of the Ministry of Health, with its own building in another part of Lilongwe. HIV-care policies are discussed in Technical Working Groups (TWGs) in which "development partners" participate. TWGs include members of the Ministry of Health, NGO representatives, consultants, physicians, and researchers in the country. In a TWG meeting for HIV care and treatment, one might see members of Médecins Sans Frontières (MSF), Baylor University, the Clinton Health Access Initiative (CHAI), Elizabeth Glazer Pediatric AIDS Foundation (EGPAF), Dignitas, Partners in Hope, University of North Carolina (UNC), Lighthouse, and more discussing policy issues with the HIV/AIDS unit. The HIV/AIDS unit takes the recommendations that emerge from TWG discussions, makes final decisions, and presents them to the principal secretary for final approval.[50] And, like other countries receiving Global Fund resources, Malawi also has a country coordinating mechanism through which stakeholders are required to participate in grant applications.

Many of the actors involved in developing Option B+ personally embodied the hybridity of policymaking. The HIV/AIDS unit itself was a hybrid space. While the technical advisors from I-TECH were part of a donor-funded NGO, they were also embedded in Malawi's public healthcare system as part of the Ministry of Health HIV/AIDS unit. In addition, each had spent years working within the Ministry of Health or in local healthcare facilities. Some were foreigners who had lived in Malawi for many years, while others were Malawian nationals with backgrounds in medicine or public health. They were all well connected in the global health field. Prior to joining I-TECH, they may have studied in leading academic institutions in the United States and Europe or worked at other major NGOs.

Some members of the Technical Working Groups had similar positionalities as the I-TECH technical advisors. While there were TWG participants who briefly visited Malawi to share new agendas from their NGO, the most active participants were NGO representatives who had been living and working in Malawi for many years. Some were foreigners working in HIV clinics, running NGO programs, or conducting research in Malawi, and some were Malawian nationals with backgrounds in medicine or public health who had started working for NGOs. HIV policymaking in Malawi includes a wide range of actors. The unique positionality of actors in this space raises questions about what it means to be a state or nonstate actor or a "global" or "local" one. While nonstate actors are a part of the policymaking process, their experiences, roles, and how they see healthcare issues vary. Many of the actors who were involved with Option B+ straddled different worlds of care, simultaneously belonging to the global HIV field and to Malawi's public healthcare system. How they understood healthcare problems and solutions was sometimes distinct from the official stances of the organizations they represented. In the story of Option B+, we will see how hybrid policymaking processes and the positionality of being between global and local institutions were instrumental for making a new policy legible to a global audience.

MAKING OPTION B+ LEGIBLE

While members of the HIV/AIDS unit may have developed the idea of Option B+, they could not adopt the policy without agreement from their "development partners." They had to come to a collective decision. In this case, Malawi's HIV/AIDS unit strategically used the hybrid structure of policymaking, promoting their idea with various nonstate representatives. Making Option B+ legible started with building consensus among the actors working in Malawi.

The HIV/AIDS unit used the Technical Working Group for HIV care and treatment to introduce Option B+. This TWG was known to be very active and had strong representation from numerous HIV NGOs in the country. The HIV/AIDS unit organizes the TWGs and always calls a meeting when the WHO releases new policy recommendations. For Option B+, they used a strategy similar to what institutional sociologists describe as brokering, when "strategic actors present themselves as neutral in a situation to mediate two groups."[51] They set up the meeting as if it were an ordinary TWG to discuss new 2010 WHO policy recommendations. NGO members described going into the TWG prepared to discuss the WHO's Option A and B, having no idea that a third option would be presented. Some already prepared presentations in favor of one of the two WHO options. By using the existing TWG format, the HIV/AIDS unit allowed participants to debate one another on Options A and B, and as they did so, many of the same issues that the HIV/AIDS unit found earlier were raised. For instance, one member of the TWG explained: "I was at the TWG and had given a presentation on Option A versus Option B. . . . Then, we had this breakout small group. . . . In that small group, we were discussing some of the implementation challenges that might happen with Option A." Another TWG member, who works at an HIV clinic, recalled that in his group's discussion, they noted problems with Option B and Malawi's fertility rates. Drawing from observations within their own healthcare facilities, he explained:

> If you go to the Bwaila general clinic, the mothers there are young, these are teen mothers. So, you know that in the coming fifteen, eighteen months, they would be coming back with another pregnancy. So, we said, "Okay, let's just move on that." So, that's when we discussed and discussed, "Okay, what else?" So, if it is beyond B, what is it?

Just as TWG participants were grappling with how to implement the WHO policy options, the HIV/AIDS unit brought up the idea of Option B+. Several participants felt that it was a natural solution. A TWG member who had given a presentation on Option A described being "totally bought in" by the idea of Option B+ because it dealt with implementation challenges that he had just discussed. Like the technical advisors in the HIV/AIDS unit, several members of the TWG had worked in Malawi for many years or were Malawian healthcare providers now working for an NGO. Problems such as lack of CD4 machines or shortages of healthcare providers were obvious because these TWG members had personally experienced them. A researcher at an HIV clinic, for instance, had worked in Malawi since the start of the country's ART program in the early 2000s. She felt that the early PMTCT policies with single doses of nevirapine (NVP) worked well because it was simple, but when policies turned toward the more complex combination therapy, that was when things "really imploded." For her, the simplicity of Option B+ made immediate sense. Similarly, another TWG member, recalled giving lectures on the 2006 policy (what would be called Option A in the 2010 guidelines) that left medical residents and nurses confused. In their program reports, they observed mistakes being made on the ground—nurses were giving out the wrong regimen. When she heard about Option B+, she thought the idea was "genius."

The format of the TWG helped create consensus around Option B+. The meetings brought together state and nonstate actors for group discussion, and while not everyone was immediately in favor of Option B+, the conversations were very persuasive. As a member of the HIV/AIDS unit, explained:

> The beauty of having these Technical Working Groups, I think, is that you bring people on board . . . So with the discussions, questions, questioning ourselves, getting a little experience from other people, then people came to be convinced slowly, slowly, slowly to the point that almost all of those who said no, later on, they understand the idea.

The HIV/AIDS unit was also ready to defend their policy. They felt they had debated the idea so many times among themselves that they could answer most questions TWG members raised. While there would always be uncertainties with adopting a new policy, they emphasized the pressing need to try something different. TWG members raised questions about women's adherence to ART or whether it was fair to give women preferential access to lifelong treatment. In response, members of the HIV/AIDS unit argued that the stakes were too high to not try. As a technical advisor said:

> All those things were coming up, but then we said, "We have to do something different." . . . [Option A is] not working. So, we need to do something to save the children's lives, and also we need to do something to save the mothers' lives as well." . . . Because, if you remember, before that, we used to give single dose nevirapine, and mothers would get nothing completely. And then came the AZT, so they would get AZT for a short period, and then it stopped. And then, they get sick, and they die, and leave an orphan. Fine, we saved a life, but the child's survival is very low when the mother dies. We all know that. We had to do something to keep the mothers alive as well. So, these were very compelling discussions that we were giving, and people got convinced that that's the way to go.

Though some NGO representatives remained skeptical, they understood the HIV/AIDS unit's desire to try something new. For instance, a member of the TWG was concerned with possible drug resistance if women did not adhere to ART, but having worked in Malawi for many years, he also knew the struggles with PMTCT firsthand. He said: "As far as I can see, there is no good alternative yet." Despite his initial skepticism, he worked closely with the HIV/AIDS unit to prepare for Option B+ implementation, for instance, retraining staff on the new policy and setting up prenatal clinics so they could provide ART. He explained that the risk of trying a new policy was worthwhile:

> The way I see it is that it's somewhat similar to the situation before, around 2000, where it was clear that there was a huge unmet need for HIV treatment in Africa. Yet there were still voices saying that this is too complicated, too expensive, and in Africa, the community is not geared up to adherence. All sorts of unfounded comments and inhibitions to start widespread treatment. And then it turned out there wasn't much difference in the success rates in Africa compared to Europe and the States. . . . So I suspect this might end up in a similar vein. Worries and lack of formal evidence that it could be done. Hopefully through organizing it well, we can turn out to be successful. So I see it quite similarly to that. In the back of my mind, that's a reason for me to engage in and support the development. Because I had seen that first step go well.

The TWG format also fostered a sense of collective ownership of Option B+. Participants had described a general sense of collaboration in these working group meetings. A representative of an international organization said:

> In the HIV sector, there isn't an "us" and a "them." There's just "us," right? And "us" is the government, it's civil society, it's international NGOs, it's the development partners. We're all in the same discussion, at the same time, at the table. We're looking after *our* collective, meaning Malawi's, interest.

Members of NGOs did not feel that they were in the meeting to approve or disapprove of the policy but instead that they were part of the *making* of Option B+. One NGO representative explained: "I think it was a really collaborative effort within the Technical Working Group. We were all talking about the idea of not stopping women." Similarly, another said: "I think I was already understanding it . . . because the key issue was the rationale for it, and I felt part of the process of discussing the rationale." The close involvement of NGOs in national policymaking processes meant that NGO representatives had a stake in Malawi's policies. Option B+ was "their" policy too.

Making Option B+ legible started with building consensus amongst the various state and nonstate actors in the country. The initial TWG meeting was the first of many formal and informal discussions on Option B+.

It was important to the HIV/AIDS unit that they build consensus with all of their NGO partners in the country. Compared to WHO policies, Option B+ was an untested policy from a small country in Africa, so they needed a "united front" against potential opposition from the WHO and donors. A technical advisor explained the importance of consensus:

> It was very important. Otherwise, if we didn't have that, the minute you go to the WHO, and they come back and ask others, the others would say, "Oh, that's their own thing." Because obviously the WHO would come back and try to engage stakeholders and find out what they think about it. So, if you don't have their buy-in, everything can be shot down. They'd say, "You guys are just working on your own. You don't even have consensus, and you want to start this thing. The rest of the country is not interested." Then we would have a problem.

Consensus with NGO partners was also helpful for promoting Option B+ outside of the country. As we will see in the next section, there was now a larger group of actors—the HIV/AIDS unit plus several NGO workers in Malawi—working together to develop strategies that would make Option B+ legible to a global audience.

Building Global Legibility

The HIV/AIDS unit and NGO representatives in Malawi occupied a unique position: They worked in local healthcare institutions and were part of the global health field. Some individuals in this coalition worked in programs funded by donors, or they were public health experts that published in academic journals and participated in WHO panels, or they had ties to academic institutions in the United States and Europe. Their knowledge of the field and professional networks within it helped them to develop a multipronged strategy for promoting Option B+. They had what organizational sociologists call "social skill," or the "ability to motivate cooperation of other actors by providing them with common meanings and identities."[52] They knew what kind of evidence actors outside the country would need to see in order to accept their policy decision.

It was clear to everyone involved that Option B+ would raise concerns. Some of the I-TECH technical advisors also participated in expert panels at the WHO. During these panel discussions, other scientists had criticized Malawi for ignoring research studies and failing to uphold the values of evidence-based medicine. One technical advisor explained that others were "put out by the fact that Malawi overtook WHO in their wisdom. We basically said, 'We can't implement that, so we'll do something else.'" In addition, they were operating within the politics of ongoing clinical trials. *If* the WHO were to recommend a policy like Option B+, which would give HIV-positive women lifelong ART, clinical trials testing the efficacy of other regimens of preventative medications might have had to stop or be redesigned, since those regimens would then be considered substandard treatment for the trial population. From the start, the HIV/AIDS unit and NGO representatives knew that they would be "under the microscope." While the WHO did not explicitly prohibit Malawi from implementing Option B+, they raised a lot of questions. A member of the HIV/AIDS unit recalled a presentation in Geneva: "They just questioned it for their understanding, at the same time giving us room . . . but with the advice that we should carefully understand what we're doing and document what we're doing and see how that is making a difference."

The HIV/AIDS unit and NGO representatives had several strategies for legitimizing Option B+. Early on, they decided to write an article that laid out their rationale. Several members of this group in Malawi were already established experts in global health; they conducted research as part of government or NGO programs and regularly published findings. In addition, they reached out to leading scholars in the HIV field outside of the country. As a technical advisor explained: "It was crucial for us to get inputs so that it doesn't look like it's just something we're just trying to do on our own. But it should be something that we know that other people have looked at." The coauthors included leaders from large NGOs, like MSF and UNAIDS, and scholars from the London School of Tropical Medicine, some with hundreds of prior publications. This was a strategy that the country has used before with earlier HIV and TB policies.[53] Eventually, Malawi's policymakers published a viewpoint article about Option B+ in *The Lancet*, a leading medical journal.[54] The article came out at a critical time, in July 2011, just before they planned to start implementation of Option B+. Policymakers felt that the article helped to bring people on board because it laid out their thinking and decision-making process in a public and reputable forum.

Policymakers in Malawi also set up research projects to immediately start gathering evidence on the outcomes of Option B+. They wanted to demonstrate that their policy could be successful as soon as possible. As part of the HIV/AIDS unit's routine monitoring of patients, they collected data on women's use of ART and outcomes for HIV transmission. Researchers from NGOs in the country also planned projects that would take place alongside Malawi's implementation of Option B+. A researcher explained:

> So there were some people who were very firmly in the camp that it wasn't evidence based enough, but as a researcher, I was in the camp that I thought it made a lot of sense. And we could just design research to go alongside of it, to be able to assess it as it's going.

Because Malawi started gathering data right away, within the first year of implementation, they were able to show increased ART initiation, which should reduce rates of maternal HIV transmission. This evidence was crucial. As a technical advisor explained: "We had to show that. Otherwise, it would be termed a failure. . . . People would come and say, 'We told you this won't work.'"

They also conducted cost-effectiveness analysis for Option B+. With the rise of neoliberalism in global health, cost-effectiveness has become a key barometer for judging the success of health programs. Option B+ would cost more than either of the two WHO options. By relying on ART, Option B+ would be much more expensive than the WHO's Option A, which uses a combination of preventative medications that are less expensive and taken for a limited time. While the WHO's Option B also relied on ART, it was temporary rather than lifelong. Additionally, Malawi needed a particular regimen of ART that is safe for pregnant women but is also more expensive. ART itself is a combination of three medications. From a previous 2009 WHO appraisal, the HIV/AIDS unit knew that switching to the new tenofovir-based ART regimen (TDF + 3TC + EFV) would increase costs significantly.[55] Policymakers wanted to show that despite higher costs initially, Option B+ would be cost-effective in the long run. The HIV/AIDS unit justified the cost of Option B+ by comparing it to the cost of what they would need to purchase if they were to adopt one of the WHO policies. For example, they calculated the price for purchasing or fixing CD4 machines, which is necessary for the WHO's Option B. By adding in the cost of CD4 machines, the difference in cost between Malawi's policy and the WHO's became smaller. As a technical advisor in the HIV/AIDS unit said: "All of a sudden, it didn't appear so much cheaper to try and do the prophylactic options. And then, all of the other programmatic, and patient benefits, that came from simplification." Doing cost-effectiveness analysis, and doing it in strategic ways, helped to justify the cost of Malawi's policy.

Finally, in order to get their policy off the ground, Malawi's policymakers needed funding to purchase the additional ART they needed. At the time, donors were ambivalent about supporting Option B+. According to members of the TWG, some of the staff members of NGOs working in Malawi pushed back against opposition from the headquarters of their own agency. One TWG member explained: "There was a lot of resistance from PEPFAR headquarters. However, in-country, the PEPFAR team advocated heavily for Option B+ and the role of donors in supporting country ownership of national programs." The team in Malawi helped the HIV/AIDS unit apply for PEPFAR funding. Malawi's policymakers in the Ministry of Health and National AIDS Commission also negotiated to use funding that had been left over from previous Global Health Rolling Continuation Channel (RCC) grants administered by the Global Fund, which provides most of the ART in the country. They reprogrammed about $30 million from "non-implemented activities" to purchase the additional ART using the tenofovir-based regimen needed for Option B+ by freezing certain activities and shortening the grant period from three to two years.[56] This was critical—without funding to buy ART, there would be no way to get Option B+ off the ground. After using those initial funds, policymakers hoped that they could demonstrate success and solicit additional funding. Their logic was that *if* their policy is successful in reducing HIV transmission, there would be momentum for more support. It would become difficult for donors to pull back without risking their reputations. One technical advisor explained:

> But the question is what's the alternative? I mean, take the foot off the accelerator, and try and slow down treatment scale-up? . . . . I think everybody

> has a fair amount of faith that the Global Fund cannot step back and say, "We don't fund you anymore." Not many will say that, but I think that's really what everybody feels. . . . The Global Fund cannot step away and say, "We let that problem stall." There are so many lives dependent on that funding, so they really have no choice.

The HIV/AIDS unit and NGO representatives who promoted Option B+ challenge how we conventionally think of local and global actors. In this case, rather than functioning as simple carriers of global norms, they were also embedded in local institutions and acted according to local interests as well as promoted these interests to the broader international field. Of course, not all NGO representatives in Malawi provided the same level of support. As a Malawian member of the HIV/AIDS unit explained, NGOs do different things for Malawi:

> It depends on how you want to look at it. I think if you want to positively look at it, you will say, "Oh, yeah, they're extra hands to help." If you want to negatively look at it, you can say, "Oh, this is neocolonialism or something." . . . There are some that you literally know that they're making a contribution, and there are others that you really wonder what they're doing.

There are many actors working in the global health field, and as this statement highlights, how much they contribute to improving healthcare in Malawi varies. Indeed, there are NGOs whose work is primarily a "cultural production"—performative actions that do more for donors and their feelings of accomplishment than for intended beneficiaries.[57] But there are also NGO actors who are long-time collaborators with the Ministry of Health, and as this case shows, will work hard—at times challenging their own agency—to promote a national policy innovation.

The support of NGO representatives not only signaled to outside observers that there was widespread consensus in Malawi around Option B+, but also expanded the range of possibilities for leveraging professional networks, gathering data, publishing articles, and negotiating with donors. This group of policymakers in Malawi, working for the state or NGOs, occupied a unique position between the global HIV field and Malawi's healthcare setting, which shaped their understanding of the problem and solution. Because of their experience working in Malawi, the challenges associated with implementing WHO policies were easily understood, and at the same time, they knew how to make Option B+ legible to the global health field. With far less authority than the WHO, Malawi faced scrutiny for their policy decision, but their strategies helped to preempt some of the criticism they would face.

Changing HIV Context

New developments in HIV research aided the efforts of policymakers in Malawi to legitimize Option B+ and, to their surprise, helped launch the policy as a new global norm. There was a new theory of treatment-as-prevention (TasP), which posited that ART also reduces patients' viral load—that is, how much of the HIV virus is present in the body—and if the viral load drops significantly, it would be difficult to transmit HIV. At the time, the HIV field distinguished between HIV prevention programs, which relied on non-pharmaceutical approaches such as education and training programs, and HIV treatment programs, which give patients ART. When Malawi's policymakers were developing Option B+, treatment-as-prevention was still theoretical, and major clinical trials were underway to test the idea. While, for Malawi's policymakers, Option B+ was about finding a practical solution to preventing maternal HIV transmission in a healthcare system with resource constraints, the design of the policy dovetailed with the new theory of treatment as prevention.

In 2011, just as Malawi was promoting Option B+, surprising results emerged from ongoing clinical trials. The interim results of a major randomized clinical trial, HPTN 052, showed an astonishing 96 percent reduction of HIV transmission among serodiscordant couples—that is, couples in which one person is HIV positive and the other is negative—when the HIV-positive partner was receiving ART.[58] Though the clinical trial had not yet finished, these results provided strong evidence that treatment does indeed prevent HIV transmission. After the release of the HPTN 052 interim results, UNAIDS director, Michel Sidibé stated: "This breakthrough is a serious game changer and will drive the prevention revolution forward. It makes HIV treatment a new priority prevention option."[59] Malawi's Option B+ happened to coincide with a major change in the HIV field toward pharmaceutical approaches for both treatment and prevention.

These new research findings gave Malawi's policymakers an opportunity to further legitimize Option B+. While the HPTN 052 trial did not provide specific evidence for preventing mother-to-child transmission, the results suggested that treatment would theoretically work in the same way. As the WHO stated, the next step would be to address the "research gaps" in whether ART as prevention works for "other populations (other than serodiscordant couples) and those with other modes of transmission."[60] Malawi's policymakers could frame Option B+ as part of the emerging treatment as prevention approach, and they could now be seen as going along with new global trends rather than acting as an outlier. A technical advisor explained:

> These [studies] were now adding more significance to what we were doing, because now there was even that TasP conference that was held in Vancouver where they were looking at treatment as prevention. So we said, "this is exactly what we are doing; this is treatment as prevention." And then the studies started coming up that if you put people on treatment you reduce their viral load, you reduce transmission. So there was a lot of, I guess, indirect evidence coming in after we had started implementing. So this was sort of like consolidating our position.

Malawi's Option B+ eventually became a new global standard for preventing mother-to-child HIV transmission. Research findings supporting treatment as prevention, along with all the efforts from Malawi's policymakers, drew global attention to the viability of Option B+. Neighboring countries were immediately interested in the policy.[61] After Malawi started implementing Option B+, Rwanda and Uganda quickly followed as early adopters, and other countries in the region expressed interest. Like Malawi, several countries had previously adopted WHO policies under donor pressure. For example, although Cameroon preferred Option B, it adopted Option A due to financial constraints and donor advice.[62] The region's rapid adoption of Option B+ suggests that these countries faced challenges with WHO policies similar to Malawi's. Given these developments, the WHO treated Malawi as a test case. As one WHO representative described, the organization "took advantage of what Malawi had already started" and worked closely with the regional office to understand how the policy was implemented and what challenges emerged. In 2013, the WHO officially listed Option B+ among their recommendations. By that time, several African countries, including Kenya, Mozambique, Tanzania, Namibia, Angola, Cameroon, and Ethiopia, were either already implementing or preparing to implement Option B+.[63]

CONCLUSION

Malawi's decision to create their own Option B+ policy was a surprising challenge to the WHO. A small country in Africa pushed back against international organizations and donors with far more resources and power. The story of Option B+ shows the tensions between global health institutions and national policymakers over how to address health problems. With the influence of neoliberalism in global health, what was legible to the WHO were medications that could prevent maternal HIV transmission. Although they acknowledged that countries faced resource constraints in their healthcare systems, such constraints were illegible to them: Donor resources could not be used to directly address these issues. To policymakers in Malawi, the practical realities of the healthcare system were a central concern. They needed policies to function within existing constraints, such as weak medication supply chains, staff shortages, and deteriorating hospital infrastructure. Option B+ was designed around the fact that donors provided HIV treatment but not resources for the broader healthcare system.

The story of Option B+ also shows how foreign aid has reshaped policymaking, bringing both opportunities and constraints. The HIV/AIDS unit in Malawi's Ministry of Health could be considered a "pocket" within the state; unlike other state agencies, it had donor resources, technical assistance, and connections to NGOs.[64] How HIV policies were made was also distinct. At the behest of donors, HIV policies had to be made in discussion with nonstate stakeholders. While these requests tended to impose conformity among countries receiving aid, in this case, policymakers used the process to promote their idea for Option B+. Spaces like the Technical Working Groups brought together state and nonstate actors for discussion, which allowed policymakers to explain their thinking, address questions, and eventually, bring others on board.

The actors who participated in these discussions were also important. Neoliberalism led to a new view of governance, according to which the state was reconceptualized as an agency led by a mix of governmental and nongovernmental actors. Malawi's policymakers reflected this change. The actors instrumental in developing Option B+ included key state actors, like the director of the Malawi HIV/AIDS unit, and the technical advisors working in the unit. Once other NGOs in the country were on board, they too helped make the policy legible to a global audience. Several policymakers straddled two worlds of care, belonging in both the HIV field and Malawi's healthcare system. Their positionality shaped how they understood and addressed the problem of PMTCT policies. Because of their work in Malawi, they had a clear understanding of the healthcare system—knowledge that was often illegible to the donors, international organizations, and NGOs they worked with. Their expertise in the HIV field and professional networks also helped to legitimize Option B+. The actions of Malawi's policymakers suggest that we need to think more carefully about what professionals in global health do. While there is a rich scholarship on the role of NGOs in global health, there has been less conceptualization of the actors working within them.[65] This chapter shows that they are not a monolithic group. Their interests and viewpoints vary and do not always reflect the official stances of the agencies they work for. In the case of Option B+, support from NGO actors stemmed less from their membership in an NGO and more from their work in Malawi and long-standing relationships with government actors. Some of those NGO actors even pushed back against colleagues in their own organization who worked in headquarter offices outside of Malawi.

Malawi's Option B+ is in many ways an optimistic story of how a small country in the global South successfully challenged powerful institutions. Though they relied heavily on donor funding for their HIV program, policymakers leveraged other resources, such as their knowledge of the field and professional networks, to promote their policy. These outcomes are rare. Strategic action was important for the policy's success—but so too were serendipitous moments, like discovering problems with past PMTCT data that pushed the HIV/AIDS unit to dig deeper and strong interim results from a clinical trial demonstrating that treatment-as-prevention works. This case also shows the dire consequences of failed global health policies. HIV programs come with donor funding and the WHO's evidence-based policy recommendations, but it is the conditions of healthcare systems that ultimately shape whether HIV policies help patients. Malawi had struggled with WHO policies. This illustrates a broader issue: Evidence-based policies with safe and effective medicines, as important as they are, fail if attention is not paid to the local healthcare systems where policies are implemented. There needs to be working supply chains, healthcare workers, and infrastructure so that medications reach clinics, are properly prescribed, and any necessary laboratory tests are run. Without these fundamental aspects of healthcare, recommended PMTCT policies cannot work effectively, leading to devastating results for maternal and child health.

Just as Malawi's policymakers work between the global HIV field and local healthcare systems, so too do healthcare providers. In the next chapter, I focus on the experiences of providers and how they manage their careers between two worlds of care.

3 Precarious Opportunities

"I'm just hoping that maybe it will take me to greater heights."

Joyce, NGO community health worker

"It's a stable job, but it cannot provide all the things I want. That's why I'm still looking for other greener pastures."

Agnes, Ministry of Health nurse

Whom and what donors and international organizations deem worthy of aid has immense consequences for the structure of healthcare in aid-receiving countries. Global health efforts to combat the HIV epidemic intersected with the rise of neoliberalism, an ideology that emphasizes the transfer of power from government to the private sector.[1] As a result, nongovernmental organizations (NGOs) assumed a significant role in implementing HIV care programs and now operate alongside public healthcare systems. Over the past forty years, a sprawling industry has emerged around HIV care. Numerous actors are involved, including donors, development contractors, international and national NGOs, research institutes, HIV clinics, and community-based organizations.[2] The influx of NGOs has had ripple effects across society—creating new employment opportunities, social networks in the HIV field, connections to foreign actors, and a cultural discourse around HIV. Their presence has also spurred the development of secondary industries, like educational programs for HIV-related subjects. These ripple effects have reached the public sector as well, since many NGO programs are implemented within public healthcare facilities, in which NGO and government providers work side by side. NGOs have also shaped personal aspirations. While wanting a better life is nothing new, the particular goals, the pathways of getting there, and the kinds of futures that are possible are deeply informed by a healthcare system transformed by foreign aid.

Structural changes in the healthcare landscape not only shape how care is provided but also the lives of people working within it. The politics of legibility that I describe in this chapter are of Malawian healthcare workers trying to improve their life circumstances amid the opportunities and constraints of a healthcare profession divided between NGOs and the public sector. To donors, NGOs are legible as program implementers, and their workers as necessary personnel whose labor is made visible through metrics that quantify progress toward program goals. However, what is illegible are the lives, aspirations, and economic struggles of healthcare workers, who are navigating a changing field of employment. In this context, how do healthcare providers think about their work and career trajectories? And to what extent have new employment opportunities with NGOs alleviated their structural vulnerabilities?

For many providers, entering the healthcare field was shaped more by chance than by deliberate choice. Faced with limited access to higher education and a small formal labor market, young Malawians often took whatever job opportunities arose—whether in the NGO or public sector. Though the differences between the sectors were not important initially, they became more salient over time. NGO work was associated with *precarious opportunities*: jobs were variable and unstable but paid better, involved higher education or skills training, and led to network connections with global actors. Public sector work, on the other hand, was associated with *stagnant stability*: a job for life, but with low pay and few opportunities to progress professionally or in terms of socioeconomic standing. For a younger generation of providers, NGO work was appealing because it spoke to their aspirations—there was a path, however tenuous, for upward social and economic mobility, whereas public sector work increasingly seemed incompatible with their aspirations. But despite significant changes in the structure of healthcare, broader economic conditions for workers have remained relatively the same. While NGOs added jobs to the labor market, with short-term contracts, they did little to alleviate the economic uncertainty that pervaded the lives of workers in one of the poorest countries in the world. Providers all wanted a future with greener pastures, but neither sector offered an ideal path.

DECISION-MAKING IN UNCERTAINTY

To understand the career decisions of healthcare workers in Malawi, I take a pragmatist approach that sees future goals and the means of achieving those goals as something that develops within contexts and is subject to reevaluation.[3] From this theoretical tradition, action is conceptualized temporally: individuals respond to emerging situations based on the present environment as well as their view of the past and arising futures.[4] A pragmatist approach differs from rational choice frameworks, which assume that actions are a manifestation of preselected goals that do not themselves change. But rationality is situational—as situations change, individuals' goals and actions toward those goals also change. Pragmatism is useful for understanding decision-making in uncertain contexts. When one's circumstances are in flux, it is often difficult to clearly imagine a future or to firmly commit to a goal.[5] For example, Johnson-Hanks explained that women in Cameroon expressed a desire for having children, but they found it difficult to commit to a concrete fertility plan.[6] Similarly, Trinitapoli and Yeatman found that, contrary to public health messages to delay or limit childbearing, women in Malawi who were uncertain about their future HIV risk were more likely to accelerate childbearing since they felt healthy in the present.[7] In uncertain contexts, actions are often not guided by preselected goals but are instead shaped by "judicious opportunism," whereby people's aspirations (ends) emerge based on the contingent and surprising opportunities (means) that arise.[8] In the narratives below, we will see career paths that suddenly and drastically change and decisions that may seem puzzling from the outside, such as pursuing precarious work. Rather than labeling decisions as "rational" or "irrational," pragmatism brings to light that individuals constantly assess and reassess their situation and that decisions make sense relative to how individuals conceptualize their past, present, and future circumstances.

Much of everyday life in Malawi is uncertain: rains may destroy one's crops; sudden illness or death may strike in the family; a generous patron may arrive or depart.[9] Economic opportunities are also uncertain. The formal labor market is small. Most work is agricultural or informal, with many contributing to family farms, taking short-term jobs, or working for themselves—for example, selling their own goods or providing services. According to an International Labor Office (ILO) survey, in 2014, only 9.3 percent of Malawi's youth, ages fifteen to twenty-nine, were considered regularly employed, meaning that they had a waged and salaried job for a duration of more than twelve months or were self-employed with employees (14.2% of men; 4.7% of women).[10] Most youth (61.1%) were irregularly employed, meaning that their positions lasted less than twelve months, or they were working on their own account or contributing to family farms or businesses (60.7% of men; 60.1% of women). And 11.3% of youth were unemployed (7.2% of men; 15.1% of women). As young Malawians transition to adulthood, they face immense challenges with finding work, and many move between short-term jobs and face periods of unemployment.

Economic uncertainty shaped the tumultuous pathways of my respondents' career trajectories. They often got to their positions after many twists and turns and unexpected downfalls and opportunities. Becoming a healthcare provider in Malawi involved a strong element of chance. Reflecting judicious opportunism, my respondents were not making career choices in the sense of deliberate, calculated decisions toward a future goal so much as taking any opportunity they could find.[11] Even as they settled into their jobs in healthcare, they approached their careers in ways that continued to be shaped by uncertainty. They compared the NGO and public sector, weighing the perceived opportunities of NGO work against the relative stability offered by the public sector. As they worked, they started side businesses to buffer themselves against the insecurities of job loss or other unexpected events that might impact their livelihoods. Plans were often vague: The appeal of an NGO or public sector job or even careers within or outside healthcare could change depending on future circumstances. Despite changes in Malawi's healthcare landscape, economic uncertainty persisted and shaped workers' experiences. How my respondents entered the healthcare profession, their present actions in their careers, and how they thought about their futures reflected judicious opportunism in contexts of uncertainty.

BECOMING A HEALTHCARE PROVIDER

The providers in Lilongwe's health centers were a mix of NGO and government workers. I interviewed providers in both sectors and across ranks (N=44; 28 NGO, 16 government). Health centers are public facilities and are usually the first point of contact for patients. If cases are more complex, patients in Lilongwe may be referred to Kamuzu Central Hospital, one of only four tertiary hospitals in the country. Because of the shortage of healthcare providers in Malawi, health centers are often understaffed and have few nurses and sometimes only one clinical officer or doctor (or none). My respondents reflected the demographics of workers at the health centers. While some of my respondents included doctors, clinical officers, and nurses with university degrees, most of my respondents were of lower rank. They had completed secondary school and worked for NGOs as community health workers (CHWs) or HIV testing counselors (HTCs), or for the government as health surveillance assistants (HSAs), data clerks, or medical assistants, who have two additional years of training. The NGO workers I interviewed were part of Tingathe, a program run by Baylor College of Medicine Children's Foundation that aims to prevent mother-to-child transmission of HIV.[12]

During childhood, young Malawians had ambitious aspirations. My respondents recalled childhood hopes for a "bright future"; they wanted to become doctors, nurses, engineers, journalists, and bankers. They saw education as the means to achieve these goals. Esther, now a CHW, described thinking as a young girl: "I know if I go to school, if I do well in school, everything is going to be okay." Emmanuel, who is now a nurse, similarly felt that education was the way to a good life. He grew up in Rumphi, a town in northern Malawi. His parents were farmers, supporting him and his five siblings with money they made selling produce, and occasionally, homebrewed beer. He recalled telling himself, "I want to have a good family and stay very well with my kids. And then, to have a happy life—it needs education. It requires education." Respondents often emphasized their hard work and that they studied day and night.

This emphasis on education is, in part, a statement of moral identity: one is virtuous because one works hard and has ambitious goals.[13] But this emphasis on education also reflects a harsh reality that there are few opportunities for formal employment. Education, which is correlated to income, is important if one is to have a life outside of farming, piecework, and, for women, staying at home.[14] However, despite their ambitions and hard work, most young Malawians found that the careers they had dreamt of were out of reach. Becoming a doctor, nurse, lawyer, or engineer requires a college degree. And Malawi has one of the lowest rates of enrollment in higher education in sub-Saharan Africa: In 2018, enrollment in tertiary education was at 2 percent for men and 1 percent for women.[15]

Entry into college marked a significant fork in the road for young Malawians. In the years immediately after secondary school, the lives of those who entered college and those who did not looked drastically different. Those who went to college described feelings of immense pride: Their hard work had culminated in being one of the select few to enter higher education. College students were able to hold onto their aspirations for a bright future, though what their educational future entailed was unknown. Becoming a healthcare provider may not necessarily be a deliberate choice. While some respondents selected medical or nursing programs as their top choices in their college applications, others were unexpectedly selected for these programs.[16] Agnes, for instance, recalled her surprise when she saw her name listed for nursing school. When she applied, she listed accounting, agriculture, and environmental health as her three choices. It was a similar situation for Emmanuel. He was not trying to go to nursing school but that was what he was picked for. He still felt happy. As he put it, "becoming a nurse is better off than none [no college degree]." In this case, being able to go to college meant accepting one's future in healthcare.

While college students focused on their studies, secondary school graduates faced a more uncertain path. Completing secondary school was still considered a major accomplishment in Malawi. Out of 1,000 children entering primary school, only 309 will attend secondary school, and of that, only 40 will graduate.[17] But there were few formal employment opportunities available to secondary school graduates without advanced degrees. Their pathways to becoming healthcare providers were filled with hopes and disappointments. When they were not selected for college, many tried pursuing one- or two-year diploma programs. But life's many uncertainties often got in the way: A family member stopped sponsoring school fees;

they ran out of money and needed to work; a spouse was no longer supportive; a family member died. Joyce, for instance, pursued several paths. When she was young, she wanted to become a nurse, but, like so many, her exam scores were not high enough for college. She had no option but to try something else. She thought about computer training but could not afford it. She then started a diploma program in sales, which seemed promising, but she did not finish. The man she had been dating for two years proposed, and after they got married, he told her he did not want a woman who goes to work. Joyce stayed home for about seven or eight years. She described how she felt after she stopped her sales program:

> It was bad. To me, having dreams being shattered. At first, I wanted to go for nursing, dreams were shattered. I wanted to go into sales, salesmanship, that dream was shattered. So, it was like, I didn't know what to do. I was like, why exactly? Why is this happening to me? But I had no choice.

For secondary school graduates, the futures they hoped for in their youth were diminished in light of the immense structural limitations they now faced. They looked for any job they could find. It was no longer about dreams, aspirations, and goals but simply about survival. Charles described that his dream of being a journalist faded into the background. He said, "Yeah, of course journalism was still in my mind, but then looking at the condition. I was eager to do anything just to survive." Blessings described moving "up and down" looking for employment. He worked as a security guard for the American Embassy and then at the Sanctuary Lodge, a hotel in Lilongwe. When that ended, he stood outside of Game, a department store, waiting to see if they had an opening. He knocked on any door he could find. He said:

> Each and every office. Show up at each and every office. So whenever they say, "Yes, we need a messenger." I'll say, "Yes, employ me." We need a cleaner. I'll say, "Yes, employ me." We need a security guard, I'll say, "Yes, employ me." What I wanted was to be employed.

Prior to becoming healthcare providers, my respondents may have worked as security guards, gardeners, welders, construction workers, factory workers, or shop clerks. While looking for jobs, men often did piecework (i.e., random short-term jobs) for some money. Women had fewer piecework options. Some worked as house cleaners or helped their families sell produce and run small businesses, while others stayed home.

Becoming a healthcare provider was a matter of taking an opportunity that presented itself. When Blessings was looking for work, a friend told him that Baylor had an ad for volunteer translators. His friend was not interested, but Blessings, who had been unemployed for six or seven months, was willing to do it, and he applied. Martha was at home and depended on her husband's income. She took her sister-in-law's daughter to the hospital and saw that there was a vacancy posted for Baylor's Tingathe program. As young adults looking for work, there was little difference between those who went to work for the Ministry of Health or for an NGO. Secondary school graduates were looking for work in general—some happened upon a vacancy at the Ministry of Health while others found an opening at an HIV-care NGO. Pilirani, who is now an HSA for the Malawi government, used to work as a primary school teacher. She was not excited about teaching since it is a low paying job, so she was open to other opportunities. She heard about the position through a parent at the school. His child would always talk about teacher Pilirani. One day, while picking up his child, he asked to meet her and mentioned that there was an opening at the Ministry of Health. She said, "I am willing to do that; I'll apply."

For many of the secondary school graduates, the job they were offered from the NGO or Ministry of Health was the only offer they received at the time. They felt both proud and relieved to have been selected. Charity, now with Baylor, explained that she was one of ten out of one hundred applicants who was selected, and among her group, the only woman. She felt lucky, "My God, this is my opportunity." The few respondents who were already employed, including Pilirani, calculated whether a healthcare position would be better than their current job. Mathews, for instance, had been processing tobacco for Amber Leaf when a friend told him there was a vacancy posted at the hospital. He read the details of the post for Baylor, washed his clothes, and got ready to show up for interviews the next day. He was offered the position for CHW. It did not pay as much as his current job, and he would have to start as a volunteer. But others who worked there assured him that if he did the work, he would eventually get a contract, and then move up the ranks. He thought to himself:

"Stamping stickers on the carton? Will my mind be maximized here? I thought no, I will remain dumb. I want to think big. I wanted somewhere where I would be by nicer things." He felt that Baylor would be a place where he could learn something, get training, and maybe go back to school one day.

In a context of uncertainty, one became a healthcare provider not necessarily by selecting a goal in advance and taking strategic action toward it but by taking a chance on a career pathway as opportunities arose.[18] At this stage in my respondents' lives, NGOs were not particularly meaningful beyond being an additional avenue for work. College students focused on their studies, and secondary school graduates focused on finding employment in general. As their careers progressed, perceptions of healthcare work and future aspirations shifted, and the divide between NGOs and the public sector became more significant.

NEW EMPLOYMENT, NEW ASPIRATIONS

Many of my respondents were of a generation of providers who grew up alongside the influx of NGOs in Malawi. Most of my respondents were younger than forty years old. The HIV epidemic had always been a part of their lives—their transition to adulthood coincided with the rapid growth of HIV-care NGOs. Since the 1990s, amid the neoliberal transition from state-led to private-led development, NGOs have played a significant role in global health and development initiatives.[19] The Council for Non-Governmental Organizations in Malawi (CONGOMA) has served as an umbrella organization for all NGOs since 1992, with HIV-focused organizations comprising a substantial portion of the sector. By the mid-2000s, more than half of all development NGOs in Malawi were dedicated to HIV care.[20] Between 2000 and 2014, donor funding supported an estimated 2,309 community-based organizations, 337 faith-based organizations, 180 national NGOs, and 20 international NGOs working on HIV.[21] After four decades of the HIV epidemic, HIV-care NGOs feel commonplace and are especially visible in Lilongwe, Malawi's capital city, where NGO offices, HIV clinics, and billboards and posters for HIV prevention and treatment programs stud the landscape.

The proliferation of HIV care NGOs came with many new employment opportunities. As Swidler and Watkins argue, global health programs depend on "brokers," local actors who do the work of implementing programs and are intermediaries who connect donors to their intended beneficiaries.[22] There is a wide array of brokers across the socioeconomic spectrum, ranging from individuals with advanced degrees from foreign universities to college and secondary school graduates, as well as those with less than a secondary school education. All of these actors have important roles to play in the HIV-care field, whether they work closely with donors to design programs, lead in-country offices of international NGOs, manage a regional team of CHWs or data collectors, provide HIV testing and counseling, or volunteer in their communities. The job opportunities that came with NGOs also shaped personal aspirations. HIV-care NGOs were often associated with money. As donor funding for HIV programs flowed into the country, newspapers wrote headlines announcing the influx of aid, for instance, "Bush Pledges $500m . . . to Help Fight HIV/AIDS" or "Canada Grants K700 Million for HIV/AIDS."[23] People working for HIV-care NGOs could also make a lot of money. While NGO work was not stable, which I describe in more detail below, it transformed the lives of some people.

In an area of healthcare fueled by donor funding, a provider could experience a rapid rise in socioeconomic status that had previously been unimaginable. Whereas in the past, college admission determined chances for socioeconomic mobility, the rise of NGOs created a new pathway. This was especially meaningful to secondary school graduates, whose career aspirations had previously been cut short when they were not accepted into college. My respondents, whether in the NGO or the public sector, could all think of someone who advanced significantly in their education and careers through an NGO job. Zione was one of them.

Zione first started working with Baylor as a volunteer translator at their pediatric HIV hospital in Lilongwe. She had been staying at home as a wife and mother, but she had completed secondary school and had the English language skills needed to translate for American doctors. The position also had personal significance, as she was living with HIV herself. Shortly after she began translating, in 2007, she was recruited as one of the first community health workers for Baylor's Tingathe program, which provided HIV testing and counseling for HIV positive women during pregnancy and breastfeeding. As Tingathe expanded from a pilot project to an established program with sites across the country, Zione's career advanced alongside it. She was promoted to site supervisor at one of health centers, where she managed a team of CHWs. Baylor then sponsored her education, providing a scholarship that paid a portion of the fees for a two-year diploma program in community development. She worked during the day and studied in the evenings, using part of her income to install electricity in her home so she could study more easily after work. During much of my fieldwork, I knew Zione as a site supervisor, but when I later returned to conduct additional interviews, Zione was gone. With her community development diploma, she had been promoted to regional manager, where she was overseeing several of Tingathe's sites. Over the course of about ten years, Zione went from being a housewife to a healthcare professional with a postsecondary education working in a managerial position. A few generations ago, a story like Zione's would have been nearly unheard of. Although stories like hers are still the exception rather than the norm, they become memorable examples of the kind of future NGOs can help create.

The influx of NGOs changed the field of employment opportunities, and along with it, people's aspirations for what their futures might look like. Stories like Zione's demonstrate how someone without the traditional markers of upward mobility, such as a college degree, can take an alternative route to higher education, career growth, and improved socioeconomic standing. As healthcare providers thought about their careers, NGOs and the public sector offered different opportunities and constraints. The differences between the two sectors were especially salient for my respondents, who had come of age alongside the proliferation of NGOs and were still early enough in their careers to weigh the implications of each path. Yet neither sector offered a truly ideal future. NGO work spoke to young Malawian's aspirations for socioeconomic mobility but was nevertheless precarious. Following in Zione's footsteps meant walking down a narrow and unstable path. While public sector work offered stability, rare in Malawi's labor market, it left providers feeling stagnant and unable to improve their life circumstances.

PRECARIOUS OPPORTUNITIES

NGO work offered *precarious opportunities*—it was possible to make money, receive more education, and connect with global actors, but in an inherently unstable field. Donors typically fund programs on short-term cycles—often one to a few years, sometimes less—and expect recipient organizations to demonstrate cost-effectiveness and clearly measurable outcomes of success within that time frame in order to receive more funding.[24] Additionally, donor interests can change, leading to certain kinds of programs being funded while others are cut. Donors also differ in the standards they apply to programmatic work, as few global employment standards exist to guide or regulate these practices uniformly.[25] NGO work reflected the unstable and variable nature of donor funding. Jobs were often based on short-term contracts and varied in salary and benefits. Some positions were voluntary while others offered high salaries and opportunities to build one's educational credentials, skill sets, and connections. Some contracts were annual while others lasted only a few months or even less. Some positions could be renewed while others were one-time gigs.

The precariousness of NGO work added to the existing economic precarity of providers' lives, especially those working in lower ranks.[26] Many HIV-care NGOs, including the one my respondents worked for, relied heavily on community health workers to provide health services. CHWs tend to have secondary school education or less. They receive training and are then responsible for a variety of medical and public health services, such as HIV testing and counseling, health education, and the collection of health data.[27] However, despite their essential role in delivering health services, CHWs are not formally recognized as medical professionals in the way that doctors or nurses are, and so, there are no global or national standards regulating their wages, benefits, and workplace protections.[28] The compensation that NGOs offer CHWs varies widely. Some NGOs pay CHWs salaries that may exceed those of their public sector counterparts and include additional benefits, like trainings and school sponsorships. Other NGO programs rely on volunteer labor, and workers may only be offered a stipend to cover travel and lunch. Organizations justify using volunteers by arguing that workers should be altruistic in helping their communities and that their programs would not be financially sustainable without volunteers.[29] But in contexts with limited resources, relying on volunteer labor turns exploitive.[30] While workers want to help others, they also need to make a living and may accept a volunteer position in the hopes that it will eventually lead to payment.

My respondents' experiences reflect this variation in the NGO field. While they were salaried workers when I met them, several had previously worked in voluntary positions that did not support their livelihoods. Before Baylor, Charity had been recruited from her local youth organization to train to become an HIV-testing counselor for an NGO. She was very excited to be selected and for the opportunity to receive training; on top of that, the program offered incentives, like lodging and meals. But after receiving her HTC certificate, she was required to work for the organization. Counselors were to volunteer and "practice" at local clinics, while submitting various reports back to the NGO until they found a job. But in Malawi's labor market, finding a job as a secondary school graduate is difficult. Charity volunteered for two years. During this time, she closed her cosmetic shop to do volunteer work, and she had to rely on her parents for financial support. She said: "It was very challenging because I had to find everything: You talk of basic needs; you talk of everything that is needed for someone to survive. My parents, my mom, supported me up to three years." Charity's obligation to the NGO that trained her was atypical, but many respondents described similar financial stress from volunteering for HIV-care NGOs. Many took volunteer positions because, as another CHW, Joyce, succinctly put it, the stipend "was better than having nothing." But the K8,000 per month stipend she received—about $65—was hard to live on.[31] She said: "I survived. I don't know how, but I survived. I think it's through the Grace of God."

Other respondents had benefited from NGO employment, but for a short time. Over the years, providers have seen NGO programs come and go. Charles, a site supervisor at one of the health centers, knew this from personal experience. He previously worked for Dignitas in its information, education, and communication (IEC) program, but funding for his position lasted for only one year. He then trained to be an HTC counselor at Lighthouse, an HIV clinic, where he stayed for three years before funding ended again. Providers were well aware that programs lose funding and that donor interests change. Signing contracts created a sense of uncertainty about the future of their work. As Charity explained:

> But when someone is on a contract job, it is very risky. Because one day, you'll not be working. You just sign one-year contract, one-year contract, one-year contract. . . . You have a good family, you have children, you have to pay school fees for your children. So, it is very challenging. Because at some time, you're not working, because the funding has stopped or the funding's off.

Similarly, Charles explained: "Yeah, for an NGO project, there's always fear. What if USAID pulls out? What if Baylor decides it's moving to Mozambique? . . . Your job is always not secure, unlike government side."

My respondents would be considered the lucky ones in the NGO field. They worked for Baylor's Tingathe program, where they were salaried workers and often received other benefits like skills trainings and school sponsorship. Many had been working with Tingathe for several years; their annual contracts were renewed every year, and the program had been successful in maintaining USAID funding for over ten years. These workers were able to achieve a provisional form of stability. Although it could change at any time, this moment of stability was valuable and helped them to pursue their goals.

PROVISIONAL STABILITY

While my respondents were working at Tingathe, they were able to make concrete improvements in their life circumstances. Their salaries allowed them to become breadwinners who supported their immediate and extended family. In their younger years, these providers were often the ones to benefit from a family member with more means. An uncle or aunt may have paid their school fees or hosted them in their home so they could attend school in a better district. Now, they were in a position to do the same. They paid school fees for other family members or took in their nieces and nephews so they could attend school in Lilongwe, where the quality of education could be higher than in their home village. Joyce described a feeling of responsibility to her family members. She said:

> I'm responsible for my kids, my mom, my sister, I have—my late sister, she left her kids—I'm also responsible for those kids. Because my mom doesn't do anything; she has no income. So all those people, they look up to me. So I have to make sure every month I send something to my mom so she can take care of my sister's kids, whilst here I'm with my kids.

Reciprocity is a common practice in Malawi. Living a context of uncertainty, individuals support others during times of economic prosperity and seek support during times of financial hardship. My respondents' NGO salaries positioned them to be key supporters in their families, at least for the time being.

Having continuous employment at the same NGO also gave providers the space to reimagine their career trajectories. Many had come to work for Tingathe after a stressful search for any form of employment. But after a few years there, being an HIV care provider became a meaningful part of their identities. Mavuto, for instance, had pursued other opportunities in the past, such as certification to be a mechanic, but after working as a CHW for several years, he saw himself as a healthcare provider. Being a CHW reconnected him to his childhood dream of being a doctor. Mavuto described how he felt when he first got the job as a CHW:

> I was very happy because of my ambition. I always tell my mother that I need to be a doctor . . . but because of the life I have gone through, I have not managed to be a doctor. But with the field I am in right now, the CHW, now I appreciate that because it was also related a little bit.

Similarly, Chikondi felt that becoming a CHW was God's way of putting her back on course after she failed to get into college for nursing school. She said: "So, when we're saying HIV testing and counseling, we also work in the hospital. So I was like, I am now connected to my career. Wow, this is God. God makes a way." Others felt connected to HIV work through personal experience. They had family members who were HIV positive or had died from AIDS and felt that their work was a calling to help families going through a similar experience.

My respondents also aspired to advance further. Many had already received skills training from the NGO. Almost all CHWs were eventually trained to provide HIV testing and counseling, allowing them to be promoted to HTC counselors, who are certified to take blood samples for HIV testing. For example, when Blessings started, he was a volunteer, but others assured him of an upward trajectory. He said: "So I was asking, 'How did you move?' 'Ah now, easy. Don't worry. You will be at my position—don't worry.' I said, 'Ah.' So those people had to encourage me, to say, 'You're not going to remain in the same position.'" He indeed found himself moving up. He volunteered for about six months, was promoted to CHW and then senior CHW, and then trained to be an HTC counselor. While there was no formal rule, NGO workers explained that it took about two years to be selected for HTC training. My respondents were ambitious and wanted to continue climbing the promotional ladder. They may have started as a volunteer or CHW, but eventually moved up to HTC counselor, and in the future, they hoped to be the assistant site supervisor, site supervisor, or regional manager.

During their years at Tingathe, some of my respondents gained access to unique opportunities provided by the NGO. Baylor offered scholarships that paid a portion of the tuition for a one- or two-year diploma program related to HIV care, such as community development, HIV management, or public health. These scholarships were not consistently offered in the way that HTC training was, but the possibility of receiving one was significant because it gave them hope that they might be able to return to school. For providers who received scholarships, a door to education opened that they thought had closed. In Malawi, education is highly valued and is closely tied to job opportunities and income. Everyone, regardless of which sector they worked in, talked about desires for "upgrading" themselves or "moving up." At each level, workers aspired for the next degree, be it completing secondary school, earning a one- or two-year postsecondary diploma, a college degree, or a PhD.[32] When my respondents did not get into college, they felt their dreams were dashed. Some tried to pay their own tuition for a one- or two-year diploma program but found it difficult to keep up with the fees. Charles, for instance, tried to pursue a diploma in journalism. He would take a few short-term jobs for money, enroll in courses, and drop out when he needed more money. But he was not able to maintain that cycle of work and school, and never finished. Then, with Baylor's financial support, he had a real chance at completing his diploma—this time in community development. Charles, who was a site supervisor, hoped that with this diploma he could be promoted:

> Yeah as a person, I have ambitions. I wouldn't always want to be a supervisor, so I would like to go other ways. It's surely an opportunity for me to advance as a person. . . . I don't want to be a community health worker forever. I would want to become a CHPO [community health program officer], even a coordinator. I know I can go that way, and for me to go all the way, I think education would be the component that would make it suitable for me to advance.

Over time, NGO workers built a social network with other HIV care providers. These providers often met one another during training sessions or through collaborative projects. Having a social network enabled NGO providers to seek better job opportunities or secure new employment if their contracts ended. Charles described being in "the system." He explained: "I'm an HTC counselor. I'm in the HTC system—that's it. For example, there's an opening and advert in, maybe in Zomba. Yeah, I have counselor friends there. They would send me 'there's a job opportunity; you can apply.' That's the network I'm talking about." Several of my respondents were part of WhatsApp groups in which members would share information about job openings in various NGOs. Even if NGO jobs were contract based, having a network gave workers a greater sense of stability because they felt that they could be connected to more work in the field. Charity, for instance, explained that she could find work among the many NGOs in the country: "You can find a lot of different projects. Baylor, UNC, Vision Fund Project, Médecins Sans Frontières, World Vision—lots of organizations."

My respondents' past experiences reflect the variability in the NGO sector: some had taken volunteer positions, while others had a salaried position but for a short time. When I met my respondents, they were in a stage of provisional stability. The NGO program they worked for continued to receive funding, and their contracts were renewed annually. During this moment of stability, they were able to improve their life circumstances and progress in their careers. They made money and became breadwinners for their families; they felt a renewed sense of ambition as they embraced their identity as HIV care providers progressing along a career path; they went back to school; they formed a social network of HIV care providers. These changes were meaningful, especially compared to their earlier struggles finding employment.

BUILDING CASTLES IN THE AIR

However, while having provisional stability with NGO work enabled providers to meaningfully improve their life circumstances, it did not alleviate the underlying precarity of their lives. Insecurity played a major role in how NGO workers navigated their daily lives and planned for their futures. Like many in Malawi, my respondents constantly sought ways to buffer against insecurity.[33] Several respondents invested a portion of their salary into side businesses. They raised chickens and pigs and started businesses selling cosmetics, groceries, second-hand clothes, popsicles, donuts, and more. Having extra income from a side business helped workers manage everyday expenses and served as a crucial safety net in case of job loss, illness, or other unforeseen circumstances. As one CHW explained:

> I choose to start it [business] because in Malawi just to depend on the one thing—life is so hard. So, I could save my salary from the week, and the money from the business—it can make me to do something. . . . Because I can use that—this money from my business—we are going to use in our home basics like food, clothing, and so on.

Working at an NGO, my respondents earned higher salaries, making it easier for them than it was for their public sector counterparts to start businesses. Some NGO providers were especially entrepreneurial. Mathews, for instance, started two businesses—one raising and selling pigs in the village and the other importing shoes from South Africa to sell. Ruth used her income to build a house, which is considered a significant accomplishment, that she and her husband rent out. While salaries from NGO work were indeed valuable, workers' need to invest in side businesses reflected the ongoing insecurity they still faced.

Career progression within HIV-care NGOs was also unstable. NGO workers aspired to advance in their careers, but organizations did not always have clear and consistent promotional pathways. The progression that many of my respondents made from volunteer to CHW to HTC counselor is common. Many HIV-care NGOs provided training for HIV testing and counseling. While becoming an HTC counselor is an advancement and comes with a modest pay increase, it does not entail additional educational credentials, which are needed for greater socioeconomic mobility. The promotions to site supervisor and higher that my respondents aspired to were far more challenging to attain than HTC training. With only one site supervisor and one assistant site supervisor per site, there was a lot of competition among the twenty to thirty CHWs and HTC counselors working at each health center. CHWs may dedicate years to working at Tingathe without being promoted to a supervisory role, leading to frustrations and jealousy. Advancing beyond site supervisor was even rarer, as only one regional manager oversaw multiple sites, and these roles required higher educational credentials. While many were inspired by their coworker, Zione, who went from being a housewife to a regional manager at an NGO, most will never be able to follow her path.

In addition, the postsecondary diplomas that my respondents pursued did not directly lead to promotions or new job opportunities. NGO workers invested time and some of their own resources into programs that might or might not lead to career advancement. Though uncommon, in a couple of cases, workers invested in fraudulent programs that did not confer real diplomas.[34] Diplomas were a way for workers to hedge their bets—they had a potential advantage if the right job opportunity came along. For instance, Lydia, who was pursuing a public health diploma, had no immediate plans to leave her job, but was ready for an opportunity, explaining that *if* a "vacancy which will show that we want someone who has public health" opens up, "I'll apply for it." Similarly, when I asked Martha what she wanted to do after her diploma, she said "I will continue with this job." She explained: "I just want the diploma to help me *in general* [emphasis mine]. I just want it to help me with my career that I am doing here, to improve my knowledge." She would like to be promoted to site supervisor one day and hoped that her diploma might help with the promotion. The diplomas my respondents sought were legible to an NGO field that did not offer stable jobs or orderly career paths.[35] While diplomas were considered a valuable "upgrade" in education, there was not much that NGO workers could actively do with one. Workers like Martha and Lydia often found themselves waiting, hoping for a job opportunity to emerge.

NGO workers' future plans reflected judicious opportunism in contexts of uncertainty. In some ways, since working for an NGO, their life circumstances had changed—for example, they had become breadwinners—but they approached the future much as they always had. Faced with uncertainty, providers did not make clear step by step plans but instead tried to position themselves to seize opportunities as they arose.[36] When I asked my respondents where they saw themselves in five years, they often told me that they wanted "greater heights" and "greener pastures" and to be "somewhere better." How they would reach those greater heights was less clear. It was difficult to say what promotion they might qualify for within five years or when exactly they would go back to school or whether they would be at the same organization or move to another. Because the NGO field itself was not stable, their future trajectories were also unstable; their paths were contingent on their circumstances and the opportunities that emerged. When I asked Joyce about her future, she described many possible forks in the road. She explained: "It's not easy to find work, especially here in Malawi." She preferred to stay at Baylor and receive promotions there, but if her contract ended, she would have to look for work. If she had to find another job, she preferred to work in HIV care with NGOs, because she had "gotten used to the NGO life." But, if her circumstances changed and it became difficult to find an NGO job, then she would take a government job in HIV care—or any other kind of job. Unable to outline any definite plans for her work, she said, "maybe in the future, I don't know."

Plans also consisted of buffering against insecurity. If there was anything certain about the future, it was that there would be uncertainty. While my NGO respondents often spoke about their hopes of furthering their education and advancing in the field of HIV care, they were equally passionate about developing their side businesses. Establishing a second source of income was seen as crucial both for the present and for the future. They aspired to grow their businesses, to buy their own plot of land so they could farm, or to build a house that they could live in or rent. Joyce, for instance, hoped to open a butchery and grocery store. She explained that these businesses would be worthwhile investments because people need to buy food every day. In our conversation, she was passionate about her career in HIV care but also about her business goals. I asked which one she wanted to pursue further in the upcoming years. She said both. She described her career in HIV care as "building castles in the air." She still aspired to receive more education and be promoted at work but whether she would be given such opportunities felt uncertain. She wanted something grounded—to her, a successful business would provide economic stability in ways that her NGO job could not. She said:

> I might not sign the next contract, maybe I might lose the job in the future, I don't know. What do I do after I leave this job? . . . It's difficult when you don't have anything to do. You have to start from scratch, looking for something else to do. . . . So it's better to have something on the side.

NGO work had important benefits but did not fundamentally change the precarious economic circumstances in which providers lived. Much of their lives were still shaped by insecurity—they needed to establish businesses to create greater financial stability, and their decisions were guided by judicious opportunism rather than long-term planning. NGO workers hoped for upward socioeconomic mobility, but opportunities often came unpredictably, and most would never achieve their goals. The plans that they had to advance their education and receive promotions at work were, as Joyce stated, building castles in the air—more of a dream than a concrete reality. But, despite this, NGO work remained desirable because there was still a *chance* of higher salaries, skills training, and access to education, and this chance was meaningful. In comparison to NGOs, the public sector fell further in the shadows. While public sector work was stable, providers felt that there was no chance for them to advance their careers and improve their life circumstances.

DISAPPOINTING REALITIES

The job opportunities and aspirations that come with NGO work do not only affect those working in NGOs. Providers in the public sector considered their careers in comparison to the NGO sector. In contrast to the precarious opportunities associated with NGO work, the public sector was associated with stagnant stability. Public sector providers felt stuck. They received low salaries and worked under challenging conditions with shortages of staff, medicine, and supplies; they also felt that the government lacked the resources to provide training and scholarships, leaving them with few opportunities for educational and career advancement. While resource constraints in the public sector were not new, they took on new meaning when compared to NGOs. Public sector work provided job security, which is rare in Malawi, but lacked the opportunities that

NGO work appeared to offer. Providers felt that they could not achieve the socioeconomic mobility they aspired to in the public sector, which they therefore sought to leave.

Working conditions in Malawi's public healthcare system are difficult. The public sector has long struggled with resource constraints and has not benefitted significantly from donor funding. Many health facilities are severely understaffed, with the number of providers far below the WHO-recommended minimum.[37] The conditions my respondents worked in reflected larger problems in healthcare in Malawi. The nurse in charge of one of the health centers explained: "There's nothing unique with this institution. It's a busy place, yes, sometimes we lack basic resources, and the staff isn't enough. . . . Everything happens slowly because you don't have whatever you need, basically."

Working under resource constraints took a toll over time. Providers in the public sector described starting their careers energetically. Doctors, clinical officers, and nurses were part of an elite class of college graduates in Malawi and felt proud of their educational accomplishments. My respondents told me about their hard work and how they triumphed over difficult courses, an overwhelming first year, and challenging final exams. As one nurse explained, "It was very exciting because it was a dream come true. I was very excited, my mom was happy and my siblings, everyone was happy that we now have a graduate in the home." But, with the severe shortages of healthcare providers, initial excitement faded as graduates were plunged into hectic work environments. Emmanuel, a nurse, described feeling excited when he first came to the health center. He was moving from a rural area to Lilongwe and would work in one of the largest catchment areas in the city. He was also given a leadership role as the in-charge of the maternity ward. In the beginning, the workload did not bother him, as he felt he was gaining experience by seeing many patients and he was taking responsibility as a leader. But over time, working under conditions of constant shortage took a toll. Emmanuel was covering multiple departments: "Maybe three areas at once, just to check how things are operating." With talk of developing a surgical center, he worried about the possibility of an even greater workload. He described feeling exhausted at the end of the day:

> It was like brain draining because you could work in different areas. And even when you go home, the food wasn't even tasty. You always go there very tired; you would even stay without eating because of tiredness. Maybe you can eat a little bit, and then sleeping, and then tomorrow you need to rush again for work. So it was really tiresome.

Because health centers were short staffed, there was not a good way for providers to slow down without impinging on their professional values. Agnes, a nurse who worked at the ART clinic, explained that she could not turn patients away even if her shift had ended. When we spoke, the clinic had closed, but there were still patients coming by. She said, "I come here at half seven, but I am supposed to knock off at half four. But you can see there are still people who want to get the medication. So I cannot go and leave them. I have to finish." With no one to hand off work to, Agnes stayed because she was ultimately responsible for those patients. While the number of patients that came to the health center varied each day, it was not uncommon to see long lines of roughly one hundred patients at the ART or prenatal clinic waiting to see the one or two nurses on duty. Emmanuel similarly explained why he felt he could not take a break from work, saying:

> Some of them, they're emergency cases. You feel, "When I leave this one, she will die within minutes. So should I leave this one and then I should be going for my lunch? No." Another one comes, another comes. So you end up staying the whole day in the clinic and not taking your lunch. At the same time, you are destroying yourself. Yeah.

While most situations may not have been emergencies, when there were long lines of patients waiting to be seen, providers felt a professional and social obligation to keep working, regardless of how tired they felt.

The experiences of Agnes and Emmanuel are part of a larger trend in provider burnout in Malawi. A survey by Kim et al. found that more than 60 percent of their respondents met clinical thresholds for burnout, which includes feeling emotionally exhausted, cynical, and ineffective. Long work hours, high burden of responsibility, low perceived control, staff shortages, and high rates of patient morbidity and mortality set the stage for burnout, which eventually affects the quality of patient care.[38] Agnes and Emmanuel were still in the early stages of their nursing careers. Both were in their thirties and expressed excitement about learning and helping patients, but signs of burnout were already creeping in. As providers continued to work under immense resource constraints, it is perhaps not surprising that their youthful energy faded. Burnout was especially pronounced among doctors, clinical officers, and nurses, who faced the most severe staff shortages. But, while lower-level positions were generally better staffed, those workers also experienced frustrations with the conditions of the public sector, which I describe below. Resource constraints in the public sector were not new, but the larger landscape of healthcare was. With the growing presence of NGOs, an alternative career path was always in sight.

COMPARISONS WITH NGOS

Since the 1990s, the rise of donor-funded NGOs has created new employment opportunities, significantly expanding Malawi's private and nongovernmental workforce. Beyond NGOs, other non–public sector opportunities do also exist. For several decades, challenging work conditions and low pay in the public sector have contributed to the "brain drain" of medical professionals to wealthier countries.[39] Malawi also has a small sector of private for-profit healthcare practices, comprising 3 percent of service provision in the country.[40] In addition to these, the Christian Health Association of Malawi (CHAM), which was established by missionaries in 1966, provides about 37 percent of healthcare and works closely with the Malawi Ministry of Health. CHAM receives government contracts to provide the essential health package—primary, maternal, and child healthcare—predominantly in rural areas, where there are fewer public healthcare facilities.[41] But because CHAM facilities rely heavily on the government for income and drug supplies, they often face similar resource constraints as public healthcare facilities. In effect, the influx of NGOs substantially shifted the range of opportunities outside of the public sector. Today, they have a dominant presence, comprising 61 percent of private and nongovernmental health facilities.[42]

As the NGO sector has grown, comparisons between government and NGO work have become more tangible. My respondents in the public sector all had friends or classmates who worked for an NGO. At the health centers, NGO programs operated within the government facility, so NGO and public sector providers worked side by side. Kelvin, a medical assistant, described how ingrained NGOs were at his work:

> Most of them, I just see them coming here to our work. We have NGO right here. We have one called Malawi Epidemiological Intervention and Research Unit. It works here. It deals with noncommunicable diseases. And we've got UNC. UNC, which deals with family planning. We have the Baylor College of Medicine, which is dealing with pediatric HIV.

NGO activities for HIV care were incorporated into everyday practices. At the prenatal clinics, Tingathe workers provided HIV testing and counseling before women received other prenatal services, and on the ART clinic's busy days, they also worked with government providers to help manage the flow of patients, organize their files, and take vital signs. In addition, government providers were receiving training through EQUIP, a USAID funded program that sends doctors and nurses working in participating NGOs, like Baylor or Partners in Hope, to mentor government providers on how to improve their quality of HIV care.

Providers drew comparisons between government and NGO work along several lines. Workers in both sectors felt that the main benefit of government work was job security. While NGO work was insecure, a government position was often considered a job for life. Luke, a data clerk, says: "Yeah, you know, we are all civil servants, so the only advantage of being a civil servant is that the job is secure, long lasting, sorts of things like those. I feel it is secure indeed." To some providers, this advantage was important, and it made them want to stay in the public sector. But for others, it did not feel advantageous enough—security was often seen as the *only* advantage.

Public sector work came with low salaries. While this has long been the case, it was especially disappointing in comparison to what one could make at an NGO. Emmanuel explained that he and his nursing school classmates received the same training and are of the same rank, but those who worked for NGOs made at least twice as much as him. He said: "It's just two hundred thousand, two hundred thousand per month [salary]. You talk of some of our friends in NGOs, they can get maybe five hundred thousand per month. Some they can go up to eight hundred." The sting was worse when NGO providers of lower rank made more. One medical assistant described his salary as a sacrifice. He received postsecondary education for two years but makes less than some of the Tingathe workers who only completed secondary school. He said: "It's like a sacrifice. . . . Because the salaries I receive compared to the counselors of Baylor, maybe the salary of a medical assistant and the salary of counselors can be the same. But a medical assistant went to school for two years. So, in NGOs, there's a lot of money." Government providers also felt that while they earned lower wages, they worked more. Because of staff shortages, they sometimes had to work beyond their scheduled hours or cover for colleagues without additional compensation. As John, a medical assistant, described: "You can work during the night—you are not given anything. . . . It's part of the job." By contrast, he felt that NGOs and private clinics compensated providers for overtime work. He said, there, the pay "is 100 percent, unlike in government."

In addition, compared to the resource constraints in the public sector, NGOs seemed to have ample supplies and modern technologies. Kelvin explained: "I see that NGO workers are provided with everything they need so that their work should be properly conducted. That is a very great incentive because it motivates somebody, and it lets him do and achieve his work properly." Kelvin explained that his colleagues used paper to write reports, but NGO providers used computers; he rode a bicycle to travel to his catchment area (a region where a provider is responsible for health education and other services) while NGO providers had motorcycles. These perceptions may not have exactly mapped onto reality. For instance, Tingathe CHWs also ride bicycles, not motorcycles. But Kelvin's comments reflect the broader perception that NGOs are resource rich and modern, whereas the public sector is resource constrained and outdated.

Finally, public sector work could not compete with the benefits that NGOs offered. Everyone was interested in pursuing more education and training. NGOs, like Baylor, were known to occasionally sponsor their employees for continued education, covering a portion of their school fees. Government providers were frustrated with how few opportunities they had been offered. Geoffrey, a dentist at a health center, described his frustration:

> So, I don't think a chance [will come] from the government. But maybe scholarships will [come] in some way. Because I'm already seeing how it's going in the Malawian government. So over these eighteen years, I was not sponsored from the Malawi government. They'll sponsor me while I'm about to retire, to resign from work. All this time without being sponsored [for education].

Geoffrey said he continues to hope for sponsorship, but it would come from "other people, well-wishers, NGOs, whatsoever" but "not in our Malawi government."

Providers felt the uneven impact of foreign aid though their everyday work and observations. They saw the resources that went toward specific disease programs, most notably HIV, as well as the resources that went to providers working for HIV-care NGOs. They also saw how resources bypassed the public sector, which continued to struggle with shortages of staff, medicine, and basic infrastructure. For providers, the HIV epidemic is an emergency, but so too is their public healthcare system. As Kelvin explained:

> Our government is in crisis as far as our economy is concerned. . . . The government is raising the money for public services on its own, so it becomes very difficult for each and every department or ministry to be funded with enough money so that it can reach out where there is need.

While working in the public sector had never been easy, providers' disappointments sharpen in comparison to NGOs. Constant comparisons shaped providers' feelings toward their work and their career trajectory.

STAGNANT STABILITY

Like their NGO counterparts, government providers desired upward social and economic mobility. They too wanted to be "somewhere better" and to find "greener pastures" in the future. They wanted to have more money, to own a home, to have luxurious commodities, and to feel they could give their children a bright future. For instance, when Emmanuel talked about his aspirations, he said:

> At this time, we're still living in government houses, so I need to have my own house, yeah. I think maybe if they can be two—two houses, big ones, good ones. Then the other thing is maybe if possible open my own hospitals. And the other thing is maybe to do some big businesses. . . . And the other thing is, maybe for my own sake, because I don't have a car, maybe I need to have my own within a period of five years.

Also, like NGO workers, government providers saw education and further training as important steps toward achieving their goals. With higher credentials, they would be able to seize better opportunities if they arose. Pilirani, a medical assistant, described how she needed to keep stepping up in her career. Her first job in healthcare was as an HSA, which she described as "step one." When I met her, she already had two more years of training at Malawi College of Health Sciences and was promoted to the next rank of medical assistant. But she emphasized that she would not stop there. This was only "step two" for her. She was "waiting for the third step, or fourth step, or fifth." Her dream is to go to Malawi's College of Medicine and become a pediatrician. Pilirani's description of her steps was not unlike NGO workers who also hoped to climb the career ladder from CHW to HTC counselor to site supervisor and beyond. Progression with one's skills, education, and careers were important to all providers whether they worked for NGOs or the government.

However, while providers had similar aspirations, they felt differently about their ability to achieve them. Government work was stable but stagnant. Providers saw little opportunity in the public sector to advance their careers and improve their life circumstances. Due to limited resources at public healthcare facilities, providers were not able to perform all the procedures they were trained in. Over time, this could make them feel stagnant as their skills started to regress. Geoffrey explained that his dental work consisted mostly of tooth extractions, as he is unable to perform other procedures like fillings or surgical treatments. He said, "If I just stay stagnant, it means these things, I'll forget them. . . . If we forget them, then we don't have a future." In addition, without educational sponsorship from the government, providers felt that it was impossible to move to a higher ranked and paid job. As Kelvin said simply: "I feel like I am not moving." With low salaries, it was also difficult to save money to fund one's own education. As Agnes, a nurse, said: "It's a stable job, but it cannot provide all the things I want. That's why I'm still looking for other greener pastures." She wanted a master's degree but could not save enough money to pay for school fees. She explained: "I pay for my house rent, I pay for my food, I pay for my transport. It ends there. I cannot devote myself in any other way." Emmanuel felt he was stuck in a cycle of work, saying: "We can't progress. Because here we work. In government institutions, we can work more than necessary. Work, work, until you get tired." With few chances to progress in their education and careers, providers felt pessimistic about their futures.

Public sector work did not speak to providers' aspirations. Government providers felt that their friends in NGOs were moving up in life while they remained the same. Emmanuel, for instance, felt that his friends working in NGOs were living "very good" lives and that they had "gone really high." He said, "Their salaries, their families, most of the achievements that normally a person needs have been accomplished. So for us, we were just, it's like just working on the very same level. We're just constant; we're not going up." Similarly, Kelvin talked about his friend's career and how he wants to follow in her footsteps. They went to secondary school together, but she went to Skyway University for a diploma in public health and is now working at an NGO. Kelvin described her situation: "Actually, it was that when she got employed under that NGO, she said that she's at least getting enough money to gather for herself. And her experience has also grown very wide just because she's exposed to many programs." Government providers often saw their NGO counterparts achieve the goals they aspired to—more income, career progression, advanced degrees, owning a home—whereas they felt it would be difficult, if not impossible, for them to do the same while working for the Ministry of Health.

As public sector providers weighed the benefits and drawbacks of each sector, the precarious opportunities that NGOs offered were often more appealing than the stability of their current jobs. Opportunities with NGOs were unpredictable, but the fact that they existed at all was meaningful to my respondents because it meant that there was a chance for upward socioeconomic mobility. Emmanuel explained that he felt the risks of NGOs were worthwhile. He said that with NGOs, "there's the problem of security." He continued, "You can be there maybe for a one-year program, then it ends, it means you'll be out again." But there were tradeoffs with the government too. He explained: "For government institution, they pay you little, but you keep on going." For him, "the issue is about risk-taking":

> Because when you say, "No I just want to be living on the same, same level. I won't take any risk," it means you will remain on this very same level, till you get old. But, if you say, "I think I can take a risk here. Let me leave the government, join a different institution, which is well-paid, maybe for a year." It means most of my problems can be solved. Even if they say, later on, this program has now ended, you are at least on a different level.

Risk-taking was a necessary part of upward mobility—the way to progress was not through stable government work but through precarious NGO work.

Government providers often looked to NGOs for opportunities. Like their NGO counterparts, how they thought about the future reflected judicious opportunism—they were waiting for better opportunities, ideally with NGOs. For some, this meant continuing their work in the public sector but keeping an eye out for job vacancies at NGOs. Emmanuel, for instance, was not actively searching for a new job but was open to opportunities. When discussing his future, he said: "I think if everything goes well, if I find better opportunities, maybe I can get out of government institutions and then go into NGOs." Similarly, Agnes was not applying to jobs at specific NGOs but broadly views them as the means to achieve her goal of getting a master's degree. She explained that she needed to look outside the government: "If I continue being here, working with the MoH [Ministry of Health], I don't see that dream coming true." Others were in the process of interviewing for NGO jobs. Kelvin, for instance, had recently come from an interview with World Relief for a community facilitator position. He was unsuccessful but planned to keep applying.

However, it is important to note that not everyone wanted to leave the public sector for an NGO job. There were some government providers who did not want to give up their job security.[43] While they were frustrated by the low salaries and poor working conditions, the risk of an insecure NGO job was not worth it. A data clerk explained, "Their working condition, there's no security. That's the problem. One has to have job security. Otherwise, without that, no." A few of my older respondents also did not desire NGO jobs; they preferred to finish their careers in the public sector.

Malawi's healthcare providers have always desired a good life for themselves and their families. With the rise of NGOs, a new pathway to upward mobility emerged. As unstable as this path was, it was possible for NGO workers to achieve what many aspired to: higher education, high incomes, home and car ownership, international travel, private schooling for children, and luxury goods. In comparison, government work was both challenging and incompatible with aspirations for upward mobility. With low pay and few opportunities for training and educational sponsorship, providers in the public sector felt stuck, with no chance to progress in their careers. If one wanted greener pastures in the future, one had to take risks with a more precarious field.

CONCLUSION

Foreign aid for HIV care has reshaped Malawi's healthcare landscape. Donor funding supports an array of NGOs, and their presence has had ripple effects across society.[44] NGOs created new employment opportunities, social networks, cultural discourses, connections to foreign actors, and educational programs in HIV-related fields, which fostered, in turn, new aspirations and possible pathways for upward socioeconomic mobility. This chapter examined how healthcare providers thought about their careers in a profession divided between NGOs and the public sector. NGO and public sector work took on contrasting meanings—NGOs offered precarious opportunities while public sector work offered stagnant stability. Neither sector was ideal. With NGOs, the pathway to upward mobility was unstable, with few achieving their goals. While public sector jobs were secure, this benefit lost its appeal as providers faced burnout and career stagnancy. For a younger generation of providers, NGO work was often appealing because it spoke to their aspirations for upward mobility, while public sector work felt incompatible with their goals.

The politics of legibility that I described in this chapter were of Malawian healthcare workers trying to improve their life circumstances amidst the opportunities and constraints of a divided healthcare profession. Healthcare workers were partially legible to donors. Donors saw NGOs as the organizations responsible for implementing various HIV programs and workers as the staff needed to carry out program activities. Yet the lives of NGO workers—their aspirations, the economic conditions they faced, and how they navigated a changing field of employment—remained illegible, as did the lives of public sector workers. Malawi's healthcare providers, however, do not think about their work separately from their economic conditions. For them, economic precarity, limited access to higher education, and a small formal labor market were the conditions in which they struggled and eventually found work in healthcare. And as they moved forward with their careers, these conditions continued to shape their decisions and thoughts about the future.[45] Despite changes in the healthcare landscape, economic conditions for healthcare providers have remained largely unchanged. NGOs added employment opportunities, but were unstable, while the public sector remained underfunded. In this context, providers struggled to escape poverty and economic uncertainty.

This chapter also speaks to the concerns of global health scholars about the brain drain of medical professionals to wealthier countries as well as to NGOs within their home country. My findings suggest that brain drain may be exacerbated as NGOs not only offer more competitive salaries but also as aspirations and public sector work become increasingly mismatched. Moreover, brain drain to NGOs worsens the already dire staff shortages in public healthcare facilities, placing greater burden on government providers and increasing their risk of burnout. If global health initiatives are to strengthen healthcare systems, they need to consider how to make public sector work more appealing, for instance by topping up salaries and offering training for career development.[46] More broadly, global health initiatives need to consider supporting education in general. There are many energetic and ambitious young people who want to be doctors and nurses—what is holding them back is limited access to education. The next chapter continues to follow providers but takes readers into Malawi's healthcare facilities. The divide in the healthcare profession also manifests in the everyday routines within health centers. At the same prenatal clinics, two worlds of care emerge in which HIV and prenatal services were characterized by distinct sets of providers, resources, and clinical practices.

4 Two Worlds of Prenatal Care

Health center in Lilongwe—Dr. Mwale, the physician in charge of the clinic, and I walk out of his office together. Outside, I glance over to a new building on the corner. "Built by UNC!" He laughs, and says, "You Americans, we like you! What would we do without you!" He gestures toward the ART clinic for HIV patients, "Built by Baylor!"

District hospital in Kasungu—Steve, one of the hospital coordinators for PMTCT programs gives a group of visitors a tour of the facility. In the hospital's lab, he makes sure to point out all of the equipment provided by donors. A representative from the Gates Foundation was one of the visitors. "Here is where we do the malaria rapid tests"; "Here we screen for HIV and syphilis"; "This is the Gene Expert machine for TB [tuberculosis] testing"; "This is the CD4 machine, given by you guys." With a smile, he looks at the Gates Foundation representative, and adds that the machine is seven years old and may need updates.

District hospital in Kabudula—Mr. Phiri takes me to the maternity ward. It smells strongly of bleach. There are only three beds, each with the mattress cover cracking, exposing the yellow foam inside. We move to the postnatal ward, where women rest after delivery. The room is cramped—there are about ten beds, placed close together. It is completely full, and half of the narrow one-person beds have two women on them. Women face opposite directions, lying head to foot to try to find more space.

Decisions about which conditions to prioritize, what populations to target, and how resources should flow are made by donors and international organizations far beyond Malawi's healthcare institutions. The spaces in Malawi's health centers are physical manifestations of donor agendas. HIV and other priority conditions are visible in new buildings, lab equipment, NGOs, and the occasional presence of foreign visitors. What is not prioritized is visible as well—in the dark and cramped rooms, shared hospital beds, and torn fabrics. Malawi's healthcare facilities embody tensions within the global health field. While donors may focus on certain diseases, healthcare facilities do not function in disease-specific ways. Patients come to the hospital with many kinds of illnesses and injuries, and healthcare providers need to care for all patients, whether they are HIV patients, expectant mothers, men, children, or the elderly.

Prenatal clinics are a place where tensions in legibility and illegibility are particularly striking. HIV services have become integrated into prenatal care. In order to protect children from HIV, global health efforts focus on testing pregnant and breastfeeding women and monitoring the health and behaviors of those who are found HIV positive. But, while preventing mother-to-child transmission of HIV is a priority, the conditions of prenatal clinics in public healthcare facilities often are not. As neoliberalism became a global norm, donors tended to fund NGOs and set up parallel structures for specific interventions, carving out a world of care distinct from the rest of the public healthcare system.[1] To donors, what was legible was disease. And they funded NGOs for prevention of mother-to-child transmission (PMTCT) programs, whose success was measured by metrics of reduced rates of HIV transmission to children. Women were seen specifically in terms of their HIV status and ability to transmit the virus, not in terms of their overall health. The politics of legibility that I describe in this chapter concerns patients and providers whose experiences are not defined by a single disease, even when donor programs narrowly focus on one. Women living with HIV could access donor-funded PMTCT programs, but they also needed care for their pregnancy as well as other illnesses and injuries. Healthcare providers, whether working for NGOs or the government, saw the patients before them but could only offer care in limited ways: The former could only treat a specific disease group for as long as a given program was funded, and the latter could only provide limited services due to resource constraints.

How have global health programs for preventing mother-to-child transmission of HIV affected healthcare services in prenatal clinics? What are the implications for women's HIV and prenatal care? This chapter follows healthcare providers in the prenatal clinics of three health centers in Lilongwe. The ways that women were partially legible to donors through disease status created fault lines through the prenatal clinics and through patients' experiences. Within the same prenatal clinics, there were divergent healthcare practices. NGOs took on almost all aspects of HIV care, from managing the supply chain to testing and counseling to tracking ART adherence. Their practices were defined by *surveillance*: Supported by donor resources, NGOs focused on finding HIV-positive pregnant women and intensively monitoring their adherence to drug treatment. In contrast, government providers were responsible for prenatal care for all pregnant women. However, with little donor support for the public sector, they struggled with shortages of staff, medicine, and space. Government practices were defined by *rationing*: providers limited time and services for each patient in order to serve everyone. This meant that prenatal care was a cursory process and women's concerns about their health and pregnancy were often left unaddressed. While NGOs can provide high-quality care, they only worked for specific populations and on specific issues. As a result, women's health was addressed in a piecemeal way, with an immense focus on preventing mother-to-child transmission of HIV, while leaving women at risk for problems that might occur during or after childbirth.

RECONFIGURATION OF PRENATAL CARE

> "Start free, Stay free, AIDS free."
>
> UNAIDS, PEPFAR & partners (2016 initiative)

Global health institutions leading the response to the HIV epidemic set an ambitious goal to one day see a generation without HIV infection. In their initiative to end AIDS in children, adolescents, and young women, UNAIDS, PEPFAR, and their partners proclaimed, "Every child deserves an HIV-free beginning."[2] This AIDS-free future rests on pregnant women. Since the 1990s, global health interventions have targeted HIV-positive mothers, asking them, for instance, to use formula instead of breastfeeding; to bear fewer children; and to take various preventative treatments like AZT, single-dose nevirapine, and more recently, triple-combination antiretroviral therapy (ART). From a public health standpoint, prevention is critical.[3] Caring for children with HIV is difficult: prescriptions are complex, there are few alternative drug regimens to switch to in cases where initial treatments fail, and children are subjected to a lifetime of medical treatment.

Today, HIV services are incorporated into prenatal care. Since 2007, women in Malawi test for HIV when they go to the prenatal clinic, making this a strategic site for identifying HIV-positive women.[4] According to government records, 95 percent of women in Malawi go to the prenatal clinic at least once during their pregnancy.[5] Starting in 2011, Malawi's new PMTCT policy, "Option B+," further integrated HIV services into prenatal care. Any pregnant or breastfeeding woman who tests positive immediately starts lifelong antiretroviral therapy, whereas, before Option B+, HIV patients could only start lifelong ART once their illness progressed to a more advanced stage, which was determined by a CD4 lab test or clinical symptoms.[6] When women go into the prenatal clinic, they sometimes walk out with a positive HIV test, their first bottle of ART, and likely enrollment into a specialized treatment support program.

The prenatal clinic is a unique space simultaneously legible to donors as a site for preventing mother-to-child transmission of HIV and illegible as a site for global health interventions on routine prenatal services. HIV care and prenatal care may take place in the same setting, but the conditions for providing care and the kind of practices that emerge are anything but the same.

THERAPEUTIC CITIZENSHIP AND CLIENTSHIP

For patients, having a condition that is legible to powerful institutions can come with benefits. Scholars have used the term *biological citizenship* to describe the way that illness, genetics, or other biological traits become categories states use to determine legal or social membership, as well as modes by which individuals can claim rights and resources.[7] Rather than being universal, the state grants rights and resources based on biomedical criteria. Medical screening for immigrants, for instance, allows "healthy" immigrants to enter and excludes those with "inadmissible" conditions like communicable diseases, addiction, and disabilities that the state deems undesirable.[8] In some cases, the state privileges people with certain illnesses for political recognition, residency, health care and other social goods.[9] For instance, France's "illness clause" gave undocumented immigrants with life-threatening illnesses the right to stay and receive treatment while others risked deportation.[10] Biological citizenship is intertwined with inequality—using group-specific criteria to determine access to state resources inevitably privileges some over others.

In low-income countries, the state can be even more selective. Nguyen develops the concept of "therapeutic citizenship" to describe a specific form of biological citizenship that arises when states do not have the resources to guarantee healthcare and social security to all citizens.[11] With limited state resources, illness can become a crucial currency. In Nguyen's case, in the early days of the HIV epidemic in West Africa, HIV patients had access through the HIV treatment system to social services, including food aid and school fees, which others could not access. Similarly, in post-Soviet Ukraine, citizens valued "illness" because the state provided social benefits like pension, healthcare, and education for children of people affected by Chernobyl radiation, benefits that were not available to those who were "healthy."[12] With therapeutic citizenship, it is not only the marginalized that lack resources but all citizens—people become visible to the state only through illness.

In today's global health field, a similar process occurs, but rather than coming from the state, resources tend to come from international donors and NGOs that serve specific populations. Whyte et al. use the concept of *therapeutic clientship* to describe how patients become visible to donor-funded NGOs and form unique relationships with them.[13] The term "client" implies a relationship over a given period of time, rather than a one-time exchange. NGOs often enroll clients into programs meant to achieve a certain health outcome. At the health centers where I conducted my research, NGOs enrolled HIV-positive women in their counseling program during their pregnancy and breastfeeding to prevent maternal HIV transmission. Additionally, the way people negotiate access to NGOs resembles a patron–client relationship. Being a client of an NGO comes with both privileges and expectations. For instance, HIV patients can join NGO programs, which come with health and social services unavailable to most, but they are also expected to do something in return, such as participate in HIV counseling sessions, adhere to medication prescriptions, or perform certain illness narratives for program evaluators.[14] With NGOs, healthcare is not a right for all citizens but a service given by (patron) organizations to those who are eligible and in the know.[15] For countries receiving foreign aid, therapeutic citizenship—a process of differentiation undertaken by the state—has largely been replaced by therapeutic clientship. It is donors that have the power to recognize certain groups or issues as worthy of aid. The state, on the other hand, is responsible for all citizens but given its resource constraints, can only provide care in limited ways.

The concepts of therapeutic citizenship and clientship provide a helpful starting point for understanding the differences in care in Malawi. These concepts capture the way that certain groups are recognized by state and nonstate institutions and the inequalities that arise as a result. However, I find that divisions go beyond group-based criteria. Clientship is an even more limited category, as it is only a portion of oneself—one's disease status—that is legible to donors and NGOs, not the entire individual. In this way, patients are both citizens and clients, navigating belonging and care through different institutions depending on their disease status. In this case, women were legible to donors and NGOs for their HIV status and ability to transmit HIV to their children, and at the same time, illegible and left to the state as pregnant women. This partial vision helps us to make sense of why healthcare practices can vary dramatically in the same prenatal clinics. NGO and government providers may work side by side, but they have different sources of funding, supply chains, and human and material resources. Women attending prenatal clinics were divided between those who tested positive for HIV and had access to NGO programs and those who did not. The experiences of women living with HIV were also divided, as NGOs focused on the risk of maternal HIV transmission, while their pregnancy and other health concerns fell to the state. After the risk of maternal HIV transmission was over, they were no longer enrolled in the NGO programs at the health centers. In this chapter, I complicate the concepts of therapeutic citizenship and clientship by showing that individuals themselves are partially recognized by donors and that this partial recognition creates fault lines through healthcare practices and patient experiences.

CONDITIONS OF HIV CARE

HIV was legible to donors as a global emergency and was treated in an exceptional way. Globally, funding for HIV increased more than twelve-fold since the early 1990s, rising from 213 million to 2.6 billion in 2005.[16] Since the mid-2000s, donors committed significant amounts of aid to scale up antiretroviral therapy in low-income countries. By 2024, the Global Fund, one of the leading donors in global health, had invested $27 billion in HIV treatment and prevention, enabling approximately 25 million patients to access ART.[17] HIV has dominated the global consciousness and is the largest disease-specific program in the global health field. Compared to illnesses that have a similar morbidity and mortality, HIV has received more funding.[18] For instance, while the global disease burden for HIV and acute respiratory infections were similar (30% and 26%), about 50 percent of direct donor funds went towards HIV, whereas only 2.5 percent went towards respiratory infections.[19] HIV programs are not only distinct for the amount of donor resources available but also for the way in which those resources tend to flow "vertically" or outside of the state. The spread of the HIV epidemic was intertwined with the spread of neoliberal ideology. Global health initiatives, financing, and programs follow an economistic logic that prioritizes solutions that are cost-effective and emphasizes the role of the market, rather than the state, as the best distributor of social goods.[20] Since the 1990s, much of the funding for global health has bypassed the state and gone through a proliferation of NGOs that offer a variety of health and social services.[21] In a neoliberal context, nonstate institutions now have a prominent role in providing healthcare.

In Malawi, the conditions for providing HIV services differed from other aspects of healthcare. Donor resources have been vital for the country's response to the HIV epidemic. Donors provided about 95 percent of the resources for the Malawi HIV/AIDS program.[22] Since the start of Malawi's HIV treatment program in 2003, the Global Fund had committed about $677 million for ART and various NGO programs that support HIV prevention and treatment.[23] And by 2019, the US government, via PEPFAR, had invested over $800 million to the HIV response in Malawi.[24] Donor resources for HIV have been managed separately from government institutions. While the Malawian government is responsible for managing most medical supplies, for HIV, donors set up a parallel supply chain through which NGOs and private companies buy, store, and distribute HIV treatment commodities along with other priority commodities like vaccines and treatments for malaria and tuberculosis. With a parallel supply chain, money from the Global Fund and other donors goes to UNICEF to procure HIV test kits and treatment.[25] These commodities are then sent to private companies in Malawi that manage storage and distribution. For instance, HIV test kits and treatment are stored at a Manobec warehouse instead of the government's Central Medical Stores Trust (CMST) and are then delivered by SDV Malawi Ltd., a private logistics firm, to hospitals and clinics around the country.

Donor organizations also strictly monitor the supply of HIV commodities. One program manager for a drug access program run by the Clinton Health Access Initiative (CHAI) described the Global Fund as running a particularly "tight ship" when it came to drug procurement, warehouse practices, and reporting stock. In his experience working on supply chains, he felt that privately managed systems worked better than those managed by the government. Manobec warehouses organized their boxes of HIV commodities neatly on racks and had a fully electronic system for monitoring supplies. In addition, on a quarterly basis, a supervision team from the Ministry of Health HIV/AIDS unit counts the number of patients on treatment and the stock of ART in all facilities to show that donor-funded materials are properly managed and to predict the future number of drug doses that would be needed at each site.[26] On the ground, what this meant was that HIV commodities were almost always available. Although public healthcare facilities struggled with resources, there have been no major stockouts of HIV testing kits or ART in the country in recent years.[27] During my fieldwork, I often heard about shortages of other health commodities, like syphilis tests or certain antibiotics, but there were no instances in which health centers ran low on HIV tests or ART. Providers had what they needed to diagnose HIV infection and to treat HIV-positive patients.

In addition, NGOs provided a separate workforce for HIV care. In the health centers where I conducted my research, there were two NGOs, both dedicated to helping pregnant women start and stay on HIV treatment. One was the Tingathe program, which was founded in 2007 by Drs. Maria Kim and Saeed Ahmed with the Baylor College of Medicine Children's Foundation. The Tingathe program hired community health workers (CHWs) to provide HIV services at the prenatal clinic as well as follow up with women at home.[28] Another NGO, Mothers2Mothers (M2M), had similar goals. They started working in Malawi in 2008 and also provided services at the clinic and in communities. Instead of using community health workers, M2M created a "mentor mothers" program, training mothers living with HIV to provide HIV counseling. While I spoke with providers in both NGOs, I spent most of my time with the Tingathe program, which was the larger program and was responsible for most HIV services at the clinics.

NGOs took on almost all aspects of HIV care. At the prenatal clinics, both NGOs provided health education lectures, group counseling to prepare women for HIV testing, and one-on-one counseling for women who test HIV positive. Workers from Tingathe did the HIV testing for women and for HIV-exposed children starting at six weeks until they were about two years old and no longer at risk for contracting HIV from their mothers. They also helped overworked government providers during the ART clinics' busiest days. They took vital signs for women and children, matched patients' personal health records with clinic files, entered data into electronic systems, organized the flow of patients, and distributed nutritional supplements. Outside the health centers, both NGOs followed up with women in their homes to provide additional counseling and treatment support.

The NGOs were well staffed. The Tingathe program, for instance, had about twenty staff members at each of their three sites in Lilongwe. M2M, which was smaller, added another four to five workers at each site. In some sites, the number of NGO staffers for PMTCT programs was greater than the total for all government providers. This labor force was important since there are several steps involved in providing comprehensive HIV care, and each step—testing, counseling, prescriptions, recording patients, and follow up—requires workers. NGOs were also involved in mentorship programs to improve the quality of HIV care in local healthcare facilities. EQUIP, a USAID-funded program, partnered with several HIV clinics in Malawi, including Baylor, Partners in Hope, and UNC. These clinics trained their doctors and nurses in HIV care, and then sent them to local hospitals and clinics to mentor government providers. In addition to the regular Tingathe and M2M staff, EQUIP mentors also came to the health centers on a monthly basis. They often worked side by side with the clinic's doctors and nurses to see HIV patients, ideally so that when there was a complex case, the mentor could provide guidance on treatment.[29]

Legibility has structural effects—in this case, creating a system of HIV care with distinct resources, supply chains, monitoring, and NGO providers. As Buse and Waxman describe, HIV programs have become "islands of excellence in seas of under-provision."[30] These islands not only reflect donor emphasis on HIV programs but also embody neoliberal approaches to healthcare that rely on the efficiency of the market and nonstate agencies. For example, while the idea of using donor funding to strengthen Malawi's CMST was proposed at the start of the HIV treatment program in 2003, it was curtailed when the World Bank dissuaded donors from doing so.[31] Such decisions illustrate how global politics influence the flow of donor resources and, in turn, impact national healthcare systems. In the next section, I describe the distinct clinical practices and implications for women that come with this separate NGO system of care.

HIV CARE AND SURVEILLANCE

The structures of HIV care shape the practices that occur. The way that women were legible to donors through their HIV status and potential to transmit HIV to children produced particular kinds of NGO practices. NGOs were focused on finding HIV-positive women, counseling them, and monitoring their use of ART during pregnancy and breastfeeding to ensure that their child stayed HIV-free. My fieldwork took place after Malawi's 2011 Option B+ policy, which coincided with global trends toward "treatment-as-prevention" (TasP). Donors, international organizations, and national policymakers embraced ART as the magic bullet to both treat patients and prevent the spread of HIV. As a result, HIV policies increasingly reflected a pharmaceutical logic that saw medicine as the primary solution to the epidemic. In this context, having HIV was not in itself stigmatizing; rather, stigma arose when individuals failed to take ART to manage their illness, which marked the boundary between acceptable and deviant health behavior.[32] In maternal healthcare this pharmaceutical logic took on a temporal component: Women became the proxies for their children's health, and their adherence to ART was framed as essential to achieving global goals for a future HIV-free generation.

Finding HIV-Positive Women

NGOs were not about serving all women but about finding pregnant or breastfeeding women living with HIV to enroll in their programs. NGOs searched the health centers for their target population, and they found most of their clients at the prenatal clinic.

When women arrived at the prenatal clinic, they lined up on rows of benches outside. Many began their travels early, sometimes before sunrise, to get to the clinic. Usually by 8 a.m., a crowd had already formed. The clinic's day began with a health education talk by either an NGO or government provider. Some talks emphasized preventing HIV transmission to children. For instance, during one talk, providers sang a song about how HIV can attack anyone—a man, a woman, even a child. The nurse emphasized the importance of getting tested and asked the audience, "Do you want to pass HIV to your baby?" Women responded in unison, "Nooooo." "If you and your husband take ART, do you want this for your baby?" Again, they answered, "Noooooo." The nurse talked about Option B+, which was colloquially known as *pompo pompo*, meaning "now." If you test positive, you start treatment now—right away.

After the health education talk, women lined up for HIV testing. Through provider-initiated testing and counseling (PITC), all women received an HIV test as part of their routine prenatal care unless they chose to opt out. But because few women knew they had a choice, in practice, HIV testing has become compulsory, and almost all pregnant women are tested.[33] NGO staff often conducted the testing at the prenatal clinic. They first gave pretest counseling to the group, explaining the basics of HIV, the procedures for HIV testing, and how to interpret the test results. One by one, women entered a room for their test. I joined Zione, the Tingathe site supervisor, when she was testing one day. Many women had been tested before and knew the routine. A woman came in, handed her health passbook (personal medical record) to Zione, and sat down. Zione took her hand, wiped her finger with alcohol, and pricked it to get a drop of blood for the HIV test kit. While they waited for the results, Zione provided HIV counseling, asking the woman if she knew what it meant to be positive or negative. After a couple of minutes, Zione asked if she was ready for the result. Her test result was negative. Zione asked how she felt. She smiled and said she was happy. Most women tested negative. Some showed little emotion, some looked away and laughed, and some were nervous and hesitated before saying they were ready to hear their result. Before women left the room, Zione reminded them to test again next year, and to bring their partners since the country was doing a "male involvement" campaign to encourage men to come to the prenatal clinic.

Women who tested positive for the first time were taken to another room for further counseling. For an NGO, even the step between the test result and counseling was an important one. Outside of the testing room, there was a community health worker acting as the "escorter," whose task was to wait to take the patient to the NGO office. During one visit, I spent time with James while he was in the escorter role. We sat on the ledge of a table in a narrow room off to the side of the prenatal clinic. This was where the clinic's data clerk waited for women to come out so he could record their visit on the computer. The clerk would let us know if someone tested positive. Most of the day was uneventful—we sat, chatted, and sometimes got bored. But occasionally, a woman would test positive. That day, James escorted three women to the NGO office. He would give them detailed instructions on where to meet and walked separately to avoid suspicion from other patients outside. James asked for women's health passbooks and held onto them to ensure that they met him at the office. For NGOs, no HIV-positive woman can fall through the cracks. Even in the short distance from the prenatal clinic to their offices, NGOs could not risk an eligible woman leaving the clinic without enrolling in their program.

In addition to testing at the prenatal clinic, NGO workers also checked other clinic departments for any HIV-positive mothers they might have missed. Staff members would often sit outside the Under 5 clinic, where women bring their young children for routine care like vaccinations, to check the health passbooks for anyone who might be HIV positive and not already enrolled as a client. Others visited the outpatient or tuberculosis (TB) department to check the passbooks of women who appeared eligible for their program—that is, women who were pregnant or with an infant. If they found someone who was HIV positive and pregnant or breastfeeding, they immediately escorted her to their office for enrollment. NGO staff also provided HIV testing for other departments. One counselor explained that she did testing and counseling "everywhere." She said, "I do work every department, yes, but especially ANC, VCT, ART, maternity ward, male and female wards; we also go there to test clients who are willing to do so." Even though provider-initiated testing at the prenatal clinic identified the majority of HIV-positive women, NGO workers did a thorough search of the entire health center to make sure they found every possible client.

Creating "Responsible" Mothers

Once NGOs found pregnant HIV-positive women, they needed to convince them to start treatment. Counseling was a main component of NGO practices. Following global standards for confidentiality and consent, counselors took a "non-directive" approach: rather than telling women what to do, they presented the possible choices and their implications.[34] These choices, however, were not neutral—they were normatively charged. While women were technically autonomous patients who make their own treatment decisions, it was the NGO provider's role to guide them towards the "right" decision of taking ART.

HIV-positive women received extensive counseling. In addition to the pretest counseling and testing procedures, if a woman was found positive, she would then have a one-on-one counseling session with a provider to discuss starting drug treatment. Individual counseling sessions often lasted thirty minutes or more. NGO providers listened to women's reactions to their diagnosis and elicited concerns about HIV and starting ART. Receiving an HIV diagnosis and a prescription for lifelong treatment was often distressing news for women, and not everyone wanted treatment right away. Emily, a supervisor at one of the NGO sites, explained:

> You know, they'll always react because this message is not simple. They will react. Some, they cry. . . . Yeah, we still keep watching them and see what they are doing. And there comes a time whereby they're now okay. Once we see that they're okay, we ask how they feel. And we share their feelings.

During counseling sessions, NGO workers emphasized women's responsibility to take treatment for the sake of their children. Counseling turned the "therapeutic gaze" onto patients' behaviors, asking them to analyze their own health behaviors and assume responsibility for their choices.[35] In the maternal healthcare setting, being a responsible mother meant undergoing HIV testing and treatment; refusing to do so meant that one did not want a "normal" child.[36] Counselors explained the biological mechanisms of HIV and that, if they did not go on treatment, women would be putting their children at risk for HIV infection. As one provider described: "It's like we make them understand about the immune system . . . what happens with this HIV virus when it enters into the body—they [HIV virus] go against the same immunity that makes you better." In discussing the biological mechanisms, providers also described that ART can stop the process of HIV transmission and thus why women needed treatment. One provider explained:

> For helping to guide what is supposed to be done. . .at this stage, like for example, you are pregnant, you understand that the unborn baby can get infected. . .what can be done better to prevent that child to be infected is you to start ARVs [antiretrovirals]. So ARVs help your CD4 to be boost up and make the virus to be small. So if the virus is small and chances of that infant to get infected is small, so at that time you have prevented your child not to get infected.

In addition, NGO providers argued that mothers had a moral responsibility to take treatment. As one provider said: "When she tests positive, she must start ARVs even before consulting her husband . . . because she's the one carrying the baby." Children were the innocent victims of their mother's HIV infection. Regardless of women's relationships and conditions at home, she was the one with HIV and therefore the only person responsible for her and her child's life. One provider explained:

> So we give hope to the mother, and we also enlighten to her: You are also having a baby and the baby is innocent. Had it been that the baby had an opportunity to speak for herself, we would have given medication to the baby. But because the baby cannot speak for herself, you are the right person. Can we work together so that we can protect the baby not to get the virus?

Counseling efforts were persistent. NGO providers would continue to counsel women even if they had already refused to join their program. They were often frustrated when women refused. Mary, one of the NGO counselors, was testing at the prenatal clinic and was taking a long time with one woman who tested positive. She could not convince her to start ART, so she sent her to Samuel, another counselor. After more time, Samuel came out and said that he could not convince her either. She went back to see Mary to finish up her appointment. But now, Mary sounded like a different person. As she went through a list of demographic questions, her voice was no longer gentle, but curt. When the woman left, Mary was angry. She said she could sense that this woman would refuse. She had heard the same story before: "Women say, 'I don't want to take ART because I want to talk to my husband first.'" But Mary argued that if she wanted her husband to come, she could still accept her status and take the pills, do the home follow-up, and then bring her husband later. Even if you do not want ART, you should still take it for the sake of the baby. She asked rhetorically, "Do you know how hard it is to raise an HIV-positive child?"

Monitoring Adherence

Once women started ART, NGOs intensively monitored their adherence to treatment for as long as they were at risk of transmitting HIV to their child. Women needed to take treatment every day until their child was about two years old—usually when women stopped breastfeeding—and presumed to be no longer at risk for contracting maternal HIV. Every woman in the program had an assigned NGO community health worker who visited them at home to see how they were doing on ART. The first visit took place within the first week of testing positive and then occurred monthly. The CHWs carefully documented home visits. Richard, one of the CHWs, showed me the program register, going through each piece of data they collect—the date, client name, CHW name, new or known positive, partner disclosure, and ART use. He also had a checklist of questions to ask during each visit, such as whether the client has side effects, needs assistance with disclosure of HIV status to partners and family, has signs of tuberculosis, and more. He emphasized that CHWs do not go into the field with a blank mind—they have a "map," referring to the list of questions, of what they needed to cover. When he returned from his home visits, he recorded the information into the NGO's database. This information was used to monitor women's use of treatment. But it also provided CHWs with a way to deflect blame if their client was not adherent. Richard explained that if a client "defaults"—that is, stops taking treatment—they can look in the records to show that they had done everything on the checklist. If there was no record, it reflected poorly on them.

NGO providers also monitored women's adherence by counting pills. During each home visit, they counted their clients' pills to see if the number left in the bottle corresponded with their last appointment day at the clinic. Counting pills was an important part of home visits because they were an objective measure of clients' adherence over time. One CHW explained the process:

> I must visit there. Mainly we do pill count to see if she is taking medication correctly. I have to check the pill count, and I have to correlate with the dates when she is coming back. If she is adhering to the medication, I have to encourage her just to keep on taking medication. I have to highlight more on PMTCT, that if she is adhering to the drugs that means, "I am protecting my baby." If she is [not] adhering to [it], she is putting the baby at risk. On top of that, she has to understand if she is not taking the right drugs, she is putting her life at risk.

NGO providers also checked women's adherence when they came to the clinic for refills of ART. The CHWs who were taking vital signs asked women if they brought their bottles and counted pills for those who did.

Another CHW stayed inside the patient consultation room to check women's records for any missed appointments. If women missed doses of medication, NGO workers notified her assigned community health worker to follow up with her at home. Women with poor adherence were put on "maximum supervision." NGO workers would visit their clients frequently, as much as once a week, to counsel and convince them to start treatment again. Since women were responsible for their child's health, they would also be the ones to blame if their child was HIV positive. As one provider explained: "If they start on their own, they know it's them who consented to start taking ARVs. . . . So if they default, they know it is their own fault, not somebody else's fault."

NGO staff were often visibly frustrated if women did not want to take ART. Blessings, one of the CHWs, encountered one of his past clients who had stopped treatment. She was pregnant with another child, took another HIV test, and it was positive. As part of program policy, they needed to recruit her. But when Blessings saw her in the NGO office, he started yelling, "I don't want her!" Walking past me, he said she used to be his client but was "not a good one." Women who do not take treatment—the "defaulters"—were a challenge for the staff. Despite the considerable time and effort NGO providers spent visiting clients, they could not count them as treatment successes if they defaulted.

Implications for Women

NGO practices reflected the ways in which women were legible to donors. HIV-positive women were a key target population because of the risk of transmitting HIV to future generations, and PMTCT programs aimed to address this. NGOs developed various strategies to identify HIV-positive women, counsel them to start ART, and monitor their adherence to treatment. While CHWs were committed to their clients' well-being, they also faced pressure to achieve program goals of ensuring treatment adherence.

These NGO programs had mixed meanings for the women they served. According to some scholars, HIV counseling and adherence monitoring represents a "responsibilization" that disciplines women into taking medication.[37] This is especially pronounced as recent HIV-care policies and programs emphasize the use of ART as the means to both treat patients and prevent the spread of disease. In my research, NGO practices like repeated counseling sessions, pill counts, and reprimands for nonadherence could certainly feel disciplinary. For NGO providers, there was no shame in being HIV positive—they comforted patients, provided health information, and emphasized that patient could live long and healthy lives. The stigma came from refusing or stopping treatment, which was when otherwise kind and understanding counselors admonished women for being "refusers" or "defaulters."

But NGO surveillance around HIV testing, counseling, and treatment adherence was not always repressive. NGO providers made sure that women received all necessary HIV services, went to their appointments, got refills of medication, tested their children, and received laboratory results. They communicated with women, gave detailed explanations about their condition, and answered any questions they had. And, because women had regular visits from their assigned CHW, they built close relationships with them. As one CHW said, "because we know our clients better . . . so it's like there's a good connection between the community health worker and the client. Of course, the doctor just meets them during the clinic, but for us, it is a routine." Some workers, like Zione and Emily, who were site supervisors, had been with the NGO program since its founding in 2007. They had seen some of their clients through several pregnancies over the years. Throughout my fieldwork, it was common to see NGO workers talking with their clients at the clinic or joking around with their children. The amount of time that NGO providers spent with their clients and level of detail in their service provision was distinct. As we will see in the next section, government providers faced numerous resource constraints, and in that context, it was impossible to provide the same level of attention to patients.

NGO practices sometimes had broader benefits for women beyond their intended goals. NGO workers acted as liaisons and helped their clients navigate the healthcare system. When I was with Grace, who was testing infants, one of her clients looked at me and said proudly in English that she was HIV positive and her and her baby were taking medicine. She pointed to her baby's foot and told me she was here to test her baby (blood is drawn from the heel for testing). After they finished the test, Grace's client turned to her, holding the side of her own face, and explained something in Chichewa. Grace suddenly left the room. When she returned, she explained that her client had bad toothache, so she ran out to look for the clinic's dentist. After she finished with her HIV services, the dentist would be expecting her. NGO workers often talked to nurses and doctors on their client's behalf, helped them pick up lab results, and escorted them to various services. One NGO provider explained:

> So we are here to observe our patients, to know how they go in with the clinician, and to maybe . . . because some of them are shy to speak on their problems. They can tell me that, 'I'm having this, this problem.' If she asks them—the clinician—maybe she's not comfortable. I'm supposed to escort the patient to the doctor when it's clinic day so that maybe if she has forgotten the issue, I can speak on her behalf.

Donor resources can come with firm boundaries as to where funding goes, but personal relationships on the ground are messier. These spillover effects show how the boundaries of belonging get blurred in practice. While NGO providers' work was oriented around finding women with HIV and monitoring their treatment adherence, they also saw their clients beyond their HIV status. NGO providers built relationships with their clients and their clients' children, and they used their clinic connections to support them with their health concerns in general.

NGOs operate within the broader context of foreign aid, which shapes the resources available to them and the kinds of practices that take place. As described above, the practices of NGOs implementing PMTCT programs were intensive. NGO providers conducted HIV testing, thoroughly searched the clinic for possible clients, provided detailed counseling sessions, checked in on clients at home, and monitored their adherence on treatment. Because of donor funding, NGO providers consistently had the HIV test kits, drugs, and staff needed to carefully carry out each aspect of PMTCT care. Their practices also reflected the ways women were legible to donors—primarily through their HIV status and potential to transmit HIV to children. The success of PMTCT programs depended on demonstrating to donors that maternal HIV transmission was declining. This requirement traveled down to frontline community health workers, who were instructed to perform various tasks to find, enroll, and retain women in their program and to document these efforts. At times, the intensity with which CHWs monitored their clients wavered between disciplinary surveillance and genuinely caring and thorough support.

The prenatal clinic was a physical embodiment of a partial vision of health. HIV-care programs took place in prenatal clinics because they were a good site to find HIV-positive pregnant women. Here, donor resources and intensive NGO practices were meant for preventing maternal HIV transmission not for maternal health as a whole. As such, therapeutic clientship had distinct components—separate supply chains, providers, target populations, practices, and quality of care—but inclusion was limited to a specific population for a specific time. Women without HIV were not legible to donors and NGOs. And, while HIV-positive women could benefit from NGOs, the benefits had limits. NGOs only served HIV-positive women while they were at risk for transmitting HIV to children. Once they finished breastfeeding and were thus no longer at risk, they too became illegible. While women formed relationships with their assigned CHW, who sought to connect them to care beyond the NGO, these efforts were driven by personal relationships rather than formal program inclusion. But prenatal care is about more than preventing HIV transmission. Women living with HIV, like those without HIV, were also expectant mothers who wanted to have healthy pregnancies and to give birth to healthy children. However, the rest of prenatal care fell to public sector healthcare, which operated under very different conditions and with different practices.

CONDITIONS FOR STATE HEALTHCARE

While NGO and government providers worked in the same clinic, they labored under different conditions. In contrast to HIV care, there was little outside assistance for Malawi's struggling national health sector. While, after the mid-2000s, there has been increasing interest among donors and international organizations about supporting national healthcare systems, it has mostly remained in the realm of discourse.[38] In their review of organizational documents, Hafner and Shiffman found that use of the term "health system strengthening" has increased but that funding has stagnated; as funding for other initiatives, like HIV/AIDS care, has increased, this has meant that the relative proportion of funding for healthcare systems has steadily declined over the years. Others have found that what health system strengthening means in practice varies.[39] For instance, donors may take a selective approach that addresses systemic issues, for example, drug procurement and distribution—but only for the specific diseases or issues they are interested in, such as HIV care or vaccination.[40] While overtly neoliberal policies like structural adjustment policies are no longer used, this ideological influence lingers and has become embedded in organizational structures that enable or constrain certain courses of actions. In this case, despite a recognized need to strengthen healthcare systems, it remains difficult for donors to dedicate significant funding to it or to do so outside of the existing structures for disease programs. As Keshavjee argues, neoliberalism produces a systematic form of blindness.[41] While the global health field grew immensely over the past few decades, the challenges faced by public healthcare systems have persisted. The conditions I describe below of Malawi's prenatal clinics are not new.

Like many low-income countries, the Malawian government struggled with managing medical supplies. Malawi's Central Medical Stores Trust (CMST) faced numerous problems, including cumbersome World Bank procurement procedures, staff shortages, poor warehouse management, and insufficient funding to purchase a buffer supply of drugs.[42] One program manager for CHAI's drug access program described the difference between the government and private warehouses as night and day. While the private Manobec warehouses for HIV-care commodities were organized and had up-to-date data on electronic systems, CMST was chaotic. There was not always space to store boxes of medications in the CMST warehouse, so medications were often left on the ground. Boxes were not systematically organized on their shelves and the database system was split between paper and electronic records, making it difficult to track supply levels.

Healthcare facilities frequently had stockouts of various drugs, laboratory equipment, and other materials. In a survey conducted on Malawi's implementation of the Essential Health Package, which are interventions to address local disease burdens, only 27 percent of facilities had sufficient supply of co-trimoxazole—a drug that treats acute respiratory and other infections—and only 24 percent and 22 percent of facilities had enough benzathine penicillin and erythromycin—oral antibiotics used to treat several conditions.[43] Thirty-one percent of facility managers said that they had to refer patients to a higher-level clinic because they did not have the necessary drugs.[44] According to the CHAI program manager, such essential medicines were a kind of "donor orphan." While common health issues, like infectious diseases, maternal health, and nutritional deficiencies, contribute significantly to the local burden of disease, they were not considered donor priorities and thus did not receive the same level of support.

During my fieldwork, HIV-care materials were always available, but there were numerous instances when other drugs or supplies were out of stock or unusable. To provide a short list: broken X-ray machines; no reagents for TB laboratory machines; no reagents for hemoglobin tests; women doubling up on beds in the maternity ward; no syphilis tests; no standing scale; no fuel for the ambulance; broken sterilizer for surgical tools; broken microscope bulbs; no amoxicillin (antibiotic). In addition, many health centers did not have consistent running water and electricity. Infrastructure problems affect all kinds of services, including HIV care. Healthcare providers often took time out of their day to secure buckets of water so they could wash their hands after an exam, or sometimes they chose to go without. Providers also had to halt certain aspects of their work when electricity stopped. Laboratory workers were unable to run CD4 tests for HIV patients, conduct blood tests for tuberculosis, or take X-rays, and even donor-funded equipment often sat unused because there was no electricity or no reagents. Similarly, patient data could only be recorded electronically when facilities had electricity, making it difficult to imagine a full transition to computer-based records.

Malawi also has one of the worst health worker shortages in the world. As we have seen, while the WHO recommends at least forty-nine doctors, nurses, and midwives per ten thousand people, in Malawi, there are only 0.5 physicians and 5.1 nurses and midwives per ten thousand people.[45] Only 13 percent of facilities have sufficient staff.[46] Short-term efforts to solve the workforce shortage have not led to significant improvements. While Malawi received grants for health systems strengthening, such grants tended to be for selective interests. For instance, a subgrant from the Global Fund to strengthen the capacity of healthcare workers successfully provided HIV-care training to healthcare workers, but it did little to increase the overall number of providers. By the end of the grant period, only 23 percent of nursing positions were filled.[47] In the health centers, there were sometimes more NGO workers dedicated to pregnant HIV-positive women than there were nurses, doctors, and medical assistants for the entire health center. While Malawi's healthcare system was often illegible to donors and international organizations, its conditions were keenly felt by healthcare providers, shaping their everyday practices and the care they delivered.

Rationing Prenatal Care

What is or is not legible to donors for foreign aid has produced distinct kinds of healthcare within the prenatal clinics. NGOs targeted particular populations while the government was responsible for the residual populations that were not donor priorities. Unlike Nguyen's earlier conceptualization of therapeutic citizenship, in which the state only functions for certain disease groups, here the state functioned for a broader population but was limited in other ways. Government providers worked with all patients—but in conditions of constant shortages. Public healthcare was defined by rationing, where providers followed their own logic of social equity: Services were about providing some to all.

Because of staffing shortages, government providers felt that they could not devote enough time and attention to each of their responsibilities. Doctors and nurses often took on the work of several providers. One nurse explained: "Instead of having four midwives on duty, we have only one or two, who are supposed to do the same job which was supposed to be done by three or four midwives." Almost all government providers I spoke with described times when they felt alone and spread too thin. Providers often juggled tasks across multiple departments at the health centers. One nurse explained:

> If we have a shortage of staff, then that means here we have one person allocated to two places. You have to be available at labor ward, you have to be available at ART, then you have to come here and see the patient, you have

> to go there, you have to run up and down and then by the end of the day you might be doing wrong things.

Global health campaigns sometimes exacerbated staff shortages. In addition to unexpected sickness, travel, or leave, government providers were called away to train for new programs. During my fieldwork, there was a male circumcision campaign taking place across the country. Training sessions took providers away for two weeks at a time, leaving additional work for those who remained at the health centers.

Government providers limited time with each patient in the prenatal clinics so that every woman could be seen. On a busy day at the prenatal clinics, there could be close to one hundred women waiting for services but only one or two nurses working. It was important for nurses to finish the line of patients "in good time." Providers often worked continuously without a break or stopping to eat lunch. As one nurse explained: "We work under pressure so that we can finish the queue, so sometimes it is difficult to spend much time with one patient because you just feel there are a lot of patients waiting outside." The logic was simple: The more patients there are, the faster one works. Another nurse explained, "While you go in sites, you just see you are two against 250, so you just increase your pace. You cannot take time with one patient." Nurses also worked quickly because they did not want to send women home without being seen. They explained that some women travel long distances to reach the clinic, so it was better to see women quickly than to risk sending them back without services.

> Usually what happens is in our setting, Malawian setting . . . For a mother to go to antenatal clinic, it's a challenge. Some come from far away, from a distance away. So if you keep them for a long time, then definitely they will not come back during the next day of the ANC visit. So we try to squeeze time, of course. It's like the care we give, we squeeze in, yeah. Which is not okay, but for them to come back . . .

The speed at which government providers worked contrasted starkly to the time NGO workers took with each HIV-positive mother. For NGOs, each part of the process was important and took time—from pre-test counseling to the continued check-ins at home and in the clinic. For government providers, this kind of detail and time was not possible. Rationing time was not ideal for patient care, but it was a necessary response to the conditions of local healthcare facilities. While service providers everywhere improvise according to the conditions of their work, it is often accentuated in low-income countries like Malawi where resources are scarce.[48]

In addition to limiting time, nurses limited which prenatal services they provided. Because facilities had frequent stockouts of supplies, government providers did not always have the materials they needed to conduct all recommended prenatal services. Most visits consisted of abdominal palpations, which is a way of examining the baby's development through touch, and distributing antimalarial and antiworm medication. But other tests that are important for catching conditions with adverse maternal and infant outcomes like anemia or preeclampsia were not always done. Providers did not regularly have the equipment necessary for taking vital signs and blood pressure or conducting syphilis, hemoglobin, and urine protein tests. Without such supplies, providers could only give cursory rather than comprehensive prenatal care. As one nurse said:

> I can say we have limited resources. Because these women are not receiving the care that they are supposed to. We don't have a weighing scale, we don't have a BP (blood pressure) machine . . . When we are talking of a holistic approach, they are supposed to have their blood tested for syphilis. We don't have the reagents. And these women, they are supposed to be checked for HB (hemoglobin) and urine protein . . . [But] we are just doing women who are in need of that . . . But when we have all the resources, [all of] these women, they are supposed to be checked for all these things.

Privacy was another aspect of comprehensive care that government providers could not give. Clinics had limited space to accommodate the growing number of patients in Malawi's urban centers. Providers adapted by using space efficiently, sometimes adding more beds to consultations rooms. This, however, created problems for patients. As one nurse explained: "We have got two beds, which is not okay. There's no privacy—one lady is there and one woman is there; we palpate this one for three minutes, another comes in. This is not okay."

Provider Burnout

The pressure to work quickly and accommodate all patients took a toll on the limited government-provider workforce. Many government providers felt burnt out and unmotivated to work. They described feeling very tired at the end of the day and did not look forward to coming in the next day. As one nurse said, "When you are knocking off [leaving work], you are tired, you feel headache. But you just accept it." Another nurse expressed a similar sentiment, "When coming in the next day you are like, 'My God, I am going to work.' We don't enjoy most of the time. We just say, 'I am supposed to work; let me just go to work.'"

Government providers felt that burnout affected patient care. They were overwhelmed by the amount of work and number of patients they needed to see, which could lead to mistakes or deficiencies in the services provided. Throughout our conversations, they often commented, "This is not okay" or "You might be doing wrong things." One nurse explained, "Once the mind is full—and you have to think of this client, you have to see this one, you have to see this one—to some extent, we can omit, or we can neglect some other things that are supposed to be done." She later described a time when she struggled during her night shift duties. She said, "I was there alone, I worked during the night, and I had also worked during the day. So, I was like dozing, or I couldn't remember to do this other thing, or there's too much work for me to do. I couldn't do everything I was supposed to do."

The problems with burnout that providers at my field sites described were also reflected nationally. In a survey of Malawi's healthcare workers, Maria Kim and collaborators found that 62 percent met the criteria for the Maslach Burnout Inventory, which measures burnout on dimensions of emotional exhaustion, depersonalization, and sense of low personal accomplishment.[49] Amongst their respondents, more than half worked over fifty hours a week, with 36 percent reporting that they worked more than sixty hours a week. These findings are similar to those for other sub-Saharan African countries facing resource constraints.[50] Burnout was also associated with suboptimal patient care. An alarmingly high proportion of healthcare workers, 89 percent, reported engaging in some suboptimal patient care practices or adopting suboptimal attitudes. This included self-reports about making mistakes in treatment due to lack of knowledge or experience (52%), shouting at patients (45%), not performing diagnostic tests due to a desire to finish quickly (35%), and absenteeism (24%). The way providers interact with patients matters for health outcomes. When patients feel they are treated disrespectfully, they may be more likely to abandon treatment or not seek care.[51]

Implications for Women's Healthcare

In the end, rationing time and services diminished the quality of prenatal care that women received. While a woman could spend over an hour on HIV care, she spent just a few minutes with prenatal services. Prenatal care was a cursory process—government providers worked like a well-oiled machine. Constance, one of the nurses, showed me the layout of the clinic before services began. She had talked to me earlier about teamwork at the clinic and wanted to highlight that here. She pointed out that in one corner, there would be a counselor doing an HIV test; in another corner, a clerk inputs data into the electronic system; at the table, she will fill out the prenatal care register (paperback record book), write in the patient's health passbook (personal medical file), and distribute iron tablets and antimalarial and antiworm prophylactic pills. Once the clinic opened, there was a flurry of activity. A woman comes in, sits down, and gets her finger pricked for an HIV rapid test. While the test results process, Constance calls her over and tells her to lie down. She does palpations, massaging the woman's abdomen to check the progress of the pregnancy and position of the baby, and if the woman is further along, she uses a wooden funnel to listen for the fetal heartbeat. While this is taking place, the clerk fills out data on the electronic system. She yells across the room to the patient, asking for her age, residence, and other demographic information. After the palpations, Constance sits down to document the visit in the facility's register. Barely looking up, she hands the woman her health passbook and gives her a handful of pills. She tells the patient to swallow the pills and gestures to the bucket of water and empty pill container, which is used as a cup, by the door. Before the patient leaves the room, the next one is already on her way in.

In this fast-paced environment, women's concerns about their pregnancy and health were often left behind. Providers felt that they did not have time or energy to explain the services and medications they were giving. As one nurse put it:

> You need to explain to a patient that has come to your facility, and they need to go back home satisfied that they have received the care . . . It's not just dispensing the drugs, they need an explanation, they need to know what they are suffering from, what they can do to get better, or what they can do to maintain their health conditions. But because when you are tired, and you have that long queue, you only give maybe two to three words, just to counsel in a few seconds. And the person goes back without full information from the facility.

It was also difficult for women to raise their health concerns to nurses. Nurses moved quickly from one task to the next and did not elicit questions from patients. Unlike the HIV counseling provided by NGOs, there was little dialogue between providers and patients during prenatal care. Interactions were mostly instructions for women to come in, lie down, take a pill, and leave. One nurse explained, "In terms of maybe counseling, maybe sometimes they fail to ask some things; they cannot ask or they are not free to say it because we are doing it fast." Moreover, nurses often discouraged women from asking questions. When women did interject to ask a question, nurses often responded in a disparaging way, saying something curt or yelling back. As one nurse said: "It happens sometimes—maybe you are tired, maybe the clients are not cooperative—you become emotional as well. Maybe you say something you didn't mean just because you are tired and someone maybe provoked you."

Unlike the spotlight on HIV care, the public healthcare system fell in the shadows of the global health field.[52] Public healthcare functioned under conditions of scarcity; there were not enough healthcare workers or medical equipment to provide comprehensive care.[53] While the conditions of public healthcare may be illegible to donors, they were not to the providers and patients in Malawi. The way government providers worked and how they felt about their work were shaped by the numerous resource constraints they encountered. Rationing time and services were responses to these conditions. Women did not receive high-quality prenatal care—but not because government providers are inherently neglectful people. Rather, with limited donor support, public healthcare facilities did not have the means to provide the same kind of intensive monitoring for the general population of pregnant women as NGOs could for pregnant women who were HIV positive. Government providers could barely keep up with basic care, let alone take time to communicate with patients, ensure that they complete all prenatal visits, and track their progress during pregnancy.

The inequalities in care that we see between HIV-care NGOs and public prenatal care are especially consequential in a context of high maternal and infant mortality. In 2015, maternal mortality in Malawi was the twenty-ninth highest in the world with 354 deaths per one hundred thousand live births.[54] Rates of neonatal and infant mortality were also troubling—out of one thousand births, there were twenty-three deaths within twenty-eight days and thirty-nine deaths within one year.[55] In addition, women do not always have enough nutrition during pregnancy. In 2015, 16 percent of children were born with a low birthweight, which puts them at higher risk for illnesses, developmental delays, and death.[56] HIV-positive women enrolled in NGO programs received nutritional supplements, but many other women did not qualify for such benefits. While the public healthcare system was responsible for all patients, in a context of resource constraints, it was a weak form of inclusion. Rather than exceptional care for a target population, state-led care was about providing limited services to all citizens. However, fast consultations and incomplete service provision mean that problems that cause adverse maternal and infant health outcomes might not be caught in time.

CONCLUSION

The way that disease status was legible to donors created fault lines that ran through clinics and through patient experiences. Healthcare practices within the same prenatal clinics diverged. NGO and public healthcare were distinct in many ways: They had different resources, staff members, target populations, practices, and in the end, outcomes for patients. NGOs took on HIV care, and their work was characterized by surveillance around finding HIV-positive women and monitoring their adherence on ART. With NGO programs, women living with HIV received comprehensive services for preventing mother-to-child HIV transmission and sometimes developed close relationships with their NGO providers, who advocated for them at the health centers. Meanwhile, government providers were relieved of some HIV services and focused on prenatal care. However, under resource-constrained conditions, public healthcare was defined by a system of rationing. Unlike the intensity of NGO surveillance, government providers limited time and services for each woman in order to serve everyone. As a result, women received cursory prenatal services, and their concerns about their pregnancy and health were often left behind.

The promise of global health programs to provide care and relieve suffering takes place under conditions of inequality and exclusion. The influx of foreign aid has redefined who state and nonstate organizations are responsible for. As scholars writing about therapeutic clientship describe, NGOs offer unique access to health and social goods to populations that are of interest to donors.[57] In this context, therapeutic citizenship takes on new meaning, as differentiation is driven more by donors and NGOs than by the state, which is left to serve the residual populations excluded from donor priorities. But dividing the patient population leaves no one truly enfranchised. While NGOs offered higher-quality care, only a specific group of pregnant and breastfeeding HIV-positive women could benefit and only for as long as the risk of maternal HIV transmission was present. While prenatal care was provided by the government as a service for all citizens, with severe resource constraints, women regardless of their HIV status received limited care. They were not counseled on prenatal care; their health was not monitored over time; and once they left the clinic, they were no longer the responsibility of the state or NGOs. While the state is meant to serve all, its inclusivity loses significance when what it can provide is extremely limited.

The politics I described in this chapter were of patients and providers whose healthcare needs and professional responsibilities are not defined by a single disease. While donor-funded PMTCT programs have been successful in reducing HIV transmission, these successes are limited to one aspect of women's health. In this context, the time that NGO providers spent with patients was exceptional, given a healthcare system otherwise characterized by rationed and fast-paced services. NGO providers used a range of techniques—searching clinics to find their target population, counseling, monitoring pill counts, tracking adherence over time—to ensure that women started and stayed on treatment. These efforts proved effective. From studies conducted before and after Option B+, mother-to-child transmission dropped from 13.5 percent in 2009 to 3.7 percent between 2014 and 2016.[58] But for HIV patients, the exceptional resources targeted towards their condition were not a panacea that transformed their lives. Women came to the prenatal clinic not just at risk for maternal HIV transmission but as expectant mothers wanting a healthy pregnancy and child. More generally, women's lives are not easily divided into disease categories. While women living with HIV had access to treatment and specialized programs, many aspects of their lives remained the same. Patients, for instance, struggled with other illnesses, hunger, job insecurity, and poverty. The next chapter will dive further into the implications of global health programs for women's lives. While women's HIV status was legible to global institutions, other aspects of their lives—their social, economic, and cultural conditions—often were not. Yet what was not legible was crucial for their decisions to take HIV medications.

5 The Uncertainty of Treatment

Grace was thirty-four years old and the mother of five children. She had always been conscientious about her health. With every pregnancy, she went to the prenatal clinic, and she had been getting HIV tests since the early 2000s when Malawi started their HIV treatment program. In 2007, at the age of twenty-seven, she found out she was HIV positive. At the time, she was not eligible to start antiretroviral therapy (ART)—drug treatment for HIV. Malawi was following WHO guidelines according to which patients could start ART only after their immune system was compromised. And Grace was still healthy. She had accepted her HIV status and knew that one day she would be able to start treatment. That day came five years later. She was pregnant with her fifth child, and when providers saw that she was HIV positive, they told her that there was a new policy, and she could start lifelong ART right away. That day, Grace spoke to counselors at the clinic—she understood everything and felt that all her questions were answered. When she was given her first bottle of ART, she felt ready to start. But after three months, she stopped taking her medications. And she was still not taking her medications two years later when I met her. What had happened? Why did she stop?

Grace was prescribed treatment in a context in which pregnant women were seen as the means to protect future generations from HIV. As we saw in chapter 2, Malawi's policymakers developed Option B+, which gave pregnant and breastfeeding women lifelong ART as soon as they tested positive for HIV. This simple test-and-treat approach was their solution for preventing mother-to-child transmission of HIV (PMTCT) after past WHO policies had failed. For Malawi's policymakers, it was about creating a PMTCT policy that they could feasibly implement in their healthcare setting—a setting with immense donor resources for HIV testing and treatment but not for the rest of the public healthcare system. At the same time, in the global health context, Malawi's policy coincided with new evidence that ART could prevent HIV transmission, and it dovetailed with a broader biomedical turn in which donors preferred targeted pharmaceutical and technological interventions over those that focused on communities or healthcare systems.[1] For different reasons, ART was embraced by national policymakers and international donors as the magic bullet solution to treat and prevent HIV infection. However, while the benefits of ART were obvious to global health institutions, as Grace's story suggests, taking ART may not be so simple for patients.

This chapter centers the experiences of women living with HIV who started treatment during their pregnancy through Option B+. How do women decide whether to take HIV medications? Why, despite the increasing availability of ART, do women refuse or stop treatment? Like others in this book, HIV patients were also situated between worlds that were legible and illegible to donors. In this case, women were legible to global health institutions through their HIV status and potential to transmit disease to future generations, and as such, they were asked to take ART to prevent HIV transmission. But women's lives are more than their HIV status. Malawian women work and provide for their families; they have romantic relationships; they are mothers, daughters, siblings; they live in communities and have their own understandings of health. This broader aspect of women's lives was not legible to national policymakers and international donors, though it was ultimately crucial for their experience with ART. Social, economic, and cultural conditions shaped how women made sense of their HIV diagnoses and their decisions for taking medications.

Taking HIV medications for preventative purposes transformed the experience of HIV from an acute to a chronic condition: Both the symptoms of disease and the efficacy of treatment could be unclear. Women assessed the cost and benefit of taking ART by looking for evidence of the drug's efficacy through their personal experience with illness and drug-taking. For some women, the benefits of the drug were clear: They interpreted past illnesses as signs of HIV infection that warranted starting treatment and felt healthier and more economically productive afterwards. For others, however, the benefits were less apparent. Taking ART sometimes led to marital problems, and side effects made them feel worse and disrupted their ability to work and make a living. While women understood the health benefits of taking ART, treatment did not always make sense when it had costly physical and economic repercussions. The particular challenges women faced with ART were a reflection of their legibility as HIV subjects. Seeing HIV as a disease that can be treated and prevented through biomedical intervention alone is a partial vision of health, one that sidelines illness experiences and the social and economic conditions in which patients live, all of which shape how patients take (or do not take) their medications. Women's decisions to start, refuse, stop, and restart treatment were an embodied politics: Though not necessarily conscious or articulated, women struggled with and pushed back on policies that only partially recognized their life circumstances.

THE MEANING OF MEDICINE

From a biomedical perspective, HIV is a virus that alters biological functioning, but for patients, illness can mean much more than that. As Arthur Kleinman argued, illness is "the innately human experience of symptoms and suffering."[2] Illness includes the experience of physical and psychological symptoms; the way people categorize and explain their suffering; the ways that family members and wider social networks respond to illness; and the ways people cope with distress, including adopting behaviors like following prescriptions and changing one's lifestyle.[3] All these experiences of illness shape how patients take medication. Peter Conrad argued that instead of labeling a patient as compliant or noncompliant, we should instead take a patient-centered perspective and analyze the meaning of medication in their lives. A patient who stops taking their prescription may be doing so for a variety of reasons, such as to test the efficacy of the drug, to assert control and avoid dependency, or to feel normal rather than sick or different.[4] Altering prescriptions is not an uncommon practice. We see it across contexts and especially among patients with chronic conditions who need to take medication on a regular basis for long periods of time. The way women in Malawi consider taking ART can echo surprisingly with the experiences of patients managing very different conditions, such as epilepsy, rheumatoid arthritis, and sleep disorders.

Focusing on patients' experiences helps with understanding their perspective. This is important to emphasize in the medical field, where doctors are often seen as the authorities and patients who do not follow doctors' orders are labeled as deviant and stigmatized as "noncompliant," or as I sometimes heard in Malawi's clinics, a "defaulter" or "refuser." Additionally, focusing on patients' experiences centers their agency—their ability to make decisions based on the circumstances they are in. Public health scholarship often frames patients' use of treatment in terms of barriers and facilitators. In the HIV-care field, researchers have described barriers such as: insufficient knowledge of HIV and ART, fear of treatment, religious beliefs, poor drug management, difficulty in reaching the clinic, HIV stigma, fear of disclosure, relationship with partners, poor treatment by healthcare providers, poverty, and gender inequality.[5] This framework implicitly assumes that patients should want treatment but that something gets in the way—whether that be their own fear, misunderstandings, partner, or poverty. While these are indeed issues that may be salient in women's lives, to conceptualize women's use of treatment in terms of barriers and facilitators obscures their own perception of illness and the process by which they make treatment decisions.

Illness experiences also intersect with social and economic conditions. As William Cockerham has argued, decisions involve an interaction between one's "life choices" (agency) and one's "life chances" (structure).[6] For instance, a diabetic patient who operates heavy machinery may choose to delay or forgo a dose of insulin because he is concerned that low blood sugar could cause an accident, whereas a patient who works in an office and has a flexible schedule may find it easier to take insulin as prescribed.[7]

While patients everywhere might weigh the costs and benefits of treatment in their lives, the issues they consider salient to their decisions reflect their social circumstances. In Malawi, economic pressures to work, uncertainty about the future, and cultural understandings of health can shape treatment decisions in unique ways.[8]

Moreover, in countries supported by global health programs, patients make treatment decisions in a healthcare setting transformed by foreign aid. In my research, HIV-positive women have become hypervisible targets for intervention, and their use of ART is seen as the means to ensure a future AIDS-free generation. As we saw in the previous chapter, women's HIV status can grant them unique access to treatment and to NGO programs that offer assiduous care unavailable to most patients. But this privileged status also reflects a partial vision of health. From the perspective of global health institutions, women are legible through their disease, which can be easily solved by a prescription of ART, whereas their illness experience—the meaning of medication in their lives—remains illegible. Yet it is this illegible world that ultimately matters for whether and how women take their medications. I argue that the tension between global health policies and women's lived experiences produces unintended consequences and challenges with taking ART.

BEING DIAGNOSED WITH HIV

With the help of a Malawian research assistant, I interviewed women who became eligible for ART under Malawi's new Option B+ policy (N=65). Most had received their HIV diagnosis after the policy change in 2011 (N=40). Some had been diagnosed with HIV earlier, but they did not start ART until they were pregnant and could start treatment under the new policy (N=25). The women ranged in age from eighteen to forty-four, and the average age of my respondents was twenty-nine years old. Most women were married or in a relationship (N=51) and already had children; only two of the women interviewed were in their first pregnancy. About half had some primary school education (N=38), and a quarter had some secondary school education (N=18). While a few of the women were from rural districts outside of Lilongwe (N=7), most lived in the urban center (N=58).[9]

HIV testing is now a routine part of prenatal care. When women first arrive at the clinic, they receive an HIV test. Though technically women may choose to opt out, few know of this option, so testing feels compulsory.[10] Women understood the significance of an HIV diagnosis. When they recalled their initial reactions, one of the first things that came to mind was concern for their child. One respondent explained: "The only worry I had was 'When my child will be born, is he going to be fine?'" Another mother felt that it was unfair for her child to be at risk, saying: "Yeah, I was really worried for the child . . . It's like for it to be born with HIV, while it is not guilty." Some were also concerned about their health and ability to raise their child to adulthood. One respondent said, "So my main worry was to the children with my short life. I worried how they were going to be raised without my presence." Many women felt reassured when counselors told them that ART would help protect their child from HIV infection.

In general, women were quite knowledgeable about HIV. When we asked respondents what they knew about HIV before testing positive, many expressed a basic understanding of the virus and the benefits of treatment. They said, for instance, that HIV "destroys the body's defense system," "attacks the immune system," and "destroys the body," and that ART "increase[s] the protection in one's body" and "put[s] back the defense mechanism." ART, they explained, allows people to resume their normal lives. As one woman put it, a "person who is taking ARVs is like any other person and they live longer, and the person does not get sick regularly, and they are energetic, and they work as before." A few respondents knew about Malawi's Option B+ policy. One respondent stated:

> What I heard in the past, when you are found positive . . . what happens is that they do CD4 count so they don't give you medication right there and then. It can happen that I have been found positive, just like the way it has happened, perhaps they may give me or not give me instantly, then the virus continues to multiply, then it doesn't take long for you to start getting sick. What is happening nowadays is that things have changed . . . So what I have observed now is that when you are found positive you should start taking medication instantly so that your life continues.

It is not surprising that most women understood how the HIV virus operates and why treatment is beneficial. Malawians have been living with the HIV epidemic for several decades, and most people know someone who has HIV or has passed away from AIDS. And as ART has become more accessible, they have also witnessed its therapeutic benefits—HIV patients were living longer, healthier lives and accomplishing life goals such as marriage and childbearing.[11] In addition, women who tested positive at the prenatal clinic received detailed counseling from NGO community health workers (CHWs). Almost all my respondents reported that their provider talked to them about the benefits of ART for their child and for their own long-term health. Many also mentioned messages about eating nutritious foods to support their immune system, using condoms with their partners, and the potential side effects of treatment. They were also enrolled in an NGO program, where CHWs provided extensive counseling and treatment support at the clinic and during home visits for the duration of their pregnancy and breastfeeding. But, while women understood the health benefits of ART, taking medications every day for life was not easy. As we will see in the following sections, taking ART did not always align with women's subjective experiences of illness, economic needs, and romantic relationships.

NEW UNCERTAINTIES WITH ILLNESS

When Malawi first started the Option B+ policy, a concerning trend emerged: There was a sudden increase in the rate of women dropping out of HIV care. The percentage of women who initially started ART but did not return for follow up care and medication was 17 percent sixty days after starting ART and rose to 24 percent six months after starting ART.[12] In other words, nearly a quarter of all pregnant and breastfeeding women who were prescribed ART through this new policy stopped coming back to the clinic during the study timeframe. This rate was about five times higher than women who started ART for their own health (not pregnant or breastfeeding). In part, this trend likely reflected a period of adjustment as the country started implementing a new policy. But as we will see in women's narratives, the trend also reflected new uncertainties and unexpected personal and economic repercussions from taking ART.

The way women were being asked to take ART produced new uncertainties about taking medication. When ART first became available in the early 2000s, treatment produced a "Lazarus effect": It seemed to bring patients on the brink of death back to life. As ART became more accessible, the effect was less extreme, but patients nonetheless saw an improvement in their symptoms. The Option B+ test-and-treat approach meant that, unlike in the past—when patients only became eligible for ART once their disease progressed to a certain severity—women could be asked to begin treatment before they felt any symptoms. The experience of HIV became more like a chronic condition that one manages through medication rather than an acute condition that medication treats. Robert Aronowitz explains that with chronic conditions, risk and disease converge. Patients are subject to medical surveillance, whether through treatments, procedures, or regular clinic visits, to prevent future health problems.[13] In this case, HIV-positive women were asked to take ART to reduce the risk of transmission to their unborn child and future children. Taking medication to manage risk produces new uncertainties: Often times, neither the physical symptoms of illness nor the effects of medication are immediately clear. A patient, for instance, who manages their blood pressure with medication may not physically feel symptoms or the effects of medication on a day-to-day basis; they take medication to mitigate the risk of a future heart attack, stroke, or other serious conditions.

This shift in the HIV illness experience is particularly salient in Malawi. Not only does it differ from collective memories of ART transforming patients' condition, but it also differs from how people tend to conceptualize illness. From a biomedical perspective, HIV is a virus that disrupts one's immune function and that can be transmitted in-utero from mother to child. The HIV test result indicates disease and ART is the treatment that manages that disease. But for patients, being healthy or sick was not marked by laboratory tests alone but also by physical feeling. When women talked about health and illness, they described experiences they could see and feel. Sickness was feeling pain, becoming weak, or losing weight. Health, in contrast, was being fat, beautiful, strong, and capable of work. For instance, one respondent described health in the following way: "It is how a person looks. Health is when you are not weak, malnourished and the like . . . There are also some people, like those who engage in some sporting activities, you actually see they are healthy." When it comes to sickness, she explained: "I know, I feel it in my body." Or it is visible: "You cannot miss someone suffering from malaria. They look weak. They show that things are not okay with this person."

In a context where health and illness are largely defined by tangible and bodily experiences, the lack of physical symptoms weighs more heavily. Feeling asymptomatic is not surprising given that HIV has a long latency period; though the virus continues replicating, patients may experience few or no symptoms for years after infection. Without ART, infection usually advances to AIDS between eight to twelve years.[14] While women understood that ART could prevent HIV transmission and benefit their health, they also assessed how the medication worked in their lives. Such interpretive practices are common. Conrad argued that patients with chronic conditions often "self-regulate" medication. Among epilepsy patients in the United States, he observed that some stopped or reduced their medication to see if seizures would come back or if the change would make them feel more or less normal.[15] It is not necessarily that patients are distrustful of physicians' prescriptions; rather, when symptoms and the effects of medication are uncertain, patients look for evidence of the benefits and costs through their own experience with self-regulation. In Malawi, women evaluated the efficacy of ART through bodily experiences, using past and present signs of sickness as important evidence.

SEARCHING FOR SICKNESS

Most of my respondents were surprised by their HIV diagnosis. They had come to the prenatal clinic for a regular visit, and they felt healthy and did not expect to test positive. To make sense of their diagnosis, women often searched for physical signs of sickness in their past. They constructed narratives about how they became infected, what the early signs were, and what effect it is having on their lives.[16] For some women, the benefits of ART were apparent when they interpreted past illnesses as signs of HIV infection. Previous bouts of malaria, colds, coughs, and fatigue could all be considered evidence of HIV-related illness. While women may not have thought much about these illnesses before, after their HIV diagnosis, they reinterpreted them as signs of HIV infection and worsening health. One respondent described:

P: I was not feeling as healthy as I used to. I can say my body was not looking good. I used to get sick often.

I: How do you know that you are sick?

P: Well, maybe the body temperature gets too high, coughing, mm.

Whether or not these conditions objectively indicate HIV-related illness is less important than their subjective meaning. The reinterpretation of past events like fevers or coughs as indications of HIV was a way for women to find concrete signs of sickness and a stronger reason for starting ART. Constructing narratives of illness is common across many chronic conditions in which symptoms are not always clear. For example, in a completely different setting, Navon found that US adults diagnosed with deletion syndrome, a genetic disorder, who had mild to no symptoms, frequently reinterpreted aspects of their past—such as academic performance or height—as possible signs of their disorder.[17]

Past events were also compared to assess the efficacy of ART. Women looked for changes in their health, comparing the frequency of sickness and their physical strength before and after treatment. For some, treatment worked the way they expected. They felt that they were sick or weak in the past and that they were better after taking ART. For instance, Sara, who had been diagnosed with HIV when she was pregnant with her fourth child, talked about her transformation. She said:

> Malaria used to catch me too often, and I could open bowels as well every now and then. Now I am good. I don't usually go through that anymore. And about sickness—it is a thing of the past . . . People used to ask, "What is wrong with you? What's going on in your life?" I failed to answer them, but I knew what was wrong with me. But when I started taking drugs, little by little, I felt alive and whole again like how I am now. My body was transformed, and I showed no signs whatsoever of illness. Now I live a normal and happy life.

Another respondent described similar changes in energy and stamina. She said, "Because as for me, before I started taking ARVs, I would differentiate. When I walked, I would feel weak, and when I ran for a short distance, I would be panting heavily and my heart would beat very fast . . . But then I had observed that when I started taking ARVs, I was able to run without any problems." These comparisons between past and present conditions were one way that women found evidence that ART was working for them.

For other women, however, signs of sickness were not as clear. They described feeling healthy and did not expect to be diagnosed with HIV. Alinafe, for instance, described her initial surprise when she tested positive. She went with friends to Macro, a clinic in Lilongwe, though it was not her intent to be tested. One of her friends suggested it while they were walking through town. When she heard her test result, she said: "I questioned myself, where is this infection coming from? Since I don't have multiple sexual partners." Her results were confirmed a second time when she went to Bwaila hospital when she became pregnant with her youngest child. She told providers at Bwaila that she had been suspicious of her prior test results, "I thought it was false. I cannot be HIV positive depending on how healthy I was, so it was impossible." She explained, "If I compare myself with my friends, then I was suspicious that my friends can be HIV positive . . . Some had skin rashes and so many things . . . but my skin was smooth, and I looked healthy . . . During that time, I was strong." Alinafe was surprised by her HIV status because she did not recall past signs of sickness and did not feel sick in that moment. She felt that she did not look or feel the way she thought someone with HIV would. Though Alinafe eventually accepted her diagnosis, her experience illustrates the friction that can arise between biomedical labels of disease and subjective understandings of illness.

Moreover, the benefits of treatment could also be unclear. For some women, treatment seemed to lead to worse, rather than better, health outcomes. Side effects were the most common reason women gave for stopping treatment (N=13/26). For instance, one respondent struggled to eat because of nausea. She said, "I was very worried that my child was going to be infected because I was not even eating . . . My body was just aching. I was failing to take water, I was even failing to take porridge, so I was also failing to swallow the medicines." Another respondent explained that the dizziness and vivid dreams she had were too much for her to handle. She said, "I was thinking I was going to die. Sometimes when you are seated, you dream about being dead; they are burying me at the graveyard . . .

I was even becoming afraid to sleep, I was really afraid." From a biomedical provider's perspective, problems like nausea and nightmares are side effects of medication—and should be tolerated because the medication effectively prevents HIV transmission. But for women, these side effects could be quite meaningful—they conflicted with their expectations of treatment and disrupted their everyday lives.

The physical effects of medication were sometimes more tangible than those of HIV infection. While women may not have had symptoms before starting treatment, after taking ART they clearly felt sick from side effects. Like other patients with chronic disease, women experimented with ART to evaluate the drugs' effects. Grace, for instance, described starting and stopping ART several times. She said:

> So when I met the doctors, they gave those drugs. We take one pill per day. So, I felt dizzy after taking the pill. I was even failing to walk, and I was crawling. Then I decided not to take the drugs for three days, and then I was feeling better.

After she stopped taking ART, a counselor visited her at home and asked her to come back to the clinic. She returned and refilled her prescription. But her side effects were still a problem. She explained:

> I began taking the drug, but the side effects continued. So, I asked myself: since I quit this treatment, I was feeling well, but now that I am taking these drugs, the side effect is back. I gained courage to continue taking the drugs, but it was not helping.

After the side effects returned, she decided to quit again. When we met, she said she had stopped ART over a year before, and that she had probably started and stopped treatment at least three times. She found that she felt better when she was not on ART: "I was not feeling better for the whole month, and if I decide to miss the treatment, I was feeling better. Then later on I decided to quit the treatment; I didn't take the drugs. After quitting the treatment, I never felt pain anywhere in my body."

The way that women evaluated and experimented with ART was not due to lack of knowledge or distrust of medical professionals. My respondents all knew about HIV transmission and that ART was a treatment that could save patients' lives. Their uncertainty around ART was tied to the particular way they were asked to take medications—as a way to prevent maternal HIV transmission, even if they were asymptomatic. Taking ART as prevention made the experience of HIV similar to other chronic conditions, in which both symptoms and the immediate effects of medication may be unclear. Like many patients, women in Malawi understood their prescription but wanted to see how treatment worked in their lives. For them, physical signs of sickness—something they could see and feel—were important. They compared their past and present conditions and sometimes self-regulated their treatments to see how ART was working. From the standpoint of global health institutions and Malawi's policymakers, ART was a straightforward intervention that protected mothers and their children. But, in women's illness experiences, ART did not always produce straightforward benefits. Treatment did not necessarily lead to clear improvements in physical health, and sometimes made women feel worse than before. Subjective understandings of health and illness and patients' evaluation of how ART worked in their lives were important for whether and how they took their medications.

TREATMENT IN ECONOMIC UNCERTAINTY

Women's experiences of illness and treatment are also impacted by their broader social and economic circumstances. Living situations in Malawi are constantly in flux. As Trinitapoli and Yeatman describe, HIV is just "one additional layer of uncertainty in an environment characterized by sudden (and often inexplicable) mortality, natural disasters, and the more mundane and universal hardships of daily life."[18] At some point, a woman might be married, working, and have a good harvest, while at other times, she might find herself divorced and depending on family for basic needs. Many women and their husbands did not have consistent work, and they sometimes had to sell land and other goods to buy food. These uncertain economic conditions affected the embodied experience of taking ART as well as how women assessed the drawbacks and benefits of treatment in relation to their everyday lives.

Several respondents described sudden life changes. Madalitso, a mother of two, talked about a difficult moment in her life when her husband lost his job. They had to move frequently because they could not afford rent, and sometimes they also could not afford food:

> We stayed for one month without paying the rent, so the landlord chased us away from the house . . . The landlord removed my belongings from the house, and I moved to Mudzi where I found a house and its rent was K2000. So, I sold my clothes to pay for the house, and after paying the fee, I started staying in that house. I was living a miserable life in that house, such that sometimes I was going to bed without taking any food. The landlord was feeling sorry for the children, and they began eating food at the landlord's [house] from morning to afternoon.

Like Madalitso, another respondent also struggled when her husband lost his job. Her family depended on her small business selling groceries and firewood. But she suddenly lost her income when a fire burned down the local market where she would sell her goods, creating a moment of extreme precarity in an already precarious context.

These moments of economic downturn could affect how women took their medications. Food insecurity was a regular problem in Malawi. It was not uncommon for women to miss meals or worry about the future availability of food. Job loss, another financial need, or low agricultural yields could all disrupt food supplies. Providers encouraged women to eat nutritious and protein-rich foods for their health, such as meat, beans, and nutrient-rich vegetables. But simply having enough food to take with ART could be a challenge. Some women described feeling concerned when they heard those messages from providers. One respondent said: "My mind was on the food at home. I know food is scarce at home, [and] these drugs require someone to eat a lot."

Economic conditions are intertwined with the experience of ART treatment. For some women, side effects worsened during times of food shortage. For instance, Chimwemwe had accepted her HIV status and prescription for ART, but she sometimes stopped taking the pills when she did not have enough food. She said, "with the new drugs, I usually feel hungry, and I feel dizzy when I have not taken any food." Her husband was not working, so it was challenging for her to find money. She sometimes went to her family in the mornings for a meal, but she did not always have money or a place to eat in the afternoons. According to her prescription, she should take ART at the end of the day. But this was difficult when she was unable to eat. On those days, she felt as if she "hits the walls" from the combination of hunger and the dizziness caused by her medication.

In Chimwemwe's case, not taking ART had little to do with her knowledge of HIV or concern about her future health. She accepted her diagnosis at the clinic and felt thankful that she could start medication. Her husband, who also tested positive, tried to support her with her medication, often reminding her to take her pills. He was concerned when she stopped but felt constrained since he could not provide her with the food she needed. "He said, 'What can I do since I don't have money?'" She understood the consequences of missing treatment: "But then I know that this thing will cause big problems one day, since if I miss today, tomorrow then it will be difficult for the drug to start working in the body, and eventually I will die." Chimwemwe was confronted with an impossible choice: She had to weigh the future benefits of treatment with her immediate food insecurity.

While the prescription for ART asks women to take medications on a regular basis, women's lives were not characterized by regularity. Women sometimes managed their ART prescription while also managing a range of other needs, like housing, income, and food. Moreover, they started ART during their pregnancy. For some, the combination of events was overwhelming. Jane, who was twenty-nine years old and a mother of three, explained why she stopped treatment. When she was diagnosed with HIV, her husband accused her of infidelity and left while she was still pregnant. She was not working at the time and could not immediately find a job when her husband left. She explained:

> And many times, I face challenges. That's one reason why I stopped taking medication . . . Sometimes you find yourself without food, so [going] until up to evening without food, then to take them again and with pregnancy, things were not okay for me. I could feel dizzy, vomit at times. When I finished the two bottles I was given, I stopped taking them.

Without a stable home, income, or food, taking ART was challenging. Jane was often so sick from the medication that she could barely walk during the day. When she stopped taking ART, she felt better; and though she was still going through a lot in her life, she could at least eat without vomiting. Jane felt that if her circumstances were different, she would take ART: "My husband evicted me out of the house. Had it been that I was still in the house, I don't think I could stop. I could be taking them without any difficulty; even coming here to get the drugs could not be a challenge."

Sudden changes in one's circumstances, such as losing a home or job, create an unstable environment in which to take daily doses of ART and to manage side effects. Moreover, sudden changes are often associated with food insecurity, which has a unique impact in the context of HIV. As Ippolytos Kalofonos argues, HIV and hunger are linked. Malnutrition is often a cofactor of the HIV pandemic, and it can create a desperate scenario. Individuals who are HIV positive often need more calories to offset greater nutritional deficiencies, but at the same time, they often cannot afford more food because they struggled to find regular work.[19] While scaling up ART is an important goal, the social and economic context in which patients take their medications is often overlooked. For global health institutions, addressing mother-to-child HIV transmission means providing ART to expectant mothers. Food insecurity is considered one of many mundane problems relating to poverty rather than something that needs to be addressed directly through foreign aid. While there are donor initiatives to address hunger, food insecurity remains widespread in Malawi. As women's narratives show, these "mundane" problems can significantly shape their experiences of illness and treatment.

Economic Impact of ART

Social and economic conditions also shape how women assess the costs and benefits of treatment in their everyday lives. The physical effects of treatment could have economic implications. Women wanted to be able to work and provide for their families. How they felt on ART, and the extent to which treatment helped or hindered their work, influenced their decisions to take their medications.

Work in Malawi is often precarious. Formal employment opportunities are extremely limited.[20] Jobs that are considered more stable, such as work in healthcare, teaching, and banking, require a secondary-school certificate and often postsecondary education, which is out of reach for most Malawians. School attrition rates are extremely high: Nationally, less than half of primary school students go on to enroll in secondary school, even fewer graduate, and just 8 percent of secondary school graduates pursue further education.[21] Among my interview respondents, about half had some primary school education (N=38), and a quarter had some secondary school education (N=18), but few had completed secondary school (N=5), and only one had postsecondary education.

Like many Malawians, my respondents participated in the informal labor market, doing "piecework"—that is, various short-term jobs. Some found a job gardening or cleaning for another family. Others ran a small business, such as selling vegetables, cooked food, or local brew at the market. Women also tended to their own family farms and gardens, which was an important source of food for the family. They also moved between jobs. As one respondent explained: "I do piece jobs. As you can see, I don't have a husband. So when there is piecework somewhere, I go and do it, and so on. And sometimes when I get some money, I cook fritters and sell them. Then if that business goes down, I go look for more money by piecework. I look after myself, my health, and like that, I survive." Women who were married had additional support from their husband's income, but this too was insecure. While Malawian men tend have more job opportunities, those opportunities were not necessarily stable.[22] Work in industries such as construction, tobacco, and security, as well as migrant work abroad, was often seasonal or contract-based. Sometimes women financially supported the family when their husbands struggled to find work.

Feeling strong and energetic was important for women's ability to work. Piecework, running small businesses, as well as everyday tasks like gathering firewood and water were physically intensive. One respondent described a typical day running a small business selling home brewed beer. She said: "I wake up at three a.m., then I check the fire to see if it's enough, then I make sure that [the brew] has started to boil like the *chibuku* [traditional beer]." She brews and sells all morning, and then takes a break in the afternoon. "When it gets dark, then I start working again. Now I start cooking, preparing *nsima* [a staple food]. We go to bed at nine, yes, when we finish eating." At the end of the day, she explained: "I feel very exhausted, maybe feeling some pains all over my body. When I am done with the alcohol, I take a bath, but when I see that I'm still experiencing some pain, I buy some drugs . . . The reason is that tomorrow I should wake up with strength."

Being healthy and being able to work were often intertwined. When women described how they felt from illness or treatment, they often talked about their physical strength and work productivity. A change in one's ability to work would signal illness. For instance, one respondent describing her HIV infection said:

> HIV deals with the immune system, and when it is down, you cannot do your usual things as you used to. . . . And you know life in the rural communities, right? Whether going to the mountains to pick firewood, pounding maize. I do all those things, but when the immune system is down, you feel weak. And that is why they then provide these drugs.

For some women, everything lined up. With ART, they felt that their health improved, and that they were more capable of work. Treatment aligned with their subjective understanding of health and illness as well as their economic needs. As one respondent explained,

> Now, I don't get sick regularly and I do all my activities at home and even at the estate. You know, working at the estate is laborious. You go at five and you knock off [leave work] at six. Yeah . . . weeding tobacco or tilling the land. But I don't see any problem. Yeah, I do everything and return home. I don't get sick, and I also go to work the following day, and I don't get sick at all.

This ability to work felt like a return to normalcy. Another respondent explained: "I don't get sick as often, that is all I can tell you for now. I do go to the garden without any difficulty. As everyone else, I am able to look after my children and husband, so I am normal." Instead of being in the sick role[23] with ART, the women fulfilled their gendered obligations to care for their families and contributed to their household income.

For others, however, treatment not only made them feel worse, but it also disrupted their ability to work. Women described numerous challenges with side effects that impacted their work, such as feeling drunk while farming, falling down in the garden or kitchen, being too weak to work after vomiting, being unable to carry vegetables to sell at the market, and being too dizzy to bike to work. Esther, a mother of four, described how difficult it was to continue her business:

> When I arrived home in the afternoon, it was getting dark, so I had to take the pills. I prepared *nsima*, and we ate. My business was ready for tomorrow's sales, and then we slept. At night, I was totally asleep. I didn't even wake up to notice that it was dawn. I woke up when it was already late morning . . . But for me to leave the room or to rise up from the mat, it was difficult. I forced myself to wake up to the extent that I hit the wall. Then I arrived at the fireplace and set the fire. I put the pot on the fire while seated. It was difficult for me to carry sweet potato for sale; someone did it for me. I didn't feel good that day. It was like the pill is stuck here . . . So I thought about it, that the whole day is spent on the mat.

Esther's husband helped her return to the clinic. The counselor there encouraged her to continue ART, saying that her body was just getting used to the pills. She tried again, but still felt weak and eventually stopped treatment. Taking ART sometimes had an economic cost. Side effects meant that women could not go to work, run their small business, or do their daily tasks. As one respondent stated: "When the sun is rising in the morning, I didn't want to stay idle, rather I want to be working."

Women's interpretations of treatment intersected with their economic conditions. While patients everywhere consider whether and how medication works in their everyday lives, what they consider to be salient reflects their broader circumstances. In this case, the physical effects of treatment were important given women's definition of health and illness—but so too was their need to perform physically demanding work. While taking one pill a day sounds simple, it can be difficult in an economically precarious context, where food is scare and work needs to be done. ART addressed women's HIV infection but not their daily survival. And it was often concerns about daily survival—having enough food, being able to work, taking care of family—that shaped how women assessed the costs and benefits of ART and made treatment decisions.

MANAGING TREATMENT AND RELATIONSHIPS

An HIV diagnosis affects patients but also their romantic partners. All of my respondents were married or in a relationship when they tested positive. Women managed their diagnosis and prescription for ART while they dealt with questions about their relationship. These questions were not always easy—a positive test result might bring up past sexual partners, blame for infection, and accusations of infidelity. A woman's relationship with her partner is another important aspect of the illness experience—relationships at home can provide more or less supportive conditions for managing HIV treatment.

Women were often the ones to start the conversation about HIV. In general, women have been prioritized as targets of HIV interventions.[24] Many of my respondents had been tested previously as part of provider-initiated testing at clinics or through NGO programs. In the context of pregnancy, women receive an HIV test as part of their routine prenatal care. While Malawi started a "male involvement" campaign to encourage partners to come to the prenatal clinic and test as a couple, few men actually came. At my field sites, most women came to the clinic alone. As Dovel et al. argue, men have been largely excluded from HIV testing and treatment strategies. Outside of prenatal clinics, provider-initiated testing and counseling for men is poor and inconsistent.[25] The few men who do accompany their partners to the prenatal clinic will find that they are usually ignored in health education talks, and their participation is framed by health workers as benefiting their partner rather than an action that also benefits themselves. While men in Malawi do get tested for HIV, testing is not as frequent as for women, nor is it an expected part of their healthcare services.

Almost all of my respondents told their husbands about their HIV diagnosis (N=53). These conversations usually took place on the same day, or sometimes a few days or weeks afterwards. Women were nervous to share their diagnosis. When they described their initial reactions to their test result, one of the first things that came to mind was how they would tell their husbands. One respondent described her concerns:

> Yes, I was worried because whenever we were listening to some HIV/AIDS program on the radio, we could hear cases of some women—their marriage ending because maybe she has been found HIV positive. So, I pondered in my head about how my husband would react, and I feared that he was going to chase me out of the house.

Women were worried about being blamed for bringing HIV to the family or what would happen if their husband was negative or whether their marriage would end. They worried: "He would blame me for bringing the infection in our family"; "My husband was not found with it, so I thought the marriage is no more"; "You just have that fear, and you tend to wonder because these are difficult issues."

Conversations about HIV infection were not easy. In some cases, women's concerns were alleviated. One respondent recalled: "He said, 'Don't worry about it. These days, everyone is tested HIV positive.'" This reaction may reflect new attitudes as the HIV epidemic enters its fourth decade, in which HIV is no longer seen as deadly, but as a chronic illness that one takes medication for.[26] It may also be a strategy to avoid blame in either direction, since one partner's HIV status likely reflects the other's, and discussing the source of infection can be uncomfortable. Still, in many cases, an HIV diagnosis raised questions about where the infection came from. Sometimes women felt it was clear that their husbands were at fault. One respondent explained that she had not discussed HIV before getting married. She laughed and said: "You know, when you are in love, you forget considering other things." But she had taken several HIV tests in the past, which always came back negative; it was after her marriage that she tested positive. In her mind, her husband was clearly to blame.

In addition to potential blame for infection, talking about HIV often brought up questions about other sexual partners and fidelity in marriage. Takondwa's diagnosis, for example, led her husband to reveal that he was HIV positive and had been unfaithful. When she came home from the prenatal clinic, she started to cry. Her husband asked why she was crying. "What is the matter? Can you come here?" He looked in her bag and saw her health passport with her HIV-positive status listed on it. She explained what happened at the clinic. He then revealed to her that he was HIV positive as well. Takondwa said: "That's when he became open to me. He said you can really blame me since I am the one who brought this virus here. He explained how he contracted the virus outside the family." While Takondwa's husband did not reveal all the details of his other relationships, she had suspicions of what happened. She said:

> At some point he left me home with the kids. He went to the field. And he even became open to me. He said: "It is really true, my wife, when I was at the field, I think I contracted the virus at the field." He went to Ntcheu and there is a certain bar there, and that's where he was spending his nights, and he met a certain lady there. Then he arrived home . . . So that's how I contracted the virus. So I was very frustrated since he didn't reveal it to me all this time, yeah.

She suspected that he was taking medication at his sister's house. In the past, she found it strange that he would immediately go to sleep after dinner. But now, she felt she understood. Because ART can make patients feel dizzy, it made sense that they would want to go to sleep after taking it.

Despite these difficult conversations, many couples stayed together. In Takondwa's case, though she was angry, she continued her relationship with her husband. She said that since their conversation, her husband has brought his medication home. They take ART together at night, and often remind each other. Other women had similar experiences with partners who accepted their status. Sometimes their partners revealed their HIV-positive status; others went for HIV testing after learning of their wife's diagnosis; and some were encouraging of their wife's use of ART but did not want to know their own status. Women in more supportive relationships described various ways that their partners helped them. Many said that their husbands reminded them to take ART each day. Others provided money for transportation to go to the clinic or to buy more nutritious foods. Their husbands were also there to help when they felt sick from ART side effects and provided general encouragement to continue treatment. One respondent explained:

> So, when they gave me those drugs, I went home. And on my first day I didn't want to take them, but my husband encouraged me to take them so that I see what would happen. So, when I took it, I felt dizziness. I fell down when I woke up to urinate outside. My husband picked me up. I became angry such that I decided to quit, but then my husband said "No, you need to protect the unborn baby; it will not be fair to quit taking the drugs. You need to go and report this to the doctor." So, I went to report to the hospital.

Of course, a supportive partner is not the only thing that matters. As we saw earlier, some women's partners were encouraging, but with little food at home or stressful economic circumstances, taking ART could still be difficult. However, in a context where much of life can feel uncertain, being in a stable relationship with a partner who accepts their HIV status helped make a new prescription easier to manage.

ART in an Unsupportive Relationship

For others, disclosing one's HIV status led to serious problems in their relationship. While women may accept their status and ART prescription, arguments, separation, and potential divorce were disruptive life events that could make it difficult to take medications on a regular basis. Alice and her husband fought over who brought HIV into their relationship, and they eventually divorced. She was twenty-one years old at the time and had one child with her husband. She started the conversation after he returned home from work. She had cooked dinner but was too nervous to eat. When they were going to bed, he asked her about her trip to the clinic. She started to explain and showed him her health passbook. He laughed and said: "I am negative, but I don't know your status, so you will follow your own way." Alice was suspicious. Her husband's reaction seemed too quick and careless. She thought that he must have known he was positive but was hiding it from her. She recalled that, when she asked him to test before their marriage or recently for her trip to the prenatal clinic, he had refused. Alice pressed her husband on his HIV infection. During one argument, her husband told her not to take ART because it causes side effects. She explained:

> Yeah, he said these drugs cause headache, and when you wake up the body becomes weak. So I was surprised, and I asked him, "How do you know that they cause headache?" . . . I told him to tell me the truth . . . He said, "I don't know that." He just told me you are going to solve it. Then he left. He came in the morning, and I asked him, "Where did you sleep?" He told me not ask him about that, so I waited for him. He took the bath, ate, and he left for work. He returned home, then I reminded him that the issue didn't end. Can you tell me the truth please?

It was difficult for Alice to take ART. The fighting with her husband escalated, and he sometimes threw away her medicine. She explained:

> The issue became so difficult that he got all his belongings and left me alone at home while pregnant. When I receive the drugs here, he was throwing the drugs away. But I was still coming here to collect those drugs, and I started hiding them from him. But once he finds them, he could take them and throw them away. He moved to Mgona, and I am staying alone, mm.

In addition to her relationship problems, Alice experienced side effects from ART. At home, she did not have a supportive partner to remind her to take ART or to help her get up from bed when she was dizzy. She said she had been "careless" with her medication at that time. Though her husband eventually came back to ask for her forgiveness, Alice felt it was too late. After they divorced, she stayed with her family. In a different environment, Alice found it easier to take ART. Her sister encouraged her to take her medications regularly, and since then, she has been on treatment.

In more extreme cases, like Alice's, women's partners actively disrupted their use of ART by taking away their medications. For others, relationship problems exacerbated other challenges, which made it difficult for women to prioritize treatment. Memory was twenty-nine years old when she tested positive during her third pregnancy. Her husband went for an HIV test, but his result was negative. He said he did not want to live with her and sent her to another home he rented. While she had a place to stay, she struggled to find a job, and her husband stopped leaving her money for food. Like others, she experienced side effects from ART. Her provider told her to continue treatment, saying that the side effects would pass. She continued ART, but the side effects persisted, and so she stopped. She explained: "The reason why I stopped was because I felt uncomfortable in my body every time I took them, and because the marriage was in tatters, I did not care." While they have not divorced, she says that more than six months have passed, and he has not forgiven her: "It feels like I am not even married." For Memory, many life challenges coincided with her HIV diagnosis. Her relationship deteriorated, which led her to worry about money and food, and she had little support at home when she felt sick from her medication.

Women's social relationships, of course, were not limited to their husbands. They often disclosed their HIV status to family members, and sometimes close friends or pastors. Women described their family members as people they could turn to if they felt sick and needed help with tasks or to pick up medication. Their community could also be a source of support. For instance, one respondent who was active in her church explained: "My church is important to my life. If I get sick suddenly, the church rushes to you and sympathizes with you so that you don't lose hope." But women's romantic relationships were particularly salient. They lived with their husbands, and how their partners responded to their HIV diagnosis could provide more or less supportive environments for taking ART. With the test-and-treat approach to PMTCT, women managed several major events at once—a pregnancy, a surprising diagnosis, a new prescription, and disclosing their status to their partners. As women were just starting ART, a loving relationship provided stability. And while actions like reminding someone to take ART may seem small, they were helpful at the start of treatment when women experienced side effects and were still adjusting to new medication routines. In contrast, relationship problems could compound challenges, leaving women to manage side effects alone or thrusting them into precarious economic situations. Women's lives are embedded in social relationships. While it is women's HIV infection that is the target of global health interventions, it was their relationships, along with their social, cultural, and economic conditions, that were important for how they experienced their illness and made decisions to take their medications.

CHANGING TREATMENT DECISIONS

Treatment decisions can change. The narratives above capture moments in women's lives. At the time of the interview, many women had already changed their initial treatment decision. About half of my respondents who initially accepted ART stopped for some period (26/55), and of those who stopped, about half started treatment again (16/26). Of the respondents who initially refused, about half started treatment later (4/10). On average, my respondents stopped ART during pregnancy for a few months before starting again, though the pause varied widely, ranging from a few days to over two years. From a medical or public health perspective, many of my respondents would be considered "noncompliant" or "nonadherent" patients because they had refused or stopped treatment at some point. From a patient-centered perspective, however, changes in women's use of ART reflected their self-regulation of treatment.[27] Women living with HIV understood the prescription for ART, but they made sense of it in light of their experiences of illness and changing life circumstances.

Over time, fluctuations in treatment use may subside. Research that has tracked the impact of Malawi's Option B+ policy shows that most women return to care and stay on ART.[28] Rates of adherence—defined as taking ART on 90 percent or more days—were lowest amongst pregnant women, especially in the first six months, at 65 percent adherence; but the rates rose after six months of pregnancy to almost 80 percent adherence.[29]

These quantitative findings resonate with descriptions in this chapter. The early stages of treatment may be a uniquely challenging time. With Option B+, women managed HIV testing, diagnosis, prescription, and disclosure to their partners at the same time as their pregnancy. One respondent said she did not start ART right away simply because she was "thinking about it too much." She said:

> I was like, "I am only nineteen years, never born a child, and I am starting the ARVs at nineteen years." I was thinking if I reach thirty years and am still taking medicines, am I going to be fine? . . . I could cry each time I was about to take the drugs. Yeah, actually crying, my brother. I was like, "Should I live a life of medicines?"

Option B+ has been considered a public health success. Studies conducted before and after the implementation of Option B+ in 2011 indicate a decline in mother-to-child HIV transmission rates, from 13.5 percent in 2009 to 3.7 percent between 2014 and 2016.[30] However, the difficulties women faced with treatment have long-term consequences for their health. Stopping ART leads to a rebound of the HIV virus, which increases the risk of HIV transmission as well as the risk of drug resistance as virus replication can produce mutations. It does not take long for the HIV virus to rebound. One study showed that it took an average of twenty-two days off ART for virus levels to go from undetectable to viral rebound (>1000 HIV RNA).[31] While public health outcomes for PMTCT are optimistic, it is equally important to address the challenges women face, as interruptions in treatment pose risks to health over time.

Why some women are "unsuccessful" in staying on ART is not indicative of any personal shortcomings. There are not two distinct types of women: adherent and nonadherent. Rather, the way that ART works in women's lives changes, and they may weave in and out of treatment. Some women who restarted treatment after stopping did so because of a life change. For instance, they felt that their health declined, left an unsupportive partner, or had greater access to food, which lessened their side effects. In Malawi, circumstances can change frequently and suddenly.[32] Thus, it was difficult for women who were on ART to know for certain if they would still be taking their medications years down the line. These healthcare decisions take place in relation to broader social structures. The situations patients live in, their past experiences, present opportunities, and projected futures, affect how they think about health and their dispositions toward action.[33] This is true of patients in Malawi and elsewhere. Moreover, social structures shape what people consider to be salient for their treatment decisions. In this case, women's changing decisions were deeply informed by a context of uncertainty.

CONCLUSION

Women living with HIV embodied tensions between legible and illegible worlds of care. They were legible to global health institutions because of their HIV status and as an embodied risk to future generations. From a policy standpoint, the test-and-treat approach offered a simple and efficient way to prevent maternal HIV transmission, and it stood to benefit women's long-term health. But outside of their HIV status, women's *illness experience* was largely illegible. And it was their illness experience—how they made sense of their illness and treatment given their social and economic circumstances—that was ultimately crucial for their treatment decisions. As this chapter showed, taking ART was not always easy. For some women, the benefits of ART aligned neatly. Treatment had both physical and material benefits; women felt healthier and more productive at work. For other women, however, the costs for taking ART were too high. Taking ART could threaten a marriage, and side effects often made them feel sicker than before, disrupting their ability to work. While women understood the health benefits of ART and wanted to give birth to an uninfected child, treatment did not always make sense in their immediate life circumstances.

In part, the illness experiences described in this chapter reflect new uncertainties that emerged with the test-and-treat approach. ART was used to prevent HIV transmission, which transformed the experience of HIV from an acute to a chronic condition. In the past, patients were eligible for ART when a CD4 count showed immune system decline or when they presented with clinical symptoms, like rashes, fatigue, or certain infections. Now, HIV-positive pregnant women started ART right away. Many of my respondents felt healthy and had no symptoms related to HIV infection.

While they understood the future benefits of ART, the medication's immediate results could be unclear or even deeply unpleasant. Experiencing HIV as a chronic condition in which symptoms and the efficacy of medication were not always clear produced new uncertainties in a context in which health and illness are often defined in physical terms.

The challenges women had with treatment were also tied to a longer history of development and fraught international interventions. Economic challenges and food insecurity affected the embodied experiences of ART as well as how women weighed the costs and benefits of treatment in their lives. These problems are not new but are tied to the lingering effects of neoliberal policies that worsened economic outcomes and exacerbated insecurities with work and food. In an economically precarious context, losing days of work due to treatment side effects can devastate one's livelihood, whereas under more stable conditions, patients can take more time away from work. Similarly, as difficult as it is to process a diagnosis and disclose one's HIV status, the possibility of losing one's partner weighs more heavily when there is a risk of being thrust into dire economic straits.

Women's narratives provide a different vantage point from which to view HIV-care programs. For global health institutions, HIV is a disease and ART is a magic bullet solution that could both treat HIV and prevent its spread. For Malawi's policymakers, relying on ART was strategic. The extreme simplicity of the Option B+ test-and-treat approach allowed them to use a donor-funded ART program while managing challenges with resource constraints in the public healthcare system. In an ideal situation, policymakers would have wanted to give all patients more individualized care and treatments. But the illegibility of Malawi's public healthcare system to donors meant that policymakers had to approach public health in a way that fit their context. With limited staff, medicine, and infrastructure, Malawi's public health approach was one that emphasized simplicity and solutions that could fit most rather than all. Over time, policymakers were indeed successful in reducing overall rates of mother-to-child HIV transmission. But seeing HIV as a disease separate from patients' illness experiences limits the success of global health programs. Women's narratives reveal that taking medication was not always a smooth process. From the vantage point of patients on the ground, taking ART was just one of many life concerns. Side effects, food insecurity, precarious work, and marital tensions are not captured by official health metrics, yet they were central to women's experiences. This is not to say that access to ART is unimportant—ART is essential for the health of people living with HIV. However, it is not a magic bullet. Even in the context of HIV care, women have needs that extend beyond access to treatment. Global health programs are less effective at retaining women in care when they overlook the social and economic realities that shape their lives.

Conclusion

PARTIAL RECOVERIES

UNEQUAL WORLDS OF CARE

In recent years, global health experts have debated whether the "end of AIDS" may be in sight. Over the past forty years, donors have invested significantly in HIV care programs. Between 2010 and 2020, there was roughly $20 billion available each year.[1] These resources have transformed HIV care for countries receiving aid. In Malawi, the transformation is visible. This is a landscape where donor-funded NGOs and HIV clinics have proliferated; where foreign doctors, consultants, researchers, and volunteers have come to work; where HIV information is on billboards, posters, radio shows, and other cultural objects; and where citizens become targets of various HIV care interventions. But, while HIV is now seen as a global emergency worthy of exceptional aid, many other aspects of healthcare in the global South are not. HIV care programs sit alongside a public healthcare system that has long struggled with shortages of medicine, staff, and infrastructure. While HIV is the largest disease program in the global health field, healthcare systems rarely garner the same global attention and resources. While there are numerous HIV-focused NGOs working on policies, supply chain management, research, HIV care, prevention education, and treatment support programs, there are few organizations addressing health worker education and retention, building new hospitals and laboratories, or ensuring the supply chain of essential medicines. While patients with HIV can access lifesaving medication, those with other diseases may struggle to find care.

What donors and international organizations see as legitimate and worthy of aid is codified in resources, policies, and programs. Legibility includes the way certain diseases or target populations are prioritized for aid—in this case, HIV is the largest disease program by far. But legibility also includes an overarching vision of what health is and how best to address it, a vision that enables and constrains certain courses of action. At a global scale, neoliberalism, which emphasizes the transfer of power from government to markets, has shaped the direction of the global health field.[2] While there are several possible ways to address public health, relying on NGOs to design targeted disease interventions becomes the "rational" approach to healthcare, whereas working to improve the public sector is not. Over time, this approach has shaped the structure of healthcare in countries receiving aid. HIV care came with donor funding and operated largely outside of the public sector through parallel structures and NGOs. In a neoliberal context, what is legible to donors carves care into distinct worlds outside of the public healthcare system.

Policymakers, providers, and patients in Malawi are situated between different worlds of care. Though illegible to donors, Malawi's public healthcare system, and more broadly the social conditions that shape health behaviors, are very much seen and felt by local actors. Policymakers must implement HIV care policies in Malawi's healthcare system; providers consider both NGOs and the public sector for their careers; and patients have a range of health concerns, including but not limited to HIV, for which they require care. Being situated between legible and illegible worlds produces what I call a *politics of legibility*, in which actors struggle with and respond to global health programs that only partially recognize their social conditions and experiences. How these politics manifested differed depending on social location. The politics of policymakers manifested as direct political resistance. They went against WHO recommendations and developed their own Option B+ policy, prescribing pregnant and breastfeeding women lifelong ART as soon as they tested positive, which they believed would work better in their healthcare context. The politics of HIV patients were embodied. When women living with HIV refused, stopped, or restarted treatment, they were pushing back on health policies that recognized their disease status but not their illness experience. For providers, politics manifested in struggles to provide care and sustain their livelihoods in a divided healthcare landscape. NGO providers, backed by donor funding, offered comprehensive HIV care but only to HIV positive women and only while they were at risk for maternal HIV transmission; public sector providers served all women but, given resource constraints, could only provide cursory prenatal care. Providers also struggled with their careers. Between NGOs that offered potential for career growth but were precarious and public sector work that provided stability but had low wages and limited advancement opportunities, providers had few reliable paths out of poverty and economic uncertainty.

The unequal worlds of care described in this book speak to the broader implications of global health programs. To be sure, the HIV care field has been successful in many ways. Global ART coverage is at an all-time high, with 76 percent of people living with HIV on treatment in 2022, compared to only 9 percent in 2006.[3] Patients are now living longer and healthier lives. In Malawi, attitudes around HIV have shifted considerably from widespread fatalism to optimism as ART improved patients' health and allowed them to live "normal" lives that included sex, marriage, and childbearing.[4] In addition to medication, NGOs provide valuable prevention education and treatment support, and research organizations gather important data on public health outcomes and the trajectory of the epidemic. But efforts to address HIV, as extraordinary as they are, have failed to recognize that disease, patients, and health workers are embedded in public healthcare systems and social structures. This failure not only limits the work of HIV care programs, but also what an AIDS-free future would mean. Ending AIDS would be a monumental achievement, but it would not put an end to the fact that patients suffer and die from other illnesses, many of which could be prevented or treated with improved public healthcare systems. What is recognized as worthy of attention and aid is a social and political question—the response to which has produced immense inequalities in care.

PARTIAL RECOVERIES

The idea of recovery has a normative trajectory and temporality, progressing from illness, to repair, and finally recovery. In a neoliberal context, global health institutions have sought recovery through targeted biomedical interventions that operate largely outside the state. In this book, I have shown that these efforts are disembedded from the healthcare systems and social conditions in which policymakers, providers, and patients are situated. Disease is disembedded from illness experience; healthcare work is disembedded from livelihood; policies are disembedded from the healthcare system where they are implemented. As a result, recovery is partial, unequal, and constrained. More broadly, the possibilities of recovery are politically constructed. HIV came to be seen as an exceptional condition that warrants an exceptional response. Collective action from activists, healthcare professionals, and governments of countries affected by HIV/AIDS pushed donors to invest in HIV care in ways that were previously unseen in the global health field. The result of this collective action is that patients have access to ART, allowing them to recover some aspects of their normal life trajectories. But in many ways, there is no return to a nostalgic normal from before the HIV pandemic. Problems in the healthcare system were a slow emergency compounded by inattention. While Malawi never had a robust health sector, the ways public healthcare failed to develop were produced over time through repeated political decisions to limit spending or investments. In conditions of scarcity, recovery stalls, and health risks, illness, death, and precarious livelihoods are the norm in which people continue to live.

The experiences of different actors in Malawi illustrate the opportunities and constraints of recovering under global health programs. Recognizing one disease without recognizing the larger healthcare system in which people are otherwise cared for has limited the success of health policies. Prior to Malawi's development of Option B+, the country followed WHO recommendations, and they experienced devastating rates of maternal HIV transmission. About one-third of children born from mothers with HIV contracted the virus, which is about the same rate of transmission as there would be with no intervention at all.[5] While WHO policies were based on scientific evidence, they failed because they could not be implemented.

Challenges with supply chain management meant that medications were not always distributed to healthcare facilities; providers working in understaffed facilities could not remember WHO policies; CD4 machines used to determine patients' eligibility for treatment were often broken or did not have the correct reagents; and the Ministry of Health did not have a systematic way of collecting patient data. Malawi's Option B+ was far more successful in reducing rates of maternal HIV transmission. Its test-and-treat approach leveraged donor-funded supplies of ART while acknowledging the conditions of Malawi's healthcare system. However, even the success of Option B+ came with constraints. The policy's simplicity and standardization, while necessary, rendered patients who fell outside the standard invisible. If patients experienced treatment failure on a given regimen, there were few alternatives. And while adult ART programs were well developed, programs for children were not. Preventing maternal transmission was crucial because there was little pediatric HIV care available, especially care that spoke to the unique physical and emotional needs of children and teens.[6]

For providers, what was legible and illegible to donors changed the healthcare profession in Malawi. The growth of the NGO sector provided new opportunities for healthcare work. This was especially meaningful for those without college degrees, who had few options in the formal work sector.[7] Many of my respondents described past struggles of moving between short-term jobs or attempting to pursue more education only to have their studies cut short by unexpected circumstances. NGOs were another avenue they could pursue for employment. Some who were able to stay at an NGO job for several years saw their lives change: They became breadwinners for their families and were able to go back to school. While some were able to improve their life circumstances, their progress was fragile and could be undone at any moment. NGOs amplified rather than moderated the economic uncertainty in people's lives.[8] NGO positions tended to be based on short-term contracts and varied in remuneration, with some offering high salaries and others being voluntary. In this sector, one could rise quickly and fall quickly. In contrast, public sector providers had stable work, often a job for life. But in comparison to NGO work, their careers felt stagnant. Public sector providers described how their lives stayed the same: With lower salaries and few opportunities for training and education, they felt that they could not advance their careers and socioeconomic status. For a younger generation of providers, NGO work was often more appealing because there was a chance, however risky, of upward mobility. While the structure of healthcare has changed, economic conditions for workers have remained relatively the same. Between precarity and stagnancy, neither sector offered workers true recovery from poverty and economic uncertainty.

For patients, recovery occurred in partial ways. Women living with HIV now had access to lifelong ART. The benefits of treatment cannot be understated—ART has transformed HIV from a death sentence to a manageable chronic condition. However, recognizing disease status but not women's social and economic conditions constrained the benefits that treatment could offer. ART was not a magic bullet. Women understood their prescription and wanted to protect their developing child from infection, but ART could disrupt important aspects of their everyday lives. Side effects, which often were exacerbated by food insecurity, made some women feel worse and incapable of work; and an HIV diagnosis could bring to light the micropolitics of trust between couples and threaten marriages. These issues could make it difficult for women to take ART consistently, limiting the potential protective and future health benefits that treatment offered.

Moreover, women's pregnancy and other health concerns were illegible. While women in Malawi could access ART and were now living with HIV, they were still dying from maternal mortality and other treatable conditions. Malawi's maternal mortality rate, at 100–499 deaths per 100,000 live births, is considered high to moderate. This is part of a broader regional issue, with over two-thirds (69%) of maternal deaths occurring in Africa.[9] At the prenatal clinic, women who tested positive for HIV had access to specialized NGO programs. With donor support, these programs had the resources necessary for providing comprehensive HIV care, including testing, counseling at the clinic and at home, treatment support, and monitoring of patients' health on ART. But these NGO programs existed only for those with HIV and only to address HIV-related issues. Other health issues, like pregnancy, fell to the public healthcare system that served all citizens but, with limited resources, could only provide cursory care. Providers had limited time and did not have the tools they needed, like blood pressure cuffs or hemoglobin testing, to properly assess patients' conditions. Even if patients had a condition recognized by donors, there are many other issues from which there is no recovery. Patients' lives and health needs cannot be neatly carved into disease-specific worlds. In this case, women's health was addressed in a piecemeal way: There was immense focus on preventing maternal transmission of HIV, but women were left at risk for any problems that might occur during or after childbirth.

MOVING FORWARD

Sustainability is often discussed in the global health field. It is an ideal in which donor-funded programs empower local actors to take control of their own futures such that donors can one day stop providing aid. It is synonymous with autonomy and self-reliance and is the opposite of passivity and dependence.[10] It is a discourse that supports neoliberal goals of cost-effectiveness: Programs should train rather than provide material goods; they should rely on volunteers rather than salaried workers; they should be short-term rather than long-term investments. Matthew, a Malawian public health professional who has worked in both the Ministry of Health and NGOs, laughed at the idea of sustainability. He said, "It is almost saying that Malawi shouldn't exist because it cannot be sustained." He explained that most African countries use foreign aid. If 40 percent or more of the budget comes from donors, then surely a country could not exist without it. His point was not to be critical of Malawi's "dependence" on aid. Instead, it was to turn the idea of sustainability on its head. If we accept that Malawi *should* exist, then we should accept that it exists unsustainably. Letting go of the idea of sustainability—at least in the way it is currently applied—would push donors to rethink their goals, make commitments beyond current boundaries, and continue doing so over a long period of time.

In this book, I have described the ways in which policymakers, providers, and patients navigate a healthcare landscape that has been unevenly transformed by foreign aid. Part of the unevenness stems from the influence of neoliberalism in the global health field. This ideology undergirds targeted, nonstate interventions that over time produce a structural divide in care. The findings of this book prompt a reconsideration of the ideological underpinnings of global health. Neoliberalism has been influential, but it is not the only possible ideological framework that could guide the global health field, which is a dynamic field. Historically, tensions have existed between social and economic approaches and those focused on specific diseases. The prominence of these approaches has waxed and waned with shifts in power, political climate, and the changing interests of key actors.[11] Though the vision of primary healthcare for all at the WHO's 1978 Alma-Ata conference did not come to pass, the near consensus around a multidimensional approach to health and socioeconomic development showed the possibility of a rights-based, rather than neoliberal, vision of global public health—one that the field could return to.

Large-scale transformations may be difficult and rare but are nonetheless possible. The global health field is characterized by inequalities in power. Donors and international organizations have the financial ability and global legitimacy to influence the health policies and programs of low-income countries. However, governments and citizens are not passive recipients of foreign aid; they respond, albeit in the shadows of power. The history of the HIV epidemic reminds us that collective action can influence a field in powerful ways. The work of AIDS activists, governments, and global health professionals made access to ART possible in the global South; and in doing so, they changed prior boundaries around what issues were appropriate for aid and how much donors could spend.[12] Some scholars have argued that HIV has made global health into the field we know today.[13] In the 1990s and early 2000s, it would have been unthinkable to have $20 billion available every year for HIV-care programs when the entire global health field had $5.6 billion available.[14] Yet mobilization for access to HIV treatment transformed these limits, reshaping what the global health field imagined to be possible.

Incremental changes could also be made in the current context of foreign aid. Research has shown that aid programs can go awry and do not always help the intended beneficiaries.[15] As Swidler and Watkins argue, development agencies and actors may be misguided in certain ways, but they are also altruists with a desire to help others. It is important to get to know the brokers—that is, the various local actors who do the work of implementing global health programs. Brokers' knowledge of their countries can help donors understand why certain programs may be embraced enthusiastically and others treated with subtle (or not so subtle) forms of opposition.[16] Similarly, Dionne has suggested that village headmen may be a key resource. During the AIDS epidemic, headmen were involved in mediating marital disputes, promoting HIV testing, and identifying orphans, thus embodying important knowledge about the epidemic's social impacts.[17] More work could also be done to directly ask citizens what they need. Dionne's survey of Malawian villagers showed that their priorities were clean water, agricultural development, education, and general health concerns.[18] This did not mean that villagers did not care about HIV; instead, while HIV had been addressed by donors, other important needs were not being met. Building boreholes for access to clean water or paving roads so that it would be easier to move to and from the village are incremental initiatives that would improve people's health and well-being in everyday life.[19]

My findings lend support to these suggestions at the policy level. The case of Option B+ suggests that donors and international organizations would benefit from incorporating the expertise of national actors. Despite being based on scientific evidence, WHO policies did little to change to the rate of maternal HIV transmission in Malawi because they could not be implemented in the healthcare system. Option B+ led to far greater success in preventing mother-to-child transmission not only in Malawi but also more widely in the sub-Saharan Africa region. Because of its success, Option B+ eventually became a WHO recommendation. The policy was developed by a group of Malawian policymakers and Malawian NGO staff as well as international NGO staff, technical advisors, researchers, and physicians who had worked in the country for many years. While there are many international actors in Malawi, their roles, influence, and embeddedness in the country vary substantially. The actors involved in Option B+ were situated between local healthcare systems and the global HIV field, which helped them to develop their policy idea and promote it internationally. The story behind Option B+ illustrates why the perspectives of national actors are vital. Global health policies have significant downstream effects on population health, and they are more likely to succeed when they incorporate the insights of national actors who understand both global public health and their local healthcare context.

This book has described how HIV-care programs operate in their own world of care. A significant part of what makes this world operate is the multitude of workers who implement programs on the ground. They are community health workers, HIV testing and treatment counselors, survey field researchers, and HIV-prevention educators. Many are in precarious economic positions. They tend to be secondary school graduates, who have limited opportunities in the formal job sector.[20] Because of this, some turn to volunteering. My research contributes to the critique of volunteer labor in global health.[21] Some of my respondents who had volunteered in the past expressed a desire to care for others, but they were also desperate to find work and often took volunteer positions in the hope that it would lead to paid employment. In this context, using volunteers is exploitative. The notion of paying workers for labor may seem obvious. But with neoliberal discourses of sustainability, volunteer labor is often seen as a cost-effective and sustainable way to implement programs.[22] Requiring NGOs to pay workers and to have some standards for compensation, benefits, and workplace protections, would be one step toward improving people's livelihoods.[23] While this would not resolve the precariousness of contract-based work, it would help reduce the exploitation inherent in volunteer positions.

The conditions of the public healthcare system need major attention. Shortages of staff, medicine, and infrastructure are long-standing problems that have struggled for recognition and resources. Making changes in the public sector will require a larger-scale reframing of what is considered legitimate for foreign aid. But in recent years, there has been renewed attention and ideas around strengthening health systems. While it is unclear whether this discourse will lead to practical changes, it suggests that the global health field is dynamic and changing.[24] An example of an idea for strengthening healthcare system is something scholars in the global health field have called taking a "diagonal approach." Rather than conceptualizing health interventions as an either-or choice between "vertical" disease programs or "horizontal" health-systems strengthening, global health institutions could simultaneously focus on major disease concerns, like HIV, while building up fundamental components of healthcare systems, like supply chain management and the health workforce.[25]

There is evidence that diagonal approaches work. At the start of Malawi's ART program in 2004, donors funded a dual initiative, the Emergency

Human Resources Program (EHRP), to address the "double burden" of health worker shortages.[26] The program boosted salaries by 52 percent for all health workers, expanded preservice training, recruited doctors and nurses from abroad, and added incentives like rural allowances, housing, and transport to improve retention.[27] By the end of the program in 2009, the number of trained health workers had increased, retention rates were higher, and the provider-patient ratio reached closer to their goal of Tanzanian levels. Efforts like the EHRP need to be sustained over time so that the availability of healthcare providers reaches the WHO minimum threshold and beyond. While donors today may be hesitant to fund public sector workers, past programs like the EHRP demonstrate that such programs are successful in addressing health worker shortages. In contrast, the current strategy of task shifting, according to which tasks normally assigned to higher-ranked providers are shifted to lower-ranked ones, contributes to the problem of provider burnout.[28] In Malawi, 89 percent of providers reported engaging in some suboptimal patient care practices or adopting suboptimal attitudes due to burnout.[29] Moreover, when providers are burned out, they are unable to incorporate training from global health initiatives to improve specific aspects of care, whether for HIV, maternal health, or other issues.[30]

Within the world of HIV care, donors supported systemic changes to improve HIV service provision. Although HIV programs often operate in isolated ways, their successes provide a roadmap for expanding efforts beyond specific disease programs. To scale up ART, donors created a parallel supply chain in which NGOs and private companies were responsible for procuring, storing, managing, and distributing HIV commodities. With a strong supply chain, there have been few stockouts of ART in Malawi's healthcare facilities.[31] Donor funding could similarly be used to provide essential medicines and improve the government's Central Medical Stores Trust (CMST), which manages health commodities for the public sector—an idea that emerged at the start of Malawi's ART program.[32] At the CMST, this improvement would involve hiring and training workers, expanding warehousing space, increasing distribution capacity, and establishing data systems for tracking medication supplies.[33] This has been done already for the ART supply chain, but through NGOs—the same initiatives are needed within the public sector. Donors have also built new healthcare facilities or buildings for HIV service provision, while public healthcare facilities have deteriorated.[34] Improving healthcare facilities and the underlying infrastructure, such as water and electricity, is fundamental for numerous aspects of care, including HIV care. For instance, when laboratories struggle with broken machines, missing reagents, and power outages, they cannot use X-rays, conduct tuberculosis screenings, or measure HIV CD4 counts or viral loads. Expanding physical infrastructure projects would have wide-ranging benefits because they can be used to address many conditions.

There are many magic bullet narratives in global health—claims that a single medication or intervention can eliminate disease and dramatically improve quality of life. These narratives are understandably appealing. Not only are such approaches simple, but they also resonate with neoliberal goals of cost-effectiveness, sustainability, and privatized technological solutions.[35] But the findings of this book suggest that there is no magic bullet. By rendering healthcare systems and broader social conditions illegible, global health programs are constrained in their ability to improve people's lives. Moving forward will require transforming at a large-scale the ideas and discourses that underlie global health programs. But progress can also include many incremental changes, which will improve the outcomes of programs for patients and those working in this field. While change is often difficult, past and present initiatives provide valuable roadmaps and expansive ideas of what is possible.

A NEW PANDEMIC

In the spring of 2020, the world was struck by another pandemic—COVID-19. Like HIV, COVID-19 was a novel virus, and in a short time, it drastically changed life in many countries. While the effects of COVID-19 brought unprecedented changes to our global society, the new pandemic also surfaced familiar patterns. Just as public healthcare systems are fundamental for providing care to patients, they are also fundamental for addressing new disease threats.

In the early stages of the pandemic, reports from Malawi showed that the country did not have adequate supplies to care for COVID-19 patients. The Malawi Emergency and Critical Care (MECC) Survey found there were only sixteen working ventilators across the four central (tertiary) hospitals in the country. While seven of the eight ICU facilities had reported adequate oxygen, only five of thirteen outpatient or emergency departments had adequate oxygen.[36] In addition, laboratory facilities could not conduct COVID-19 testing because of poor infrastructure, irregular water supply, insufficient electricity, and lack of equipment and reagents.[37] Inconsistent electricity also made it a challenge to store certain vaccines, such as the mRNA-based Moderna and Pfizer-BioNTech vaccines, which required low-temperatures.[38] These shortages were considered an emergency during COVID-19. But they have long been part of the slow emergency of the public sector.

During lockdown in the summer of 2020, three research assistants kept journals on conversations they had or overheard about COVID-19.[39] Conversational journals are a kind of "insider ethnography" in which individuals document their own lives, and they allow for research on everyday conversations in natural settings without the presence of an outsider ethnographer or interviewer.[40] While these journals are not representative of Malawi as a whole, they provide insight on people's experiences during the pandemic.

Community members felt the constraints of their healthcare system. In the context of COVID-19, problems in healthcare facilities, like overcrowding and poor sanitation, were not merely "resource constraints" but potential risk factors for spreading infection. Esther, one of the "journalists," described her experience taking her niece to the hospital when the pandemic started. There were no beds when they arrived, so they both slept on the floor until one became available. When they were finally admitted, they felt nervous about the number of people in the room. There was little space for Esther and the other family members who accompanied their loved ones. One woman said to her:

> Look at our room that we are staying in. Is this a room to be occupied by more than twenty people? The room is small. We have eight beds for patients with different diseases, and we are more than eight guardians here breathing on each other. Are we protected from COVID-19?

That same day, Esther heard other family members talk about how soap was available in the "early days" but now the dispensers were empty. They were also concerned about inconsistent supplies of personal protective equipment (PPE) at the hospital. Nurses talked about how they ration their PPE, for instance, by wearing shorter aprons while keeping the longer ones in storage for suspected COVID-19 cases. In these conditions, patients and family members did not feel safe. As one guardian said: "If we get infected here, we carry the viruses back home and spread it to our families." Another responded: "So if the nurse is worried about her life, yet she is a health worker, and she received other protecting resources including masks, aprons, and gloves, what about you and me who have nothing? Are we going to survive?" Community members did not feel safe within their own healthcare facilities.

While patients and providers in Malawi have long been critical of state healthcare, COVID-19 became yet another reminder of inadequacies in care. Government hospitals were often described as a "graveyard" and a "place for people to die." At the market, a woman said to Esther:

> We have nothing here, so if the disease is spread to us, I hope all of us can die within seconds because we have nothing to protect ourselves from the disease. And we have no money for building better hospitals for saving lives for patients with coronavirus.

Similarly, at the hospital, guardians echoed these concerns: "They are doing nothing because the hospitals have no resources for them to use when helping patients." Another responded: "This is why we say that the hospital is a place for people to die and not for one to get healed." These fatalistic attitudes are tied to the structure of the global health field. While improvements like a new ART clinic or maternity ward might be made, public healthcare facilities have generally faced resource constraints. Citizens have experienced these issues for a long time and did not trust their government to manage the new pandemic.

NGOs provided valuable emergency support but could only do as much as donor funding allowed. HIV-care NGOs in Malawi helped distribute emergency resources like COVID-19 tests, PPE, and hand-washing materials.[41] HIV community health workers also provided information about COVID-19 vaccines and assisted with vaccine distribution.[42] But these efforts were necessarily ad hoc and depended on donor attention. In the early stages of the pandemic, wealthy donor countries were struggling with their own pandemic responses. Esther described a conversation at the market, where one person said to her: "If the disease is killing many people from the rich countries including America that are well equipped, what about Malawi?" Countries were turning inward, closing borders and focusing on protecting their own citizens. While global alliances for vaccine distribution were starting to form, they seemed unlikely to lead to equitable access as wealthy countries jockeyed among themselves to hoard vaccine supplies. After years of global health initiatives, there have been few improvements to Malawi's public healthcare system. The country needed donors to provide even basic protective materials, which in an uncertain time, came in an inconsistent manner.

COVID-19 also compounded disadvantages in an economically precarious context. Community members expressed concerns about whether they could afford protective measures for their family. Purchasing items, such as washing pails and soap, could stretch a family's budget. For instance, Frank, another journalist, described a conversation with his wife: She told him that she bought a pail for their family to use outside of the toilet, but she could not afford the more expensive ones with a tap for running water. She also hid bars of soap to prevent others from stealing them. In addition, work became more unstable during the pandemic. Frank's wife told him about her conversation with a friend on the struggles of small businesses. He wrote:

> She went on saying that with this era of COVID-19 things are worse. She added, saying that most of her friends, who were running small businesses at the trading center, saw their businesses collapse . . . She met the wife of Mavuto, who has just gone to South Africa and left his wife with a small business of selling tomatoes. She said tomatoes used to be a good business because each and every day people want to eat *nsima* [a staple food], and no one prepares *nsima* without preparing relish first. And that requires tomatoes. She was complaining that she doesn't see any difference compared to those who are just staying at home, running no business.

It was hard for community members to imagine how they could support themselves and their families when shelter-in-place and other public health measures are put into effect. Esther described someone at the market saying to her: "Every day we go to look for piecework for survival, so what will happen to us if we are in a lockdown situation?" Moreover, with less work available, food security becomes a serious concern. Outside the village bank, one person said to Frank: "We eat through hand to mouth, so we cannot stay locked into our houses even for three days." In response to the pandemic, Frank described how he and his wife tightened their budget. His wife suggested cutting out tea, sugar, cassava, and sweet potato, which were now considered luxury items. People were concerned about both health and economic suffering. One man at the bank said to Frank: "This COVID-19 is really and absolutely going to make people suffer a lot, not only suffering from the disease itself, but also we are going to be affected and severely hit by crucial poverty."

The illegibility of public healthcare systems created familiar problems during this new pandemic. As Ferguson argues, repeated failure often suggests that there is an ideology that transcends any individual program.[43] A neoliberal approach to health, which has resulted in disease programs run by NGOs, carves care into worlds outside the state. As I have argued in this book, approaching health in these partial and divided ways limits the potential of global health programs to improve healthcare and people's lives. The world of public healthcare, and more broadly the social conditions in which people live, affects multiple aspects of care, including policymaking, healthcare careers, everyday service provision, and patient experiences with illness and treatment. The challenges that emerged with managing COVID-19 were another reminder of this. The pandemic revealed the vulnerabilities that inhere in systems dependent on foreign aid that may go unnoticed during times of stability. Because funding often bypassed the public sector, Malawi was left with few lasting structures in place when donor priorities shifted inward toward their own countries. Just as the illegibility of public healthcare limits the potential of ongoing global health programs, it also limits the ability of countries to prepare for and manage new disease threats.

Acknowledgments

This book is the product of nearly a decade of research and writing. As a first book, it truly took a village, and I am deeply thankful for the many people who supported me throughout this journey. Above all, I owe gratitude to the people of Malawi. This project would not have been possible without the generosity of patients, healthcare workers, government officials, and NGO staff who took the time to speak with me and share often deeply personal aspects of their lives. Your stories form the heart of this work. Out of respect for privacy, I do not mention individuals by name, but I am thankful to the health workers at my field sites. Your willingness to not only participate in this research but also to welcome me into your daily routines—sharing meals, conversations, and guidance on navigating both the clinics and life in Lilongwe—has taught me so much. I also value the meaningful connections we formed during our time together, which go beyond the research itself.

This book began as a dissertation in the Sociology Department at UCLA. I am immensely grateful to my advisor, Stefan Timmermans, whose expertise in medical sociology and steadfast mentorship were instrumental in shaping my development as a scholar. As a first-year student, I nervously emailed Stefan to ask for book recommendations. He instead suggested that we meet to talk about what drew me to sociology—a conversation that would mark the beginning of a long-term mentorship that shaped this and many other projects. I also thank Ching Kwan Lee, Edward Walker, and Susan Watkins for forming an intellectually rich and supportive committee. Each of them pushed my thinking in distinct ways, strengthening my work and encouraging me through the inevitable moments of fatigue and frustration that come with conducting research. At a time when I was ready to give up on part of this project, CK Lee's encouragement to try again—to knock on any and all doors—reinvigorated the research that became a key section of this book. Susan Watkins's commitment to Malawi has been a source of inspiration, as has the generosity with which she shared her knowledge and mentored students, and her unrelenting intellectual curiosity. Her guidance was essential during the conceptualization of this project and my fieldwork in Malawi. I also benefited from feedback and camaraderie from my fellow UCLA students: Brooks Ambrose, Neil Gong, Zach Griffen, Ben Jarvis, Hyeyoung Oh, Eleni Skaperdas, Caroline Tietbohl, and the Health Working Group. The journal club organized by Susan Watkins provided a space for engaging conversations on international development. During these sessions, Nicole Angotti, Marie Berry, Juan Delgado, Leydy Diossa, Saskia Nauenberg Dunkell, Matías Fernández, Tom Hannan, Tara McKay, and Ann Swidler contributed insights that have shaped the direction of this project. My dissertation research was supported by funding from the National Science Foundation, UCLA Graduate Division, and the UCLA Sociology Department.

During my fieldwork, I received support from various people and organizations in Malawi. I am grateful to McDaphton Bellos, my research assistant, for conducting interviews in Chichewa, taking field notes, and generously teaching me about life in Malawi. I am also thankful to Invest in Knowledge and Umoyo+ for their transcription and translation services. A research team from the University of Bern offered me a place to stay and an opportunity to begin my research. I learned a lot by working alongside members of that team, including Andreas Haas, Malango Msukwa, and Lyson Tenthani. Conversations with Christine Chung, Ruth Ehret, Carly Farver, Tracy Han, and Molly Uebele gave me valuable insights into their work in Malawi and encouraged deeper reflection on my own. I was fortunate to meet Maria Kim during my research and to benefit from her extensive experience in HIV care. I collaborated with Maria Kim, Alick Mazenga, and others at the Baylor College of Medicine Children's Foundation to explore women's experiences with ART. Maria and Alick also facilitated valuable connections with community health workers in their Tingathe program, allowing me to understand on-the-ground healthcare practices and experiences.

After completing my PhD at UCLA, I spent a year at the Institute for Practical Ethics at UCSD, where John Evans was a generous mentor who supported this book project and my professional growth. Much of the writing for this book took place at Barnard College, Columbia University. As department chair, Mignon Moore exemplified what it means to shepherd new faculty in the early stages of their careers. I am grateful to Gil Eyal and Elizabeth Bernstein for their mentorship. Through the COVID-19 pandemic and beyond, they supported this project, engaging with the manuscript at multiple stages and providing guidance throughout. Debra Minkoff organized a book workshop that gave me feedback at a pivotal stage of the writing process. Alongside my colleagues Gil and Elizabeth, Claire Decoteau and Sanyu Mojola provided thoughtful, detailed comments, and the group discussion helped push my thinking in new and exciting directions. I appreciate the many writing communities that have sustained me along the way. A writing group with Deisy Del Real, Eli Wilson, and Hajar Yazdiha has been a vital intellectual community—my conversations with them have shaped every chapter of this book. I am also thankful to Casandra Salgado, who shared the writing journey with me and offered valuable feedback, and to Emily Yoon, who also provided steady emotional support and accountability. I am grateful to my colleagues at Barnard, Columbia, and beyond who engaged with this project at various stages: my Barnard and Columbia colleagues, Adam Reich, Angela Simms, Josh Whitford, and the Science, Knowledge, and Technology working group; the womyn's writing group with Karina Chavarria, Becca DiBennardo, Nicole Iturriaga, Mirian Martinez-Aranda, and Ariana Valle; the Recovery Working Group with Elizabeth Bernstein, Nadja Eisenberg-Guyot, Chloé Samala Faux, Rebecca Jordan-Young, Kerwin Kaye, Samuel Roberts, Jackie Orr, Gabriela Quintero, Marisa Solomon, and Miriam Ticktin; and fellow global health scholars, Sarah Fischer, Joseph Harris, Jon Shaffer, Catherine van de Ruit, Lillian Walkover, and Robert Wyrod. I may have unintentionally overlooked others, but please know that my gratitude extends to them as well.

In the final stages of writing, Elizabeth Jean Bailey's keen editorial eye sharpened both the ideas and the prose of this manuscript. K Magnusdottir McComish and Anagha Rajesh provided research assistance during the completion of this book. At University of California Press, Naomi Schneider and Aline Dolinh have been an outstanding editorial team, supporting me during the earlier stages of this manuscript and helping me grow as a first-time author. I am also grateful to the anonymous reviewers and the faculty board at University of California Press for their thoughtful feedback on the manuscript.

I am deeply thankful to my parents, Yan Cheng and Albert Zhou, for their unwavering love and support. My dad's advice—to seek to understand others before seeking to be understood—has shaped much of my sociological perspective, while my mom's support for both my work and my well-being has been a constant source of strength. My husband, Kyle Kirwan, has been by my side and has helped carry me through the highs and lows of this project. My family has been the foundation that made this work possible.

Notes

PREFACE

1. Imray, "Trump's Permanent USAID Cuts Slam Humanitarian Programs Worldwide."

2. Kenny and Sandefur, "New Estimates of the USAID Cuts."

3. Nolen, "U.S. to End Vaccine Funds for Poor Countries"; Kritz, "Gavi, the Vaccine Alliance, Has Its Billion Dollar Grant Cut by Trump Administration."

4. Ratevosian, "PEPFAR Misses Reauthorization Deadline."

5. Nolen, "U.S. to End Vaccine Funds for Poor Countries"; Sandefur and Charles, "USAID Cuts."

6. Cohen, "'A Bloodbath.'"

7. Sandefur and Charles, "USAID Cuts."

8. USAID Stop-Work, "USAID Stop-Work."

9. Malawi's ranking: UNDP, "Human Development Insights"; percentage of Malawi's population living under the poverty line: World Bank Group, "Poverty & Equity Brief: Africa Eastern & Southern; Malawi."

10. Savage, "'Devastating.'"

11. Dionne, *Doomed Interventions.*

12. Savage, "'Devastating.'"

13. Vijayakumar, "Lessons from India's Sex Worker Activists on Surviving USAID Freeze."

14. Desilver, "What the Data Says About U.S. Foreign Aid."

15. Swidler and Watkins, *A Fraught Embrace.*

16. UNAIDS, "Global HIV & AIDS Statistics."

17. Funding waivers do not include PrEP for LGBTQ people or sex workers, programs specific to girls/young women, or community-led monitoring programs. MSF, "Uncertainty Around PEPFAR Program Puts Millions at Risk."

18. McKoy, "Tracking Anticipated Deaths from USAID Funding Cuts."

19. *Al Jazeera*, "HIV and AIDS Deaths Could Increase Globally amid US Aid Freeze, UN Says."

20. Mzungu, "Malawi Economic Crisis Deepens as U.S. Cuts $177 Million in Vital Aid, New Report Reveals."

21. Swidler and Watkins, *A Fraught Embrace: The Romance and Reality of AIDS Altruism in Africa.*

22. MSF, "Uncertainty Around PEPFAR Program Puts Millions at Risk."

23. UNESCO, "Malawi: Education Country Brief."

24. Cilliers, "Data Modelling Reveals the Heavy Toll of USAID Cuts on Africa."

25. Centeno and Cohen, "The Arc of Neoliberalism."

26. Conroy, Yeatman, and Dovel, "The Social Construction of AIDS During a Time of Evolving Access to Antiretroviral Therapy in Rural Malawi."

27. Sandefur and Charles, "USAID Cuts: New Estimates at the Country Level."

28. *Al Jazeera*, "South Sudanese Children Die as US Aid Cuts Shutter Medical Services: NGO."

29. Farber, Harris, and Singh, "Reimagine Aid, Don't Destroy It."

30. Esacove, "Love Matches: Heteronormativity, Modernity, and AIDS Prevention in Malawi"; Esacove, *Modernizing Sexuality: US HIV Prevention in Sub-Saharan Africa*; Esacove, "Good Sex/Bad Sex: The Individualised Focus of US HIV Prevention Policy in Sub-Saharan Africa, 1995-2005."

31. Swidler and Watkins, *A Fraught Embrace: The Romance and Reality of AIDS Altruism in Africa*; McDonnell, *Best Laid Plans: Cultural Entropy and the Unraveling of AIDS Media Campaigns*; Dionne, *Doomed Interventions: The Failure of Global Responses to AIDS in Africa.*

32. van Lettow et al., "Uptake and Outcomes of a Prevention-of-Mother-to-Child Transmission (PMTCT) Program in Zomba District, Malawi."

33. Ooms et al., "The 'Diagonal' Approach to Global Fund Financing: A Cure for the Broader Malaise of Health Systems?"

34. Farber, Harris, and Singh, "Reimagine Aid, Don't Destroy It."

35. Farber, Harris, and Singh.

36. Swidler and Watkins, *A Fraught Embrace: The Romance and Reality of AIDS Altruism in Africa*; Dionne, *Doomed Interventions: The Failure of Global Responses to AIDS in Africa.*

INTRODUCTION: POLITICS OF LEGIBILITY

1. Steven Brown is a pseudonym, as are all the names used in this book, with the exception of policymakers speaking in official capacities.

2. World Bank Group, "Prevalence of HIV, Total (% of Population Ages 15–49)." HIV prevalence has declined in Malawi over time. In 2015, HIV prevalence was 9.6 percent and, in 2020, 7.9 percent.

3. WHO, "Population, Malawi."

4. UNAIDS, "HIV Financial Dashboard."

5. KFF, "U.S. Global Health Funding (in Millions)." In comparison maternal and child health received 10.5 percent of the US annual global health budget, nutrition received 1.4 percent, and neglected tropical diseases 0.9 percent (KFF, 2024).

6. Shiffman, "Donor Funding Priorities for Communicable Disease Control in the Developing World."

7. Epstein, *Impure Science*; Parker, "Grassroots Activism, Civil Society Mobilization, and the Politics of the Global HIV/AIDS Epidemic"; Gamson, "Silence, Death, and the Invisible Enemy."

8. UNAIDS, "AIDS Epidemic Update: December 2000."

9. Crane, *Scrambling for Africa*; Kenworthy, *Mistreated*.

10. Herbert, "Opinion: In America."

11. Smith and Watkins, "Perceptions of Risk and Strategies for Prevention"; Thornton, *Unimagined Community*.

12. WHO, "HIV/AIDS: Report by the Director-General."

13. UNAIDS, "AIDS Epidemic Update: December 2000."

14. Fassin, *When Bodies Remember*, xii.

15. Biehl, *Will to Live*; Decoteau, *Ancestors and Antiretrovirals*; Fassin, *When Bodies Remember*.

16. Fassin, *When Bodies Remember*, 229.

17. Global Fund, "Results Report 2024."

18. HIV.gov, "What Is PEPFAR?"

19. Chorev, "Changing Global Norms Through Reactive Diffusion"; Harris, *Achieving Access*.

20. Parker, "Grassroots Activism, Civil Society Mobilization, and the Politics of the Global HIV/AIDS Epidemic."

21. Packard, *A History of Global Health*; Harris, *Achieving Access*.

22. Chorev, "Changing Global Norms Through Reactive Diffusion."

23. Nguyen, *The Republic of Therapy*.

24. Moyer, "The Anthropology of Life After AIDS."

25. Assefa et al., "Leaving No One Behind"; World Bank Group, "Antiretroviral Therapy Coverage (% of People Living with HIV)."

26. Persson, "Non/Infectious Corporealities"; Persson, "'The World Has Changed.'"

27. Conroy, Yeatman, and Dovel, "The Social Construction of AIDS During a Time of Evolving Access to Antiretroviral Therapy in Rural Malawi."

28. Kenworthy, Thomann, and Parker, "From a Global Crisis to the 'End of AIDS.'"

29. Biehl, "Pharmaceuticalization"; Persson, "'The World Has Changed.'"

30. Whyte et al., "Therapeutic Clientship."

31. Morfit, "'AIDS Is Money.'"

32. Swidler and Watkins, *A Fraught Embrace.*

33. Lasker, *Hoping to Help.*

34. Benton, *HIV Exceptionalism.*

35. Brandt, "How AIDS Invented Global Health"; Grepin, "HIV Donor Funding Has Both Boosted and Curbed the Delivery of Different Non-HIV Health Services in Sub-Saharan Africa."

36. England, "Are We Spending Too Much on HIV?"

37. Shiffman, "Has Donor Prioritization of HIV/AIDS Displaced Aid for Other Health Issues?"; Yu et al., "Investment in HIV/AIDS Programs"; Rasschaert et al., "Positive Spill-Over Effects of ART Scale Up on Wider Health Systems Development"; Lordan, Tang, and Carmignani, "Has HIV/AIDS Displaced Other Health Funding Priorities?"

38. Ooms, Damme, and Temmerman, "Medicines Without Doctors."

39. Scott, *Seeing Like a State.*

40. Biruk, "Seeing Like a Research Project."

41. Shiffman, "Donor Funding Priorities for Communicable Disease Control in the Developing World."

42. Swidler and Watkins, *A Fraught Embrace.*

43. Dionne, *Doomed Interventions.*

44. Fassin, "Another Politics of Life Is Possible."

45. Esser and Bench, "Does Global Health Funding Respond to Recipients' Needs?"; MacKellar, "Priorities in Global Assistance for Health, AIDS, and Population"; Ravishankar et al., "Financing of Global Health"; Shiffman, "Donor Funding Priorities for Communicable Disease Control in the Developing World."

46. Sullivan, "Mediating Abundance and Scarcity"; Prince and Otieno, "In the Shadowlands of Global Health"; Pfeiffer, "The Struggle for a Public Sector."

47. Swidler and Watkins, *A Fraught Embrace.*

48. Suh, *Dying to Count.*

49. Boli and Thomas, "INGOs and the Organization of World Culture."

50. Biesma et al., "The Effects of Global Health Initiatives on Country Health Systems"; Okuonzi and Macrae, "Whose Policy Is It Anyway?"

51. Nguyen, "Government-by-Exception"; Ferguson and Gupta, "Spatializing States."

52. Wendland, "Estimating Death"; Oni-Orisan, "The Obligation to Count."

53. Adams, *Metrics: What Counts in Global Health.*

54. Kenworthy, *Mistreated.*

55. Dionne, *Doomed Interventions*; Dionne, "Local Demand for a Global Intervention."

56. Biehl and Petryna, *When People Come First.*

57. Swidler and Watkins, *A Fraught Embrace.* This number does not include the funding the United States gives to multilateral organizations like the Global Fund, which itself is the second largest donor.

58. Esacove, "Love Matches"; Esacove, *Modernizing Sexuality.*

59. Dionne, *Doomed Interventions.* As I discuss in chapter 2, Malawi faced several challenges with implementing WHO policies—one of which was that donors purchased CD4 machines from different companies, each requiring their own reagents, leading to mix-ups in delivering the right reagents to the right facilities.

60. McDonnell, *Best Laid Plans.*

61. Angotti, "Working Outside of the Box"; Kaler and Watkins, "Disobedient Distributors."

62. Angotti, "Working Outside of the Box."

63. McDonnell, *Best Laid Plans*; McDonnell, "Cultural Objects as Objects."

64. Centeno and Cohen, "The Arc of Neoliberalism," 318.

65. Birn, Nervi, and Siqueira, "Neoliberalism Redux"; Keshavjee, *Blind Spot*; Packard, *A History of Global Health*; Pfeiffer and Chapman, "Anthropological Perspectives on Structural Adjustment and Public Health."

66. Decoteau, *Ancestors and Antiretrovirals.*

67. Basilico et al., "Health for All?"

68. WHO, "Declaration of Alma-Ata."

69. Brown, Cueto, and Fee, "The World Health Organization and the Transition From 'International' to 'Global' Public Health"; Cueto, "The Origins of Primary Health Care and Selective Primary Health Care."

70. Ferguson and Gupta, "Spatializing States."

71. Birn, Zimmerman, and Garfield, "To Decentralize or Not to Decentralize, Is That the Question?"; Pfeiffer, "The Struggle for a Public Sector"; Rowden, *The Deadly Ideas of Neoliberalism.*

72. Rowden.

73. Brass, *Allies or Adversaries*; Kamat, "The Privatization of Public Interest."

74. Koch et al., "Keeping a Low Profile"; McCoy, Chand, and Sridhar, "Global Health Funding."

75. Packard, *A History of Global Health.* Formal recognition by the UN does not extend to the many small community-based organizations, which are difficult to count.

76. Brass et al., "NGOs and International Development."

77. Storeng and Béhague, "'Playing the Numbers Game.'" In addition, health metrics, like disability-adjusted life years (DALYs) and quality-adjusted life years (QALYs), which are necessary for monitoring health outcomes, implicitly place value on human life in market terms. Adams, *Metrics*. Rather than a public good, health has become tied to market accountability.

78. Sparke, "Austerity and the Embodiment of Neoliberalism as Ill-Health"; Storeng, "The GAVI Alliance and the 'Gates Approach' to Health System Strengthening"; Storeng and Béhague, "'Playing the Numbers Game.'"

79. Moran-Thomas, "A Salvage Ethnography of the Guinea Worm"; Cueto, "A Return to the Magic Bullet?"; Packard, *A History of Global Health*; Storeng, "The GAVI Alliance and the 'Gates Approach' to Health System Strengthening."

80. Moran-Thomas, "A Salvage Ethnography of the Guinea Worm."

81. Kenworthy, Thomann, and Parker, "From a Global Crisis to the 'End of AIDS'"; Persson, "'The World Has Changed.'"

82. Keshavjee, *Blind Spot.*

83. Feierman, "When Physicians Meet"; Adams, *Metrics: What Counts in Global Health.*

84. Hafner and Shiffman, "The Emergence of Global Attention to Health Systems Strengthening"; Ravishankar et al., "Financing of Global Health."

85. Luboga et al., "Did PEPFAR Investments Result in Health System Strengthening?"; Marchal, Cavalli, and Kegels, "Global Health Actors Claim to Support Health System Strengthening"; Storeng, "The GAVI Alliance and the 'Gates Approach' to Health System Strengthening." Although PEPFAR increased funding for systemic improvements—such as medical records, pharmacies, and lab infrastructure—these improvements were designated specifically for a separate system of HIV care (Luboga et al., 2016).

86. Benton, *HIV Exceptionalism*; Yu et al., "Investment in HIV/AIDS Programs."; Luboga et al., "Did PEPFAR Investments Result in Health System Strengthening?"

87. Sullivan, "Mediating Abundance and Scarcity."

88. Pfeiffer, "The Struggle for a Public Sector."

89. Nguyen, *The Republic of Therapy.*

90. Petryna, "Science and Citizenship Under Postsocialism."

91. Whyte et al., "Therapeutic Clientship: Belonging in Uganda's Projectified Landscape of AIDS Care."

92. Biehl and Petryna, *When People Come First.*

93. Biehl, "Pharmaceuticalization"; Burchardt, "The Self as Capital in the Narrative Economy"; Cataldo, "New Forms of Citizenship and Socio-Political Inclusion"; Meinert, Mogensen, and Twebaze, "Tests for Life Chances"; Richey, "Counselling Citizens and Producing Patronage."

94. Benton, *HIV Exceptionalism.*

95. Fan, *Commodities of Care.*

96. Rosenthal, *Health on Delivery*; Swidler and Watkins, *A Fraught Embrace.*

97. Swidler and Watkins.

98. Fan, *Commodities of Care.*

99. Kalofonos, *All I Eat Is Medicine.*

100. Farber, "'Don't Think That We Die from AIDS.'"

101. World Bank Group, "Population, Total: Malawi."

102. Geubbels and Bowie, "Epidemiology of HIV/AIDS in Adults in Malawi."

103. World Bank Group, "Prevalence of HIV, Total (% of Population Ages 15–49)."

104. UNAIDS, "Fact Sheet 2022"; WHO, "HIV/AIDS."

105. UNAIDS, "HIV Financial Dashboard."

106. Dionne, *Doomed Interventions*, 82.

107. Morfit, "'AIDS Is Money."

108. Swidler and Watkins, *A Fraught Embrace.*

109. Benton, *HIV Exceptionalism.*

110. Mattes, "'We Are Just Supposed to Be Quiet'"; Moyer, Burchardt, and Dijk, "Editorial Introduction: Sexuality, Intimacy and Counselling"; Burchardt, "Subjects of Counselling"; Vernooij and Hardon, "'What Mother Wouldn't Want to Save Her Baby?'"

111. Malawi's Human Development Index ranking: The UNDP, "Human Development Insights." Percentage of the population living under the poverty line: World Bank Group, "Poverty & Equity Brief: Africa Eastern & Southern; Malawi."

112. Swidler and Watkins, *A Fraught Embrace*; Trinitapoli and Yeatman, "Uncertainty and Fertility in a Generalized AIDS Epidemic."

113. UNESCO, "Malawi: Education Country Brief."

114. Mussa, *Labour Market Transitions of Young Women and Men in Malawi.*

115. iAHO and WHO, "Maternal Mortality."

116. Messac, *No More to Spend.*

117. WHO, "Population, Malawi"; WHO, "WHO Health Workforce Support and Safeguards List."

118. Burawoy, "Manufacturing the Global," 156.

119. Gille and Riain, "Global Ethnography."

120. Swidler and Watkins, *A Fraught Embrace.*

121. Kim et al., "The Tingathe Programme:"

122. Kim et al., "Why Did I Stop?"

123. Researchers have used conversational journals to document everyday talk on HIV/AIDS.

124. While I developed relationships during my time in Malawi, I am far freer to leave my Malawian acquaintances than they are to leave me. This is a dynamic many ethnographers describe, but in Malawi, it contributes to a larger pattern of foreign agencies and actors that come and go.

CHAPTER 1. CONSTRUCTING UNEQUAL WORLDS OF CARE

1. Piot, "Why Aids Demands an Exceptional Response"; Benton, *HIV Exceptionalism*.

2. UNAIDS, "HIV Financial Dashboard."

3. Ntonya, "So, AIDS Is Money?"

4. Morfit, "'AIDS Is Money.'"

5. Pensulo, "'Bring Your Own Syringe.'"

6. Buse and Waxman, "Public–Private Health Partnerships"; Sullivan, "Mediating Abundance and Scarcity"; Prince and Otieno, "In the Shadowlands of Global Health."

7. UNDP, "Human Development Insights"; World Bank Group, "Poverty & Equity Brief: Africa Eastern & Southern; Malawi"; IPC, "Malawi IPC Chronic Food Insecurity Report."

8. Fassin, *When Bodies Remember*.

9. Benton, *HIV Exceptionalism*.

10. Nguyen, "Government-by-Exception."

11. Decoteau, "The Entangled Emergencies of COVID-19," 107.

12. Anderson, "Emergency Futures."

13. Ravishankar et al., "Financing of Global Health."

14. Benton, *HIV Exceptionalism*.

15. Nguyen, "Government-by-Exception."

16. Nguyen, *The Republic of Therapy*; Decoteau, *Ancestors and Antiretrovirals*.

17. Decoteau, *Emergency*.

18. Nguyen, *The Republic of Therapy*; Petryna, "Biological Citizenship."

19. Berlant, "Slow Death"; Anderson, "Emergency Futures:"; Nixon, *Slow Violence and the Environmentalism of the Poor*.

20. Anderson et al., "Slow Emergencies."

21. Berlant, "Slow Death."

22. Nixon, *Slow Violence and the Environmentalism of the Poor*.

23. Decoteau, "The Entangled Emergencies of COVID-19."

24. Decoteau, *Emergency*.

25. Decoteau.

26. Hafner and Shiffman, "The Emergence of Global Attention to Health Systems Strengthening"; Ravishankar et al., "Financing of Global Health"; Storeng, "The GAVI Alliance and the 'Gates Approach' to Health System Strengthening"; Marchal, Cavalli, and Kegels, "Global Health Actors Claim to Support Health System Strengthening."

27. Marchal, Cavalli, and Kegels.

28. Decoteau, *Emergency*; Decoteau, "The Entangled Emergencies of COVID-19."

29. Decoteau; Mbembe, "Necropolitics."

30. Decoteau, "The Entangled Emergencies of COVID-19."

31. Decoteau; Decoteau, *Emergency.*

32. Biruk, *Cooking Data*; Kalofonos, *All I Eat Is Medicine.*

33. Benjamin, "Theses on the Philosophy of History"; Anderson et al., "Slow Emergencies."

34. Anderson, "Emergency Futures"; Southwood, *Non-Stop Inertia.*

35. Auyero, *Patients of the State.*

36. E.g., the Bantu migration in the fifteenth century and the Batwa in the seventeenth century. Kalinga and Pike, "A Pre-Colonial History of Malawi."

37. Wendland, *A Heart for the Work.*

38. Phiri, "Pre-Colonial States of Central Malawi"; Wendland, *A Heart for the Work.*

39. McCracken, *Politics and Christianity in Malawi, 1875–1940*; Wendland, *Partial Stories.*

40. Sindima, *Malawi's First Republic.*

41. Kalofonos, *All I Eat Is Medicine.*

42. Rain-making was an especially important function of chiefs. According to oral evidence, female chiefs were considered ritual specialists. The most famous was Mangadzi, also known as Makewana, or "mother of children," who presided over what became the central Chewa rain shrine. Leaders were considered divinely sanctioned and owners of communal charms. Phiri, "Pre-Colonial States of Central Malawi."

43. Wendland, *A Heart for the Work.*

44. Ashforth, "AIDS, Religious Enthusiasm and Spiritual Insecurity in Africa"; Ashforth, *Witchcraft, Violence, and Democracy in South Africa.*

45. Kaspin, "A Chewa Cosmology of the Body"; Wendland, *A Heart for the Work.*

46. Wendland.

47. Wendland; Decoteau, *Ancestors and Antiretrovirals*; Morris, "Herbalism and Divination in Southern Malawi"; Morris, "Medical Herbalism in Malawi."

48. Messac, *No More to Spend.*

49. Campbell, *Letting Them Die*; Decoteau, *Ancestors and Antiretrovirals.*

50. Heaton, "Health and Medicine in Colonial Society"; Vaughan, *Curing Their Ills*; Wendland, *A Heart for the Work.*

51. Hokkanen, "The Government Medical Service and British Missions in Colonial Malawi, c. 1891–1940."

52. Hokkanen; Vaughan, *Curing Their Ills.*

53. Heaton, "Health and Medicine in Colonial Society."

54. Hokkanen, "The Government Medical Service and British Missions in Colonial Malawi, c. 1891–1940."

55. Beck, *A History of the British Medical Administration of East Africa, 1900–1950*; Wendland, *A Heart for the Work.*

56. King and King, *The Story of Medicine and Disease in Malawi.*

57. Messac, *No More to Spend.*

58. Messac, "Moral Hazards and Moral Economies."

59. Messac, *No More to Spend.*

60. Heaton, "Health and Medicine in Colonial Society"; Packard, *A History of Global Health.*

61. Messac, *No More to Spend.*

62. Whitehead, *Annual Medical Report on the Health and Sanitary Conditions of the Nyasaland Protectorate for the Year Ended 31st December, 1925*; Messac, *No More to Spend.*

63. Busy, *Blantyre Government Hospitals and Dispensary General Report 1921*; Messac, *No More to Spend.*

64. Messac, *No More to Spend.*

65. Messac; Shircore, *Report on the Nyasaland Medical Service with Special Reference to a Grant Under the Colonial Development Fund.*

66. Messac, *No More to Spend*; Nyasaland, *Annual Medical Report on the Health and Sanitary Condition of the Nyasaland Protectorate for the Year Ending the 31st December 1930.*

67. Lwanda, *Politics, Culture and Medicine in Malawi.*

68. King and King, *The Story of Medicine and Disease in Malawi*; Wendland, *A Heart for the Work.*

69. Wendland, *A Heart for the Work.*

70. The first African to graduate from Blantyre Mission Hospital's training program, John Gray Kufa, became second in command to John Chilembwe, an African Baptist preacher who led a major rebellion in 1915. The rebellion was crushed, Chilembwe's Providence Industrial Mission was destroyed, and colonial surveillance of Nyasaland's educational structures subsequently increased. Wendland, *A Heart for the Work*, 42.

71. Hokkanen, "The Government Medical Service and British Missions in Colonial Malawi, c. 1891–1940."

72. Messac, "Moral Hazards and Moral Economies."

73. Messac, *No More to Spend.*

74. Wendland, *A Heart for the Work.*

75. McCracken, *Politics and Christianity in Malawi, 1875–1940.*

76. Messac, *No More to Spend.*

77. Fassin, *When Bodies Remember*; Chorev, "Changing Global Norms Through Reactive Diffusion"; Harris, *Achieving Access.*

78. Messac, *No More to Spend*, 139.

79. Messac, 142.

80. Malawi's first president, Hastings Banda, received a scholarship from the African Methodist Episcopal Church to study in the United States. He completed secondary school in Ohio, then went on to the University of Indiana and

University of Chicago for his undergraduate studies; he went to Meharry Medical College for medical school (Messac, *No More to Spend*, 84).

81. Messac, "Birthing a Nation."

82. Messac.

83. Messac.

84. Messac, *No More to Spend*; Harrigan, "Malawi"; Wendland, *A Heart for the Work*.

85. Starting in 1979, then again in 1981, 1982, and 1985 (Messac, *No More to Spend*, 173).

86. Pfeiffer and Chapman, "Anthropological Perspectives on Structural Adjustment and Public Health."

87. Chipeta, "Malawi"; Kolko, "Ravaging the Poor"; World Bank Group, "Domestic General Government Health Expenditure (% of General Government Expenditure)."

88. Turshen, *Privatizing Health Services in Africa*.

89. Wendland, *Partial Stories*.

90. Kalipeni, "Structural Adjustment and the Health-Care Crisis in Malawi."

91. Pfeiffer, "The Struggle for a Public Sector."

92. Malawi Government, International Monetary Fund, and World Bank, "Malawi: Enhanced Structural Adjustment Facility Policy Framework Paper, 1998/99–2000/01."

93. Malawi Government, International Monetary Fund, and World Bank.

94. Menon, *Famine in Malawi*.

95. Wendland, *A Heart for the Work*.

96. Based on 2004 WHO data, Tanzania had 2.3 doctors and 36.6 nurses per 100,000 people; Zambia had 6.9 doctors and 113 nurses; Ghana had 9 doctors and 64 nurses; Botswana had 28.7 doctors and 241 nurses; and South Africa had 69.2 doctors and 388 nurses. Palmer, "Tackling Malawi's Human Resources Crisis."

97. Ministry of Health and Population, "Malawi Health Facility Survey"; Palmer, "Tackling Malawi's Human Resources Crisis."

98. Leslie et al., "Training and Supervision Did Not Meaningfully Improve Quality of Care for Pregnant Women or Sick Children in Sub-Saharan Africa"; Pfeiffer, "The Struggle for a Public Sector."

99. National Statistical Office, *Malawi Demographic and Health Survey*; Palmer, "Tackling Malawi's Human Resources Crisis."

100. McCoy, McPake, and Mwapasa, "The Double Burden of Human Resource and HIV Crises"; Palmer, "Tackling Malawi's Human Resources Crisis"; Damme, Kober, and Kegels, "Scaling-up Antiretroviral Treatment in Southern African Countries with Human Resource Shortage."

101. Chimwaza et al., "What Makes Staff Consider Leaving the Health Service in Malawi?"

102. Palmer, "Tackling Malawi's Human Resources Crisis."

103. McCoy, McPake, and Mwapasa, "The Double Burden of Human Resource and HIV Crises."

104. Chimwaza et al., "What Makes Staff Consider Leaving the Health Service in Malawi?"

105. Institute for Health Metrics and Evaluation, *Financing Global Health 2017*.

106. Messac, *No More to Spend*, 183.

107. Chimwaza et al., "What Makes Staff Consider Leaving the Health Service in Malawi?"; Assefa, Damme, and Hermann, "Human Resource Aspects of Antiretroviral Treatment Delivery Models"; Zuber et al., "A Survey of Nurse-Initiated and -Managed Antiretroviral Therapy (NIMART) in Practice, Education, Policy, and Regulation in East, Central, and Southern Africa."

108. Mueller et al., "Constraints to Implementing the Essential Health Package in Malawi."

109. Chimwaza et al., "What Makes Staff Consider Leaving the Health Service in Malawi?"; Mueller et al., "Constraints to Implementing the Essential Health Package in Malawi."

110. Berlant, "Slow Death."

111. Crisis can mean different things to different groups. In Vijayakumar's case in India, to the global HIV/AIDS field, HIV was the crisis, but for sex workers, minorities, and transgender individuals in India, crisis consisted of the routine challenges in their lives—police violence, domestic violence, unlawful arrest—that were often left unaddressed. Vijayakumar, *At Risk*.

112. Wendland, *Partial Stories*.

113. Trinitapoli, *An Epidemic of Uncertainty*.

114. Dionne, *Doomed Interventions*; Harries et al., "Why Did the Scale-up of HIV Treatment Work?."

115. Dionne, *Doomed Interventions*; National Statistical Office and Macro International Inc., *Malawi Knowledge, Attitudes and Practices in Health Survey 1996*.

116. Dionne, *Doomed Interventions*; National Statistical Office, *2008 Population and Housing Census Main Report*.

117. Dionne, *Doomed Interventions*; Institute for Health Metrics and Evaluation, "GBD Compare."

118. Dionne, *Doomed Interventions*.

119. Dionne.

120. Malawi was one of nine sites in a 1994 clinical trial for zidovudine. The trial tested whether taking zidovudine during the last weeks of pregnancy would reduce rates of HIV transmission to newborns. Half received it, the other half received a placebo—and treatment stopped at delivery. This trial was later considered an ethical controversy, as patients were denied a potentially beneficial treatment (Wendland, *Partial Stories*, 168).

121. Biehl, *Will to Live*; Fassin, *When Bodies Remember.*

122. Harries et al., "Why Did the Scale-up of HIV Treatment Work?"

123. Trinitapoli, *An Epidemic of Uncertainty.*

124. Trinitapoli and Weinreb, *Religion and AIDS in Africa*; Dionne, *Doomed Interventions.*

125. Doran, "Reconstructing Mchape '95."

126. Chimwaza and Watkins, "Giving Care to People with Symptoms of AIDS in Rural Sub-Saharan Africa"; Trinitapoli and Weinreb, *Religion and AIDS in Africa.*

127. Esacove, "Love Matches"; Esacove, *Modernizing Sexuality.*

128. Zulu and Chepngeno, "Spousal Communication About the Risk of Contracting HIV/AIDS in Rural Malawi."

129. Smith and Watkins, "Perceptions of Risk and Strategies for Prevention."

130. Trinitapoli, *An Epidemic of Uncertainty.*

131. Watkins, "Navigating the AIDS Epidemic in Rural Malawi."

132. Watkins.

133. Watkins.

134. Conroy, Yeatman, and Dovel, "The Social Construction of AIDS During a Time of Evolving Access to Antiretroviral Therapy in Rural Malawi."

135. UNAIDS, "HIV Financial Dashboard."

136. USAID and IMPACT, "Malawi and HIV/AIDS"; UNAIDS, "HIV Financial Dashboard."

137. Centeno and Cohen, "The Arc of Neoliberalism"; Pfeiffer, "The Struggle for a Public Sector."

138. Mtonya et al., "System-Wide Effects of the Global Fund in Malawi"; Schouten et al., "Antiretroviral Drug Supply Challenges in the Era of Scaling up ART in Malawi."

139. McCoy, McPake, and Mwapasa, "The Double Burden of Human Resource and HIV Crises."

140. Schouten et al., "Antiretroviral Drug Supply Challenges in the Era of Scaling up ART in Malawi."

141. Palmer, "Tackling Malawi's Human Resources Crisis."

142. Conroy, Yeatman, and Dovel, "The Social Construction of AIDS During a Time of Evolving Access to Antiretroviral Therapy in Rural Malawi"; Trinitapoli, *An Epidemic of Uncertainty.*

143. Trinitapoli; Dionne, *Doomed Interventions.*

144. Conroy, Yeatman, and Dovel, "The Social Construction of AIDS During a Time of Evolving Access to Antiretroviral Therapy in Rural Malawi."

145. Trinitapoli, *An Epidemic of Uncertainty.*

146. Some organizations were large and internationally networked and others so small that there was no phone number or post office address. Swidler and Watkins, *A Fraught Embrace*, 45.

147. Morfit, "'AIDS Is Money.'"
148. Ferguson and Gupta, "Spatializing States."
149. Swidler and Watkins, *A Fraught Embrace.*
150. Swidler and Watkins; Swidler and Watkins, "'Teach a Man to Fish.'"
151. McDonnell, *Best Laid Plans.*
152. Rosenthal, *Health on Delivery*; Swidler and Watkins, *A Fraught Embrace.*
153. University of North Carolina, "UNC Project Malawi: About Us."
154. Biruk, *Cooking Data.*
155. McCoy, McPake, and Mwapasa, "The Double Burden of Human Resource and HIV Crises."
156. Harries et al., "Why Did the Scale-up of HIV Treatment Work?"
157. Rosenthal, "'Doing the Best We Can,'" 137.
158. Rosenthal, *Health on Delivery.*
159. Rosenthal; Rosenthal, "'Doing the Best We Can,'"
160. WHO, "World Health Organization Data: Population, Malawi."
161. Palmer, "Tackling Malawi's Human Resources Crisis."
162. USAID, "Malawi: Nutrition Profile."
163. Kalofonos, *All I Eat Is Medicine.*
164. Wendland, *Partial Stories.*
165. Rosenthal, *Health on Delivery.*
166. Lettow et al., "Uptake and Outcomes of a Prevention-of-Mother-to-Child Transmission (PMTCT) Program in Zomba District, Malawi."
167. Rosenthal, *Health on Delivery.*
168. Annan, "In Africa, AIDS Has a Woman's Face."
169. UNAIDS, "Country Factsheets: Malawi."
170. UNAIDS, "World AIDS Day 2023."
171. Dworkin, *Men at Risk*; Dovel et al., "Men's Heightened Risk of AIDS-Related Death."
172. Dovel et al.
173. Poulin, Dovel, and Watkins, "Men with Money and the 'Vulnerable Women' Client Category in an AIDS Epidemic."
174. Dworkin, *Men at Risk*; Wyrod, *AIDS and Masculinity in the African City.*
175. Dovel et al., "Men's Heightened Risk of AIDS-Related Death."
176. Exner et al., "HIV Sexual Risk Reduction Interventions with Heterosexual Men"; Exner et al., "Beyond the Male Condom: The Evolution of Gender-Specific HIV Interventions for Women."
177. Dovel et al., "Men's Heightened Risk of AIDS-Related Death."
178. Poulin, Dovel, and Watkins, "Men with Money and the 'Vulnerable Women' Client Category in an AIDS Epidemic."
179. Dworkin, *Men at Risk.*
180. Street, "Affective Infrastructure," 54.

CHAPTER 2. FOR THE MOTHERS AND CHILDREN OF OUR COUNTRY

1. Donnelly, "Battles with Donors Cloud Malawi's HIV Prevention Plan."
2. Donnelly.
3. Coutsoudis et al., "Is Option B+ the Best Choice?"
4. UNICEF, "Options B and B+."
5. Donnelly, "Battles with Donors Cloud Malawi's HIV Prevention Plan."
6. Schouten et al., "Prevention of Mother-to-Child Transmission of HIV and the Health-Related Millennium Development Goals."
7. Boli and Thomas, "INGOs and the Organization of World Culture"; Inoue and Drori, "The Global Institutionalization of Health as a Social Concern"; Meyer et al., "World Society and the Nation-State."
8. Boli and Thomas, "INGOs and the Organization of World Culture."
9. Frank, Hardinge, and Wosick-Correa, "The Global Dimensions of Rape-Law Reform"; Burton and Tsutsui, "Human Rights in a Globalizing World"; Meyer et al., "World Society and the Nation-State"; Swiss, "Security Sector Reform and Development Assistance."
10. Beckfield, "Inequality in the World Polity."
11. Dobbin, Simmons, and Garrett, "The Global Diffusion of Public Policies."
12. Centeno and Cohen, "The Arc of Neoliberalism."
13. Okuonzi and Macrae, "Whose Policy Is It Anyway?"
14. Biesma et al., "The Effects of Global Health Initiatives on Country Health Systems."
15. Meyer and Rowan, "Institutionalized Organizations."
16. Berkovitch and Gordon, "Differentiated Decoupling and Human Rights"; Bromley and Powell, "From Smoke and Mirrors to Walking the Talk"; Meyer and Rowan, "Institutionalized Organizations."
17 Halliday and Carruthers, "The Recursivity of Law"; Halliday, "Recursivity of Global Normmaking."
18. Chorev, "Changing Global Norms Through Reactive Diffusion."
19. Chorev; Ford et al., "The Role of Civil Society in Protecting Public Health over Commercial Interests"; Gomez, "The Politics of Receptivity and Resistance."
20. Halliday, "Recursivity of Global Normmaking," 285.
21. Seabrooke and Henriksen, *Professional Networks in Transnational Governance*; Nilsson, "Treating Market Failure Access Professionals in Global Health"; Harris, *Achieving Access.*
22. Seabrooke and Henriksen, *Professional Networks in Transnational Governance.*
23. Biruk, *Cooking Data.*
24. van Lettow et al., "Uptake and Outcomes of a Prevention-of-Mother-to-Child Transmission (PMTCT) Program in Zomba District, Malawi."

25. van Lettow et al.

26. Mueller et al., "Constraints to Implementing the Essential Health Package in Malawi."

27. Bickton and Lillie, "Strengthening Human Resources for Health in Resource-Limited Countries."

28. Manzi et al., "High Acceptability of Voluntary Counselling and HIV-Testing but Unacceptable Loss to Follow up in a Prevention of Mother-to-Child HIV Transmission Programme in Rural Malawi."

29. Manzi et al.; van Lettow et al., "Uptake and Outcomes of a Prevention-of-Mother-to-Child Transmission (PMTCT) Program in Zomba District, Malawi."

30. For exposed infants, the 2006 policy recommended sd-NVP + AZT for seven days. The 2010 policy recommended breastfeeding infants receive NVP from birth until one week after all exposure to breastfeeding and non-breastfeeding infants receive sd-NVP + AZT for four to six weeks. For breastfeeding, the 2006 policy recommended breastfeeding for six months. The 2010 policy recommended breastfeeding for six months, then introducing complementary food, and continuing breastfeeding for twelve months.

31. ART starting from fourteen weeks until delivery, and if breastfeeding, until one week after all infant exposure to breastmilk has ended.

32. WHO, "Antiretroviral Drugs for Treating Pregnant Women and Preventing HIV Infection in Infants," 1.

33. Harries et al., "Act Local, Think Global."

34. Schouten et al., "Prevention of Mother-to-Child Transmission of HIV and the Health-Related Millennium Development Goals."

35. van Lettow et al., "Uptake and Outcomes of a Prevention-of-Mother-to-Child Transmission (PMTCT) Program in Zomba District, Malawi."

36. van Lettow et al.

37. Chorev, "Restructuring Neoliberalism at the World Health Organization."

38. WHO, "Antiretroviral Drugs for Treating Pregnant Women and Preventing HIV Infection in Infants."

39. Schouten et al., "Antiretroviral Drug Supply Challenges in the Era of Scaling Up ART in Malawi."

40. Schouten et al.

41. Pfeiffer and Chapman, "Anthropological Perspectives on Structural Adjustment and Public Health"; Centeno and Cohen, "The Arc of Neoliberalism."

42. Brass, "Blurring Boundaries," 218.

43. CONGOMA, "Council for Non-Governmental Organizations in Malawi"; Malawi Government, *Non-Governmental Organizations Act.*

44. Malawi, *Malawi Growth and Development Strategy.*

45. Chorev, Rey, and Ciplet, "The State of States in International Organizations," 298.

46. Chorev, Rey, and Ciplet.

47. McDonnell, "Patchwork Leviathan."

48. Vijayakumar, *At Risk.*

49. Vijayakumar.

50. This is mostly a formality; if the TWG agrees, the policy usually gets signed off on.

51. Fligstein, "Social Skill and Institutional Theory," 399.

52. Fligstein.

53. Harries, Schouten, and Libamba, "Scaling Up Antiretroviral Treatment in Resource-Poor Settings"; Harries et al., "Expanding Antiretroviral Therapy in Malawi"; Libamba et al., "Scaling Up Antiretroviral Therapy in Africa."

54. Schouten et al., "Prevention of Mother-to-Child Transmission of HIV and the Health-Related Millennium Development Goals."

55. WHO, UNAIDS, and UNICEF, "Towards Universal Access."

56. WHO, "Implementation of Option B+ for Prevention of Mother-To-Child Transmission of HIV." The second phase of the grant was also consolidated and reprogrammed to make funds available to continue supporting implementation.

57. Swidler and Watkins, *A Fraught Embrace.*

58. Cohen et al., "Antiretroviral Therapy for the Prevention of HIV-1 Transmission."

59. UNAIDS, "Groundbreaking Trial Results Confirm HIV Treatment Prevents Transmission of HIV."

60. WHO, *The Strategic Use of Antiretrovirals for Treatment and Prevention of HIV Infection.*

61. WHO.

62. WHO.

63. Kellerman et al., "Beyond Prevention of Mother-to-Child Transmission."

64. McDonnell, "Patchwork Leviathan," 66.

65. Seabrooke and Henriksen, *Professional Networks in Transnational Governance*; Nilsson, "Treating Market Failure Access Professionals in Global Health"; Harris, *Achieving Access.*

CHAPTER 3. PRECARIOUS OPPORTUNITIES

1. Centeno and Cohen, "The Arc of Neoliberalism."

2. Swidler and Watkins, *A Fraught Embrace.*

3. Whitford, "Pragmatism and the Untenable Dualism of Means and Ends."

4. Emirbayer and Mische, "What Is Agency?"; Mische, "Projects and Possibilities."

5. Tavory and Eliasoph, "Coordinating Futures."

6. Johnson-Hanks, "When the Future Decides."

7. Trinitapoli and Yeatman, "Uncertainty and Fertility in a Generalized AIDS Epidemic."

8. Johnson-Hanks, "When the Future Decides"; Swidler and Watkins, *A Fraught Embrace*; Vijayakumar, "'I'll Be Like Water.'"

9. Swidler and Watkins, *A Fraught Embrace.*

10. Mussa, *Labour Market Transitions of Young Women and Men in Malawi.*

11. Johnson-Hanks, "When the Future Decides."

12. Kim et al., "The Tingathe Programme."

13. Frye, "Bright Futures in Malawi's New Dawn."

14. There is a positive relationship between education and wage and salaried work, especially at the top end of the education distribution; those with post-secondary training or tertiary education are more likely to be formally employed rather than self-employed. Mussa, *Labour Market Transitions of Young Women and Men in Malawi.*

15. UNESCO, "Malawi: Education Country Brief."

16. Malawi College of Medicine sometimes looks for students with strong aptitude in math and sciences. Wendland, *A Heart for the Work.*

17. Frye, "Bright Futures in Malawi's New Dawn."

18. Johnson-Hanks, "When the Future Decides."

19. Packard, *A History of Global Health*; Keshavjee, *Blind Spot.*

20. Morfit, "'AIDS Is Money.'"

21. Swidler and Watkins, *A Fraught Embrace.*

22. Swidler and Watkins.

23. Swidler and Watkins, 78.

24. Adams, *Metrics*; Erikson, "Metrics and Market Logics of Global Health"; Birn, "The Stages of International (Global) Health"; Sparke, "Austerity and the Embodiment of Neoliberalism as Ill-Health."

25. van de Ruit, "Unintended Consequences of Community Health Worker Programs in South Africa."

26. College graduates tend to find formal employment with greater ease. A nurse or a doctor may not necessarily like where they are posted, but they will be guaranteed a job in the public healthcare system.

27. van de Ruit and Zhou, "The Problem of Insecure Community Health Workers in the Global South"; van de Ruit, "Unintended Consequences of Community Health Worker Programs in South Africa."

28. van de Ruit; Mukherjee and Eustache, "Community Health Workers as a Cornerstone for Integrating HIV and Primary Healthcare."

29. Swidler and Watkins, "'Teach a Man to Fish.'"

30. Kane et al., "Limits and Opportunities to Community Health Worker Empowerment"; Akintola, "Unpaid HIV/AIDS Care in Southern Africa"; Maes, "Experts' Tools, Altruists, and Job-Seekers"; Nading, "'Love Isn't There in Your Stomach'"; Maes and Kalofonos, "Becoming and Remaining Community Health Workers"; Maes et al., "Psychosocial Distress Among Unpaid Community Health Workers in Rural Ethiopia."

31. "US Dollar to Malawi Kwacha History," https://www.exchangerates.org.uk/USD-MWK-spot-exchange-rates-history-2010.html. This estimate was based on the average 2010 exchange rate.

32. Swidler and Watkins, *A Fraught Embrace.*

33. Swidler and Watkins.

34. This happened to two NGO CHWs at my field sites.

35. Swidler and Watkins, 209

36. Johnson-Hanks, "When the Future Decides"; Mische, "Projects and Possibilities."

37. WHO, "Population, Malawi"; WHO, "WHO Health Workforce Support and Safeguards List."

38. Kim et al., "Burnout and Self-Reported Suboptimal Patient Care Amongst Health Care Workers Providing HIV Care in Malawi."

39. Wendland, *A Heart for the Work.*

40. Levey et al., "Malawi Private Health Sector Assessment."

41. Levey et al.

42. Carmona, "Malawi Private Health Sector Mapping Report."

43. There were three respondents who wanted to stay with the Ministry of Health.

44. Swidler and Watkins, *A Fraught Embrace.*

45. Johnson-Hanks, "When the Future Decides."

46. Ooms, Damme, and Temmerman, "Medicines Without Doctors."

CHAPTER 4. TWO WORLDS OF PRENATAL CARE

1. Pfeiffer and Chapman, "Anthropological Perspectives on Structural Adjustment and Public Health."

2. UNAIDS, "Start Free, Stay Free, AIDS Free."

3. Kellerman et al., "Beyond Prevention of Mother-to-Child Transmission."

4. WHO, "Implementation of Option B+ for Prevention of Mother-To-Child Transmission of HIV."

5. WHO.

6. This changed in 2016 when Malawi adopted universal test-and-treat guidelines for all HIV patients.

7. Epstein, *Inclusion*; Novas and Rose, "Genetic Risk and the Birth of the Somatic Individual"; Nguyen, *The Republic of Therapy*; Petryna, "Biological Citizenship."

8. Lakhani and Timmermans, "Biopolitical Citizenship in the Immigration Adjudication Process"; Rodriguez, "Inoculating Against Barbarism? State Medicine and Immigrant Policy in Turn-of-the-Century Argentina."

9. Fassin and d'Halluin, "The Truth from the Body"; Fassin and d'Halluin, "Critical Evidence"; Petryna, "Biological Citizenship"; Ticktin, "Where Ethics and Politics Meet."

10. Ticktin.

11. Nguyen, *The Republic of Therapy.*

12. Petryna, "Science and Citizenship Under Postsocialism."

13. Whyte et al., "Therapeutic Clientship."

14. Biehl, "Pharmaceuticalization"; Burchardt, "The Self as Capital in the Narrative Economy"; Cataldo, "New Forms of Citizenship and Socio-Political Inclusion"; Meinert, Mogensen, and Twebaze, "Tests for Life Chances"; Richey, "Counselling Citizens and Producing Patronage"; Nguyen et al., "Adherence as Therapeutic Citizenship."

15. Biehl and Petryna, *When People Come First.*

16. Shiffman, "Has Donor Prioritization of HIV/AIDS Displaced Aid for Other Health Issues?"

17. Global Fund, "HIV and AIDS."

18. Esser and Bench, "Does Global Health Funding Respond to Recipients' Needs?"; MacKellar, "Priorities in Global Assistance for Health, AIDS, and Population"; Ravishankar et al., "Financing of Global Health"; Shiffman, "Donor Funding Priorities for Communicable Disease Control in the Developing World."

19. Shiffman.

20. Keshavjee, *Blind Spot*; Sparke, "Austerity and the Embodiment of Neoliberalism as Ill-Health."

21. Koch et al., "Keeping a Low Profile"; Morfit, "'AIDS Is Money.'"

22. Dionne, *Doomed Interventions.*

23. Global Fund to Fight AIDS, Tuberculosis and Malaria, "Malawi Investments."

24. Birx, "FY 2019 PEPFAR Planned Allocation and Strategic Direction."

25. McCoy, McPake, and Mwapasa, "The Double Burden of Human Resource and HIV Crises."

26. Schouten et al., "Prevention of Mother-to-Child Transmission of HIV and the Health-Related Millennium Development Goals."

27. Schouten et al.

28. Kim et al., "The Tingathe Programme."

29. In practice, this relationship was not perfect. There was often tension between the government providers and NGO mentors. For instance, during one mentoring session, a government doctor left his office. The EQUIP mentor refused to see patients until he returned, saying that if he saw patients for him, it would defeat the purpose of mentorship and normalize the idea that mentors can do their work for them.

30. Buse and Waxman, "Public–Private Health Partnerships: A Strategy for WHO"; Sullivan, "Mediating Abundance and Scarcity."

31. Schouten et al., "Antiretroviral Drug Supply Challenges in the Era of Scaling Up ART in Malawi."

32. Ecks, "Pharmaceutical Citizenship"; Persson, "'The World Has Changed.'"

33. Angotti, Dionne, and Gaydosh, "An Offer You Can't Refuse?"

34. Moyer, Burchardt, and Dijk, "Editorial Introduction."

35. Moyer, Burchardt, and Dijk; Burchardt, "Subjects of Counselling."

36. Vernooij and Hardon, "'What Mother Wouldn't Want to Save Her Baby?'"

37. Vernooij and Hardon; Mattes, "'We Are Just Supposed to Be Quiet.'"

38. Hafner and Shiffman, "The Emergence of Global Attention to Health Systems Strengthening."

39. Storeng, "The GAVI Alliance and the 'Gates Approach' to Health System Strengthening"; Marchal, Cavalli, and Kegels, "Global Health Actors Claim To Support Health System Strengthening"

40. Marchal, Cavalli, and Kegels.

41. Keshavjee, *Blind Spot.*

42. Mueller et al., "Constraints to Implementing the Essential Health Package in Malawi."

43. Mueller et al.

44. Mueller et al.

45. WHO, "Population, Malawi"; WHO, "WHO Health Workforce Support and Safeguards List."

46. MSH, "Evaluation of Malawi's Emergency Human Resources Programme."

47. Global Fund, "Grant Scorecard."

48. Livingston, *Improvising Medicine.*

49. Kim et al., "Burnout and Self-Reported Suboptimal Patient Care Amongst Health Care Workers Providing HIV Care in Malawi."

50. Kim et al., "Factors Associated with Burnout Amongst Healthcare Workers Providing HIV Care in Malawi."

51. Kim et al.

52. Prince and Otieno, "In the Shadowlands of Global Health."

53. Sullivan, "Mediating Abundance and Scarcity."

54. World Bank Group, "Maternal Mortality Ratio."

55. World Bank Group, "Mortality Rate, Neonatal"; World Bank Group, "Mortality Rate, Infant."

56. World Bank Group, "Low-Birthweight Babies."

57. Whyte et al., "Therapeutic Clientship."

58. van Lettow et al., "Uptake and Outcomes of a Prevention-of-Mother-to-Child Transmission (PMTCT) Program in Zomba District, Malawi"; Barr et al., "National Estimates and Risk Factors Associated with Early Mother-to-Child Transmission of HIV after Implementation of Option B+."

CHAPTER 5. THE UNCERTAINTY OF TREATMENT

1. Kenworthy, Thomann, and Parker, "From a Global Crisis to the 'End of AIDS': New Epidemics of Signification."

2. Kleinman, *The Illness Narratives: Suffering, Healing, and the Human Condition*, 1-2.

3. Kleinman.

4. Conrad, "The Meaning of Medications: Another Look at Compliance"; Donovan and Blake, "Patient Non-Compliance: Deviance or Reasoned Decision-Making?"; Karp, "Taking Anti-Depressant Medications: Resistance, Trial Commitment, Conversion, Disenchantment"; Venn and Arber, "Understanding Older Peoples' Decisions About the Use of Sleeping Medication: Issues of Control and Autonomy"; Pound et al., "Resisting Medicines: A Synthesis of Qualitative Studies of Medicine Taking."

5. Colvin et al., "A Systematic Review of Health System Barriers and Enablers for Antiretroviral Therapy (ART) for HIV-Infected Pregnant and Postpartum Women"; Gourlay et al., "Barriers and Facilitating Factors to the Uptake of Antiretroviral Drugs for Prevention of Mother-to-Child Transmission of HIV in Sub-Saharan Africa: A Systematic Review"; hIarlaithe et al., "Economic and Social Factors Are Some of the Most Common Barriers Preventing Women from Accessing Maternal and Newborn Child Health (MNCH) and Prevention of Mother-to-Child Transmission (PMTCT) Services: A Literature Review"; Hodgson et al., "A Systematic Review of Individual and Contextual Factors Affecting ART Initiation, Adherence, and Retention for HIV-Infected Pregnant and Postpartum Women"; Psaros et al., "Adherence to HIV Care After Pregnancy Among Women in Sub-Saharan Africa: Falling Off the Cliff of the Treatment Cascade."

6. Cockerham, "Health Lifestyle Theory and the Convergence of Agency and Structure."

7. Lutfey and Freese, "Toward Some Fundamentals of Fundamental Causality: Socioeconomic Status and Health in the Routine Clinic Visit for Diabetes."

8. Johnson-Hanks, "When the Future Decides: Uncertainty and Intentional Action in Contemporary Cameroon"; Trinitapoli and Yeatman, "Uncertainty and Fertility in a Generalized AIDS Epidemic."

9. The majority of people in Malawi live in rural areas. Lilongwe, the capital city, is a unique site in that it is urban, its people have higher education and income levels, and it has a higher concentration of NGOs. HIV rates are also higher in Lilongwe and other city centers, which makes it a relevant place to study patient experiences. The intensity of NGO programs and resources available for women are more prominent here than in other areas of Malawi.

10. Angotti, Dionne, and Gaydosh, "An Offer You Can't Refuse? Provider-Initiated HIV Testing in Antenatal Clinics in Rural Malawi."

11. Conroy, Yeatman, and Dovel, "The Social Construction of AIDS During a Time of Evolving Access to Antiretroviral Therapy in Rural Malawi."

12. Tenthani et al., "Retention in Care Under Universal Antiretroviral Therapy for HIV-Infected Pregnant and Breastfeeding Women ('Option B+') in Malawi."

13. Aronowitz, "The Converged Experience of Risk and Disease."

14. Fauci and Desrosiers, "Pathogenesis of HIV and SIV."

15. Conrad, "The Meaning Of Medications: Another Look At Compliance."

16. Pierret, "The Illness Experience: State of Knowledge and Perspectives for Research."

17. Navon, "'The Gene Didn't Get the Memo': Realigning Disciplines and Remaking Illness in Genomic Medicine."

18. Trinitapoli and Yeatman, "Uncertainty and Fertility in a Generalized AIDS Epidemic," 936.

19. Kalofonos, "'All I Eat Is ARVs': The Paradox of AIDS Treatment Interventions in Central Mozambique."

20. According to an ILO survey, in 2014, only 9.3 percent of Malawi's youth, ages fifteen to twenty-nine, were considered regularly employed, meaning that they had a waged and salaried job for a duration of more than twelve months or were self-employed with employees (14.2% of men; 4.7% of women). Mussa, "Labour Market Transitions of Young Women and Men in Malawi: Results of the 2014 School-to-Work Transition Survey."

21. Frye, "Bright Futures in Malawi's New Dawn: Educational Aspirations as Assertions of Identity."

22. Mussa, *Labour Market Transitions of Young Women and Men in Malawi: Results of the 2014 School-to-Work Transition Survey.*

23. Parsons, "Illness and the Role of the Physician: A Sociological Perspective."

24. Dovel et al., "Men's Heightened Risk of AIDS-Related Death."

25. Dovel et al.

26. Conroy, Yeatman, and Dovel, "The Social Construction of AIDS During a Time of Evolving Access to Antiretroviral Therapy in Rural Malawi"; Mojola et al., "'A Nowadays Disease': HIV/AIDS and Social Change in a Rural South African Community."

27. Conrad, "The Meaning Of Medications: Another Look At Compliance."

28. Haas et al., "Retention in Care During the First 3 Years of Antiretroviral Therapy for Women in Malawi's Option B+ Programme: An Observational Cohort Study."

29. Women who started ART while breastfeeding or for their own health (not pregnant or breastfeeding) showed fewer changes in adherence and generally higher adherence rates than women who started during pregnancy. Haas et al.

30. van Lettow et al., "Uptake and Outcomes of a Prevention-of-Mother-to-Child Transmission (PMTCT) Program in Zomba District, Malawi"; Barr et al., "National Estimates and Risk Factors Associated with Early Mother-to-Child Transmission of HIV After Implementation of Option B+: A Cross-Sectional Analysis."

31. Li et al., "Time to Viral Rebound After Interruption of Modern Antiretroviral Therapies."

32. Trinitapoli and Yeatman, "Uncertainty and Fertility in a Generalized AIDS Epidemic."

33. Cockerham, "Health Lifestyle Theory and the Convergence of Agency and Structure"; Veenstra and Burnett, "A Relational Approach to Health Practices: Towards Transcending the Agency-Structure Divide."

CONCLUSION: PARTIAL RECOVERIES

1. UNAIDS, "HIV Financial Dashboard."

2. Centeno and Cohen, "The Arc of Neoliberalism"; Pfeiffer and Chapman, "Anthropological Perspectives on Structural Adjustment and Public Health"; Keshavjee, *Blind Spot.*

3. World Bank Group, "Antiretroviral Therapy Coverage." This is up from 2 percent in 2000, 9 percent in 2006, and 35 percent in 2012.

4. Conroy, Yeatman, and Dovel, "The Social Construction of AIDS During a Time of Evolving Access to Antiretroviral Therapy in Rural Malawi."

5. Without intervention, MTCT rates are 25 to 35 percent. van Lettow et al., "Uptake and Outcomes of a Prevention-of-Mother-to-Child Transmission (PMTCT) Program in Zomba District, Malawi."

6. Rosenthal, *Health on Delivery.*

7. Mussa, "Labour Market Transitions of Young Women and Men in Malawi."

8. Swidler and Watkins, *A Fraught Embrace.*

9. iAHO and WHO, "Maternal Mortality."

10. Swidler and Watkins, "'Teach a Man to Fish.'"

11. Brown, Cueto, and Fee, "The World Health Organization and the Transition From 'International' to 'Global' Public Health."

12. Chorev, "Changing Global Norms through Reactive Diffusion"; Harris, *Achieving Access*; Benton, *HIV Exceptionalism.*

13. Brandt, "How AIDS Invented Global Health."

14. UNAIDS, "HIV Financial Dashboard"; Ravishankar et al., "Financing of Global Health: Tracking Development Assistance for Health from 1990 to 2007."

15. McDonnell, *Best Laid Plans*; Farber, "'Don't Think That We Die from AIDS'"; Angotti, "Testing Differences"; Dionne, *Doomed Interventions.*

16. Swidler and Watkins, *A Fraught Embrace.*

17. Dionne, *Doomed Interventions.*

18. Dionne, "Local Demand for a Global Intervention"; Dionne, *Doomed Interventions.*

19. Swidler and Watkins, *A Fraught Embrace.*

20. Mussa, "Labour Market Transitions of Young Women and Men in Malawi."

21. Swidler and Watkins, *A Fraught Embrace*; Maes and Kalofonos, "Becoming and Remaining Community Health Workers"; Maes, "Volunteerism or Labor

Exploitation?"; Maes et al., "Psychosocial Distress among Unpaid Community Health Workers in Rural Ethiopia."

22. Maes and Kalofonos, "Becoming and Remaining Community Health Workers."

23. van de Ruit and Zhou, "The Problem of Insecure Community Health Workers in the Global South"; van de Ruit, "Unintended Consequences of Community Health Worker Programs in South Africa."

24. Marchal, Cavalli, and Kegels, "Global Health Actors Claim To Support Health System Strengthening"; Storeng, "The GAVI Alliance and the 'Gates Approach' to Health System Strengthening"; Hafner and Shiffman, "The Emergence of Global Attention to Health Systems Strengthening."

25. Ooms, Damme, and Temmerman, "Medicines without Doctors"; Ooms et al., "The 'Diagonal' Approach to Global Fund Financing."

26. Palmer, "Tackling Malawi's Human Resources Crisis"; McCoy, McPake, and Mwapasa, "The Double Burden of Human Resource and HIV Crises"; Chimwaza et al., "What Makes Staff Consider Leaving the Health Service in Malawi?"

27. Chimwaza et al.

28. Assefa, Damme, and Hermann, "Human Resource Aspects of Antiretroviral Treatment Delivery Models"; Zuber et al., "A Survey of Nurse-Initiated and -Managed Antiretroviral Therapy (NIMART) in Practice, Education, Policy, and Regulation in East, Central, and Southern Africa"; Chimwaza et al., "What Makes Staff Consider Leaving the Health Service in Malawi?"

29. Kim et al., "Burnout and Self-Reported Suboptimal Patient Care amongst Health Care Workers Providing HIV Care in Malawi"; Kim et al., "Factors Associated with Burnout Amongst Healthcare Workers Providing HIV Care in Malawi."

30. Leslie et al., "Training and Supervision Did Not Meaningfully Improve Quality of Care for Pregnant Women or Sick Children in Sub-Saharan Africa"; Pfeiffer, "The Struggle for a Public Sector."

31. Schouten et al., "Antiretroviral Drug Supply Challenges in the Era of Scaling up ART in Malawi."

32. Schouten et al.

33. Mueller et al., "Constraints to Implementing the Essential Health Package in Malawi."

34. Street, "Affective Infrastructure"; Street, *Biomedicine in an Unstable Place.*

35. Cueto, "A Return to the Magic Bullet?"; Parker and Allen, "De-Politicizing Parasites."

36. Sonenthal et al., "COVID-19 Preparedness in Malawi."

37. Munharo et al., "Challenges of COVID-19 Testing in Low-Middle Income Countries (LMICs): The Case of Malawi."

38. Nachega et al., "Scaling Up Covid-19 Vaccination in Africa."

39. The entries are part of the Malawi Journals Project—a longitudinal collection of ethnographic journals on local responses to the HIV epidemic, and more recently, to COVID-19. The "journalists" write about conversations they have had or overheard about COVID-19; they do not conduct interviews or do other forms of research. Kaler, Watkins, and Angotti, "Making Meaning in the Time of AIDS: Longitudinal Narratives from the Malawi Journals Project."

40. Kaler, "AIDS-Talk in Everyday Life"; Watkins and Swidler, "Hearsay Ethnography"; Ashforth and Watkins, "Narratives of Death in Rural Malawi in the Time of AIDS."

41. Loembé et al., "COVID-19 in Africa"; Fund, "Global Fund Supports 11 Countries in Response to COVID-19."

42. Nachega et al., "Scaling Up Covid-19 Vaccination in Africa."

43. Ferguson, *The Anti-Politics Machine.*

Bibliography

Adams, Vincanne. *Metrics: What Counts in Global Health*. Duke University Press, 2016.

Akintola, Olagoke. "Unpaid HIV/AIDS Care in Southern Africa: Forms, Context, and Implications." *Feminist Economics* 14, no. 4 (October 2008): 117–47. https://doi.org/10.1080/13545700802263004.

Al Jazeera. "HIV and AIDS Deaths Could Increase Globally amid US Aid Freeze, UN Says." March 24, 2025. https://www.aljazeera.com/news/2025/3/24/hiv-and-aids-deaths-could-increase-globally-amid-us-aid-freeze-un-says.

Al Jazeera. "South Sudanese Children Die as US Aid Cuts Shutter Medical Services: NGO." April 9, 2025. https://www.aljazeera.com/news/2025/4/9/us-aid-cuts-leave-south-sudan-children-dead-as-medical-services-collapse.

Anderson, Ben. "Emergency Futures: Exception, Urgency, Interval, Hope." *The Sociological Review* 65, no. 3 (February 27, 2017): 463–77. https://doi.org/10.1111/1467-954X.12447.

Anderson, Ben, Kevin Grove, Lauren Rickards, and Matthew Kearnes. "Slow Emergencies: Temporality and the Racialized Biopolitics of Emergency Governance." *Progress in Human Geography* 44, no. 4 (August 2020): 621–39. https://doi.org/10.1177/0309132519849263.

Angotti, Nicole, Kim Yi Dionne, and Lauren Gaydosh. "An Offer You Can't Refuse? Provider-Initiated HIV Testing in Antenatal Clinics in Rural Malawi." *Health Policy and Planning* 26, no. 4 (June 21, 2011): 307–15. https://doi.org/10.1093/heapol/czq066.

Angotti, Nicole. "Testing Differences: The Implementation of Western HIV Testing Norms in Sub-Saharan Africa." *Culture, Health & Sexuality* 14, no. 4 (April 2012): 365–78. https://doi.org/10.1080/13691058.2011.644810.

Angotti, Nicole. "Working Outside of the Box: How HIV Counselors in Sub-Saharan Africa Adapt Western HIV Testing Norms." *Social Science & Medicine* 71, no. 5 (September 2010): 986–93. https://doi.org/10.1016/j.socscimed.2010.05.020.

Annan, Kofi. "In Africa, AIDS Has a Woman's Face." *The New York Times*, December 29, 2002.

Annual Medical Report on the Health and Sanitary Condition of the Nyasaland Protectorate for the Year Ending the 31st December, 1930. Government Printer, 1931.

Aronowitz, Robert. "The Converged Experience of Risk and Disease." *The Milbank Quarterly* 87 (June 4, 2009): 417–42. https://doi.org/10.1111/j.1468-0009.2009.00563.x.

Ashforth, Adam. "AIDS, Religious Enthusiasm and Spiritual Insecurity in Africa." *Global Public Health* 6, no. S2 (2011): S132–47. https://doi.org/10.1080/17441692.2011.602702.

Ashforth, Adam. *Witchcraft, Violence, and Democracy in South Africa*. University of Chicago Press, 2005.

Ashforth, Adam, and Susan Watkins. "Narratives of Death in Rural Malawi in the Time of AIDS." *Africa* 85, no. 2 (April 24, 2015): 245–68. https://doi.org/10.1017/s0001972015000017.

Assefa, Yibeltal, Wim Van Damme, and Katharina Hermann. "Human Resource Aspects of Antiretroviral Treatment Delivery Models: Current Practices and Recommendations." *Current Opinion in HIV and AIDS* 5, no. 1 (January 2010): 78–82. https://doi.org/10.1097/coh.0b013e328333b87a.

Assefa, Yibeltal, Peter S. Hill, Wim Van Damme, Judith Dean, and Charles F. Gilks. "Leaving No One Behind: Lessons from Implementation of Policies for Universal HIV Treatment to Universal Health Coverage." *Globalization and Health* 16, no. 1 (February 24, 2020): 17. https://doi.org/10.1186/s12992-020-00549-4.

Auyero, Javier. *Patients of the State: The Politics of Waiting in Argentina*. Duke University Press, 2012.

Barr, Beth A Tippett, Monique van Lettow, Joep J. van Oosterhout, Megan Landes, Ray W. Shiraishi, Ermias Amene, Erik Schouten, et al. "National Estimates and Risk Factors Associated with Early Mother-to-Child Transmission of HIV after Implementation of Option B+: A Cross-Sectional Analysis." *The Lancet HIV* 5, no. 12 (December 2018): e688–95. https://doi.org/10.1016/s2352-3018(18)30316-3.

Basilico, Matthew, Jonathan Weigel, Anjali Motgi, Jacob Bor, and Salmaan Keshavjee. "Health for All? Competing Theories and Geopolitics." In

Reimagining Global Health: An Introduction, edited by Paul Farmer, Jim Yong Kim, Arthur Kleinman, and Matthew Basilico, 74–110. University of California Press, 2013.

Beck, Ann. *A History of the British Medical Administration of East Africa, 1900–1950*. Harvard University Press, 1970.

Beckfield, Jason. "Inequality in the World Polity: The Structure of International Organization." *American Sociological Review* 68, no. 3 (June, 2003): 401–24. https://doi.org/10.2307/1519730.

Benjamin, Walter. "Theses on the Philosophy of History." In *Illuminations*, 253–64. Schocken, 1968.

Benton, Adia. *HIV Exceptionalism: Development Through Disease in Sierra Leone*. University of Minnesota Press, 2015.

Berkovitch, Nitza, and Neve Gordon. "Differentiated Decoupling and Human Rights." *Social Problems* 63, no. 4 (October 18, 2016): 499–512. https://doi.org/10.1146/annurev.so.13.080187.002303.

Berlant, Lauren. "Slow Death (Sovereignty, Obesity, Lateral Agency)." *Critical Inquiry* 33, no. 4 (2007): 754. https://doi.org/10.1086/521568.

Bickton, Fanuel Meckson, and Tamsin Lillie. "Strengthening Human Resources for Health in Resource-Limited Countries: The Case of Medic to Medic in Malawi." *Malawi Medical Journal* 31, no. 1 (March 31, 2019): 99–101. https://doi.org/10.4314/mmj.v31i1.17.

Biehl, João. "Pharmaceuticalization: AIDS Treatment and Global Health Politics." *Anthropological Quarterly* 80, no. 4 (2007): 1083–126. https://doi.org/10.1353/anq.2007.0056.

Biehl, João. *Will to Live: AIDS Therapies and the Politics of Survival*. Princeton University Press, 2007.

Biehl, João, and Adriana Petryna. *When People Come First: Critical Studies in Global Health*. Princeton University Press, 2013.

Biesma, Regien, Ruairi Brugha, Andrew Harmer, Aisling Walsh, Neil Spicer, and Gill Walt. "The Effects of Global Health Initiatives on Country Health Systems: A Review of the Evidence from HIV/AIDS Control." *Health Policy and Planning* 24, no. 4 (June 19, 2009): 239–52. https://doi.org/10.1093/heapol/czp025.

Birn, Anne-Emanuelle. "The Stages of International (Global) Health: Histories of Success or Successes of History?" *Global Public Health* 4, no. 1 (November 3, 2009): 50–68. https://doi.org/10.1080/17441690802017797.

Birn, Anne-Emanuelle, Laura Nervi, and Eduardo Siqueira. "Neoliberalism Redux: The Global Health Policy Agenda and the Politics of Cooptation in Latin America and Beyond." *Development and Change* 47, no. 4 (July 2016): 734–59. https://doi.org/10.1111/dech.12247.

Birn, Anne-Emanuelle, Sarah Zimmerman, and Richard Garfield. "To Decentralize or Not to Decentralize, Is That the Question? Nicaraguan Health

Policy Under Structural Adjustment in the 1990s." *International Journal of Health Services* 30, no. 1 (January 2000): 111–28. https://doi.org/10.2190/C6TB-B16Y-60HV-M3QW.

Biruk, Crystal. *Cooking Data: Culture and Politics in an African Research World*. Duke University Press, 2018.

Biruk, Crystal. "Seeing Like a Research Project: Producing 'High-Quality Data' in AIDS Research in Malawi." *Medical Anthropology* 31, no. 4 (2012): 347–66. https://doi.org/10.1080/01459740.2011.631960.

Birx, Deborah. "FY 2019 PEPFAR Planned Allocation and Strategic Direction." January 16, 2019. https://www.state.gov/wp-content/uploads/2019/08/Malawi.pdf.

Boli, John, and George M. Thomas. "INGOs and the Organization of World Culture." In *Constructing World Culture: Institutional Nongovernmental Organizations Since 1875*, edited by John Boli and George M. Thomas, 13–49. Stanford University Press, 1999.

Brandt, Allan M. "How AIDS Invented Global Health." *The New England Journal of Medicine* 368 (May 28, 2013): 2149–52. https://doi.org/10.1056/nejmp1305297.

Brass, Jennifer N. *Allies or Adversaries: NGOs and the State in Africa*. Cambridge University Press, 2016.

Brass, Jennifer N. "Blurring Boundaries: The Integration of NGOs into Governance in Kenya." *Governance* 25, no. 2 (October 3, 2011): 209–35. https://doi.org/10.1111/j.1468-0491.2011.01553.x.

Brass, Jennifer N, Wesley Longhofer, Rachel S Robinson, and Allison Schnable. "NGOs and International Development: A Review of Thirty-Five Years of Scholarship." *World Development* 112 (December 2018): 136–49. https://doi.org/10.1016/j.worlddev.2018.07.016.

Bromley, Patricia, and Walter W. Powell. "From Smoke and Mirrors to Walking the Talk: Decoupling in the Contemporary World." *The Academy of Management Annals* 6, no. 1 (June 2012): 483–530. https://doi.org/10.1080/19416520.2012.684462.

Brown, Theodore M, Marcos Cueto, and Elizabeth Fee. "The World Health Organization and the Transition From 'International' to 'Global' Public Health." *American Journal of Public Health* 96, no. 1 (January 2006): 62–72. https://doi.org/10.2105/ajph.2004.050831.

Burawoy, Michael. "Manufacturing the Global." *Ethnography* 2, no. 2 (June 2001): 147–59. https://doi.org/10.1177/14661380122230867.

Burchardt, Marian. "Subjects of Counselling: Religion, HIV/AIDS and the Management of Everyday Life in South Africa." In *AIDS and Religious Practice in Africa*, edited by Felicitas Becker and Wenzel Geissler, 333–58. Brill, 2009.

Burchardt, Marian. "The Self as Capital in the Narrative Economy: How Biographical Testimonies Move Activism in the Global South." *Sociology of*

Health and Illness 38, no. 4 (November 19, 2015): 592–609. https://doi.org/10.1111/1467-9566.12381.

Burton, Emilie M. Hafner, and Kiyoteru Tsutsui. "Human Rights in a Globalizing World: The Paradox of Empty Promises." *American Journal of Sociology* 110, no. 5 (March 2005): 1373–1411. https://doi.org/10.1086/428442.

Buse, Kent, and Amalia Waxman. "Public–Private Health Partnerships: A Strategy for WHO." *Bulletin of the World Health Organization* 79 (August 6, 2001): 748–54. https://doi.org/10.1186/1744-8603-4-6.

Busy, Raymond. *Blantyre Government Hospitals and Dispensary General Report 1921*. Government Printer, 1922.

Campbell, Catherine. *Letting Them Die: Why HIV/AIDS Prevention Programmes Fail*. The International African Institute, 2003.

Carmona, Andrew. "Malawi Private Health Sector Mapping Report." Strengthening Health Outcomes Through the Private Sector Project. January 2013.

Cataldo, Fabian. "New Forms of Citizenship and Socio-Political Inclusion: Accessing Antiretroviral Therapy in a Rio de Janeiro Favela." *Sociology of Health and Illness* 30, no. 6 (September 2008): 900–12. https://doi.org/10.1111/j.1467-9566.2008.01124.x.

Centeno, Miguel A., and Joseph N. Cohen. "The Arc of Neoliberalism." *Annual Review of Sociology* 38, no. 1 (2012): 317–40. https://doi.org/10.1146/annurev-soc-081309-150235.

Chimwaza, Angella F., and Susan C. Watkins. "Giving Care to People with Symptoms of AIDS in Rural Sub-Saharan Africa." *AIDS Care* 16, no. 7 (October 2004): 795–807. https://doi.org/10.1080/09540120412331290211.

Chimwaza, Wanangwa, Effie Chipeta, Andrew Ngwira, Francis Kamwendo, Frank Taulo, Susan Bradley, and Eilish McAuliffe. "What Makes Staff Consider Leaving the Health Service in Malawi?" *Human Resources for Health* 12, no. 1 (2014): 17. https://doi.org/10.1186/1478-4491-12-17.

Chipeta, Chinyamata. "Malawi." In *The Impact of Structural Adjustment on the Population of Africa: The Implications for Education, Health and Employment*, edited by Aderanti Adepoju, 105–18. James Currey, 1993.

Chorev, Nitsan. "Changing Global Norms Through Reactive Diffusion: The Case of Intellectual Property Protection of AIDS Drugs." *American Sociological Review* 77, no. 5 (September 30, 2012): 831–53. https://doi.org/10.1177/0003122412457156.

Chorev, Nitsan. "Restructuring Neoliberalism at the World Health Organization." *Review of International Political Economy* (July 2012): 1–40. https://doi.org/10.1080/09692290.2012.690774.

Chorev, Nitsan, Tatiana Andia Rey, and David Ciplet. "The State of States in International Organizations: From the WHO to the Global Fund." *Review (Fernand Braudel Center)* 43, no. 3 (2011): 285–310. http://www.jstor.org/stable/23631060.

Cilliers, Jakkie. "Data Modelling Reveals the Heavy Toll of USAID Cuts on Africa." Institute for Security Studies, February 28, 2025. https://issafrica.org/iss-today/data-modelling-reveals-the-heavy-toll-of-usaid-cuts-on-africa.

Cockerham, William C. "Health Lifestyle Theory and the Convergence of Agency and Structure." *Journal of Health and Social Behavior* 46, no. 1 (March 1, 2006): 51–67. https://doi.org/10.1177/002214650504600105.

Cohen, Jon. "'A Bloodbath': HIV Field Is Reeling After Billions in U.S. Funding Are Axed." *Science*, February 28, 2025. https://www.science.org/content/article/bloodbath-hiv-field-reeling-after-billions-u-s-funding-axed.

Cohen, Myron S., Ying Q. Chen, Marybeth McCauley, Theresa Gamble, Mina C. Hosseinipour, Nagalingeswaran Kumarasamy, James G. Hakim, et al. "Antiretroviral Therapy for the Prevention of HIV-1 Transmission." *New England Journal of Medicine* 375, no. 9 (2016): 830–9. https://doi.org/10.1056/nejmoa1600693.

Colvin, Christopher J., Sarah Konopka, John C. Chalker, Edna Jonas, Jennifer Albertini, Anouk Amzel, and Karen Fogg. "A Systematic Review of Health System Barriers and Enablers for Antiretroviral Therapy (ART) for HIV-Infected Pregnant and Postpartum Women." *PLoS One* 9, no. 10 (October 10, 2014): e108150. https://doi.org/10.1371/journal.pone.0108150.s006.

CONGOMA. "Council for Non-Governmental Organizations in Malawi." Accessed February 4, 2025. https://www.congoma.mw/.

Conrad, Peter. "The Meaning of Medications: Another Look at Compliance." *Social Science & Medicine* 20 (March 25, 1985): 29–37.

Conroy, Amy, Sara Yeatman, and Kathryn Dovel. "The Social Construction of AIDS During a Time of Evolving Access to Antiretroviral Therapy in Rural Malawi." *Culture, Health & Sexuality* 15, no. 8 (September 2013): 924–37. https://doi.org/10.1007/s10461-011-0089-6.

Coutsoudis, Anna, Ameena Goga, Chris Desmond, Peter Barron, Vivian Black, and Hoosen Coovadia. "Is Option B+ the Best Choice?" *Lancet* 381, no. 9863 (January 26, 2013): 269–71. https://doi.org/10.1016/s0140-6736(12)61807-8.

Crane, Johanna Tayloe. *Scrambling for Africa: AIDS, Expertise, and the Rise of American Global Health Science*. Cornell University Press, 2013.

Cueto, Marcos. "A Return to the Magic Bullet?: Malaria and Global Health in the Twenty-First Century." In *When People Come First: Critical Studies in Global Health*, edited by João Biehl and Adriana Petryna, 30–53. Princeton University Press, 2013.

Cueto, Marcos. "The Origins of Primary Health Care and Selective Primary Health Care." *American Journal of Public Health* 94, no. 11 (2004): 1864–74.

Damme, Wim Van, Katharina Kober, and Guy Kegels. "Scaling-up Antiretroviral Treatment in Southern African Countries with Human Resource Shortage: How Will Health Systems Adapt?" *Social Science & Medicine* 66, no. 10 (May 2008): 2108–21. https://doi.org/10.1016/j.socscimed.2008.01.043.

Decoteau, Claire Laurier. *Ancestors and Antiretrovirals: The Biopolitics of HIV/AIDS in Post-Apartheid South Africa*. University of Chicago Press, 2013.

Decoteau, Claire Laurier. *Emergency: COVID-19 and the Uneven Valuation of Life*. University of Chicago Press, 2024.

Decoteau, Claire Laurier. "The Entangled Emergencies of COVID-19." *Sociological Theory* 42, no. 2 (June 2024): 97–113. https://doi.org/10.1177/07352751241247567.

Desilver, Drew. "What the Data Says About U.S. Foreign Aid," February 6, 2025. https://www.pewresearch.org/short-reads/2025/02/06/what-the-data-says-about-us-foreign-aid/.

Dionne, Kim Yi. *Doomed Interventions: The Failure of Global Responses to AIDS in Africa*. Cambridge University Press, 2018.

Dionne, Kim Yi. "Local Demand for a Global Intervention: Policy Priorities in the Time of AIDS." *World Development* 40, no. 12 (December 2012): 2468–77. https://doi.org/10.1016/j.worlddev.2012.05.016.

Dobbin, Frank, Beth Simmons, and Geoffrey Garrett. "The Global Diffusion of Public Policies: Social Construction, Coercion, Competition, or Learning?" *Annual Review of Sociology* 33, no. 1 (August 2007): 449–72. https://doi.org/10.1146/annurev.soc.33.090106.142507.

Donnelly, John. "Battles with Donors Cloud Malawi's HIV Prevention Plan." *Lancet* 378, no. 9787 (July 16, 2011): 215–16. https://doi.org/10.1016/s0140-6736(11)61110-0.

Donovan, Jenny L., and David R. Blake. "Patient Non-Compliance: Deviance or Reasoned Decision-Making?" *Social Science & Medicine* 34 (March 1992): 507–13. https://doi.org/10.1016/0277-9536(92)90206-6

Doran, Marissa C. M. "Reconstructing Mchape '95: AIDS, Billy Chisupe, and the Politics of Persuasion." *Journal of Eastern African Studies* 1, no. 3 (2007): 397–416. https://doi.org/10.1080/17531050701625573.

Dovel, Kathryn, Sara Yeatman, Susan Watkins, and Michelle Poulin. "Men's Heightened Risk of AIDS-Related Death." *AIDS* 29, no. 10 (June 19, 2015): 1123–5. https://doi.org/10.1097/qad.0000000000000655.

Dworkin, Shari. *Men at Risk: Masculinity, Heterosexuality and HIV Prevention*. New York University Press, 2015.

Ecks, Stefan. "Pharmaceutical Citizenship: Antidepressant Marketing and the Promise of Demarginalization in India." *Anthropology & Medicine* 12, no. 3 (2005): 239–54. https://doi.org/10.1080/13648470500291360.

Emirbayer, Mustafa, and Ann Mische. "What Is Agency?" *American Journal of Sociology* 103, no. 4 (January 1998): 962–1023. https://doi.org/10.1086/231294.

England, Roger. "Are We Spending Too Much on HIV?" *BMJ* 334, no. 7589 (February 15, 2007): 344. https://doi.org/10.1136/bmj.39113.402361.94.

Epstein, Steven. *Impure Science: AIDS, Activism, and the Politics of Knowledge*. University of California Press, 1996.

Epstein, Steven. *Inclusion: The Politics of Difference in Medical Research.* University of Chicago Press, 2007.

Erikson, Susan L. "Metrics and Market Logics of Global Health." In *Metrics: What Counts in Global Health*, edited by Vincanne Adams, 147–62. Duke University Press, 2016.

Esacove, Anne. "Love Matches: Heteronormativity, Modernity, and AIDS Prevention in Malawi." *Gender & Society* 24, no. 1 (February 2010): 83–109. https://doi.org/10.1177/0891243209354754.

Esacove, Anne. *Modernizing Sexuality: US HIV Prevention in Sub-Saharan Africa.* Oxford University Press, 2016.

Esacove, Anne W. "Good Sex/Bad Sex: The Individualised Focus of US HIV Prevention Policy in Sub-Saharan Africa, 1995–2005." *Sociology of Health and Illness* 35, no. 1 (January 2013): 33–48. https://doi.org/10.1111/j.1467-9566.2012.01475.x.

Esser, Daniel E., and Kara Keating Bench. "Does Global Health Funding Respond to Recipients' Needs? Comparing Public and Private Donors' Allocations in 2005–2007." *World Development* 39, no. 8 (August 2011): 1271–80. https://doi.org/10.1016/j.worlddev.2010.12.005.

Exner, Theresa M., Shari L. Dworkin, Susie Hoffman, and Anke A. Ehrhardt. "Beyond the Male Condom: The Evolution of Gender-Specific HIV Interventions for Women." *Annual Review of Sex Research* 14, no. 1 (2003): 114–36. https://doi.org/10.1080/10532528.2003.10559813.

Exner, Theresa M., P. Sandor Gardos, David W. Seal, and Anke A. Ehrhardt. "HIV Sexual Risk Reduction Interventions with Heterosexual Men: The Forgotten Group," *AIDS and Behavior* 3, no. 4 (December 1999): 347–58. https://doi.org/10.1023/a:1025493503255.

Fan, Elsa. *Commodities of Care: The Business of HIV Testing in China.* University of Minnesota Press, 2021.

Farber, Reya. "'Don't Think That We Die from AIDS': Invisibilised Uncertainty and Global Transgender Health." *Sociology of Health & Illness* 45, no. 1 (January 2023): 196–212. https://doi.org/10.1111/1467-9566.13563.

Farber, Reya, Joseph Harris, and Renu Singh. "Reimagine Aid, Don't Destroy It." *Studies in Comparative International Development* (2025) https://doi.org/10.1007/s12116-025-09475-1.

Fassin, Didier. "Another Politics of Life Is Possible." *Theory Culture and Society* 26, no. 5 (September 2009): 44–60. https://doi.org/10.1177/0263276409106 3.

Fassin, Didier. *When Bodies Remember.* University of California Press, 2007.

Fassin, Didier, and Estelle d'Halluin. "Critical Evidence: The Politics of Trauma in French Asylum Policies." *Ethos* 35, no. 3 (September 2007): 300–29. https://doi.org/10.1525/eth.2007.35.3.300.

Fassin, Didier, and Estelle d'Halluin. "The Truth from the Body: Medical Certificates as Ultimate Evidence for Asylum Seekers." *American*

Anthropologist 107, no. 4 (December 2005): 597–608. https://doi.org/10.1525/aa.2005.107.4.597

Fauci, Anthony S, and Ronald C. Desrosiers. "Pathogenesis of HIV and SIV." In *Retroviruses*, edited by John M. Coffin, Stephan H. Hughes, and Harold E. Varmus. Cold Spring Harbor Laboratory Press, 1997. https://www.ncbi.nlm.nih.gov/books/NBK19374/.

Feierman, Steven. "When Physicians Meet: Local Knowledge and Global Public Goods." In *Evidence, Ethos and Experiment: The Anthropology and History of Medical Research in Africa*, edited by P. Wenzel Geissler and Catherine Molyneux, 171–96. Berghahn, 2011.

Ferguson, James. *The Anti-Politics Machine: "Development," Depoliticization and Bureaucratic Power in Lesotho*. University of Minnesota Press, 1994.

Ferguson, James, and Akhil Gupta. "Spatializing States: Toward an Ethnography of Neoliberal Governmentality." *American Ethnologist* 29, no. 4 (November 2002): 981–1002. https://www.jstor.org/stable/3805165.

Fligstein, Neil. "Social Skill and Institutional Theory." *American Behavioral Scientist* 40, no. 4 (February 1997): 397–405. https://doi.org/10.1177/0002764297040004003.

Ford, Nathan, David Wilson, Onanong Bunjumnong, and Tido von Schoen Angerer. "The Role of Civil Society in Protecting Public Health over Commercial Interests: Lessons from Thailand." *The Lancet* 363 (February 14, 2004): 560–63. https://doi.org/10.1016/S0140-6736(04)15545-1.

Frank, David, Tara Hardinge, and Kassia Wosick-Correa. "The Global Dimensions of Rape-Law Reform: A Cross-National Study of Policy Outcomes." *American Sociological Review* 74, no. 2 (April 2009): 272–90. https://doi.org/10.1177/000312240907400206.

Frye, Margaret. "Bright Futures in Malawi's New Dawn: Educational Aspirations as Assertions of Identity." *American Journal of Sociology* 117, no. 6 (May 2012): 1565–624. https://doi.org/10.1086/664542.

Gamson, Josh. "Silence, Death, and the Invisible Enemy: AIDS Activism and Social Movement 'Newness.'" *Social Problems* 36, no. 4 (October 1989): 351–67. https://doi.org/10.1525/sp.1989.36.4.03a00030.

Geubbels, Eveline, and Cameron Bowie. "Epidemiology of HIV/AIDS in Adults in Malawi." *Malawi Medical Journal* 18, no. 3 (2006): 111–33. https://doi.org/10.4314/mmj.v18i3.10917.

Gille, Zsuzsa, and Seán Ó Riain. "Global Ethnography." *Annual Review of Sociology* 28, no. 1 (August 2002): 271–95. https://doi.org/10.1146/annurev.soc.28.110601.140945.

Global Fund to Fight AIDS, Tuberculosis and Malaria. "Global Fund Supports 11 Countries in Response to COVID-19." The Global Fund: News & Stories, March 20, 2020. https://www.theglobalfund.org/en/news/2020-03-20-global-fund-supports-11-countries-in-response-to-covid-19/.

Global Fund to Fight AIDS, Tuberculosis and Malaria. "Grant Scorecard," August 12, 2014.

Global Fund to Fight AIDS, Tuberculosis and Malaria. "HIV and AIDS," 2024. https://www.theglobalfund.org/en/hivaids/.

Global Fund to Fight AIDS, Tuberculosis and Malaria. "Malawi Investments: Signed," 2023. https://data.theglobalfund.org/location/MWI/signed/treemap.

Global Fund to Fight AIDS, Tuberculosis and Malaria. "Results Report 2024." 2024. https://www.theglobalfund.org/en/results/.

Gomez, Eduardo J. "The Politics of Receptivity and Resistance: How Brazil, India, China, and Russia Strategically Use the International Health Community in Response to HIV/AIDS; A Theory." *Global Health Governance* 3 (May 30, 2009): 1–29.

Gourlay, Annabelle, Isolde Birdthistle, Gitau Mburu, Kate Iorpenda, and Alison Wringle. "Barriers and Facilitating Factors to the Uptake of Antiretroviral Drugs for Prevention of Mother-to-Child Transmission of HIV in Sub-Saharan Africa: A Systematic Review." *Journal of the International AIDS Society* 16, no. 1 (January 2013): 1–21. https://doi.org/10.7448/ias.16.1.18588.

Grépin, Karen A. "HIV Donor Funding Has Both Boosted and Curbed the Delivery of Different Non-HIV Health Services in Sub-Saharan Africa." *Health Affairs* 31, no. 7 (July 2012): 1406–14. https://doi.org/10.1377/hlthaff.2012.0279.

Haas, Andreas D., Lyson Tenthani, Malango T. Msukwa, Kali Tal, Andreas Jahn, Oliver J. Gadabu, Adrian Spoerri, Frank Chimbwandira, Joep J. van Oosterhout, and Olivia Keiser. "Retention in Care During the First 3 Years of Antiretroviral Therapy for Women in Malawi's Option B+ Programme: An Observational Cohort Study." *The Lancet HIV* 3, no. 4 (April 2016): e175–82. https://doi.org/10.1016/s2352-3018(16)00008-4.

Hafner, Tamara, and Jeremy Shiffman. "The Emergence of Global Attention to Health Systems Strengthening." *Health Policy and Planning* 28, no. 1 (January 2013): 41–50. https://doi.org/10.1093/heapol/czs023.

Halliday, Terence C. "Recursivity of Global Normmaking: A Sociolegal Agenda." *Annual Review of Law and Social Science* 5, no. 1 (December 2009): 263–89. https://doi.org/10.1146/annurev.lawsocsci.093008.131606.

Halliday, Terence C., and Bruce G. Carruthers. "The Recursivity of Law: Global Norm Making and National Lawmaking in the Globalization of Corporate Insolvency Regimes." *American Journal of Sociology* 112, no. 4 (January 2007): 1135–202. https://doi.org/10.1086/507855.

Harries, Anthony D., Nathan Ford, Andreas Jahn, Erik J. Schouten, Edwin Libamba, Frank Chimbwandira, and Dermot Maher. "Act Local, Think Global: How the Malawi Experience of Scaling Up Antiretroviral Treatment Has Informed Global Policy." *BMC Public Health* 16, no. 1 (September 6, 2016): 938. https://doi.org/10.1186/s12889-016-3620-x.

Harries, Anthony D, Edwin Libamba, Erik J Schouten, Andrina Mwansambo, Felix M Salaniponi, and Rex Mpazanje. "Expanding Antiretroviral Therapy in Malawi: Drawing on the Country's Experience with Tuberculosis." *BMJ* 329, no. 7475 (November 11, 2004): 1163–6. https://doi.org/10.1136/bmj.329.7475.1163.

Harries, Anthony D, Simon D Makombe, Edwin Libamba, and Erik J Schouten. "Why Did the Scale-up of HIV Treatment Work?: A Case Example from Malawi." *Journal of Acquired Immune Deficiency Syndromes* 57, no. S2 (August 1, 2011): S64–67. https://doi.org/10.1097/qai.0b013e31821f6bab.

Harries, Anthony D., Erik J. Schouten, and Edwin Libamba. "Scaling Up Antiretroviral Treatment in Resource-Poor Settings." *The Lancet* 367, no. 9525 (June 2006): 1870–2. https://doi.org/10.1016/s0140-6736(06)68809-0.

Harrigan, Jane. "Malawi." In *Aid and Power: The World Bank and Policy-Based Lending*, volume 2, *Case Studies*, edited by Paul Mosley, Jane Harrigan, and John Toye, 201–69. Routledge, 1991.

Harris, Joseph. *Achieving Access: Professional Movements and the Politics of Health Universalism*. Brown University Press, 2017.

Heaton, Mathew. "Health and Medicine in Colonial Society." In *The Palgrave Handbook of African Colonial and Postcolonial History*, edited by Martin S. Shanguhyia and Toyin Falola. Palgrave Macmillan, 2018.

Herbert, Bob. "Opinion: In America; Refusing To Save Africans." *The New York Times*, June 11, 2001.

hIarlaithe, Micheal O., Nils Grede, Saskia de Pee, and Martin Bloem. "Economic and Social Factors Are Some of the Most Common Barriers Preventing Women from Accessing Maternal and Newborn Child Health (MNCH) and Prevention of Mother-to-Child Transmission (PMTCT) Services: A Literature Review." *AIDS and Behavior* 18, no. S5 (April 2, 2014): 516–30. https://doi.org/10.1007/s10461-014-0756-5.

HIV.gov. "What Is PEPFAR?," December 7, 2021. https://www.hiv.gov/federal-response/pepfar-global-aids/pepfar.

Hodgson, Ian, Mary L. Plummer, Sarah N. Konopka, Christopher J. Colvin, Edna Jonas, Jennifer Albertini, Anouk Amzel, and Karen P. Fogg. "A Systematic Review of Individual and Contextual Factors Affecting ART Initiation, Adherence, and Retention for HIV-Infected Pregnant and Postpartum Women." *PLoS One* 9, no. 11 (November 5, 2014): e111421. https://doi.org/10.1371/journal.pone.0111421.

Hokkanen, Markku. "The Government Medical Service and British Missions in Colonial Malawi, c. 1891–1940: Crucial Collaboration, Hidden Conflicts." In *Beyond the State: The Colonial Medical Service in British Africa*, edited by Anna Greenwood, 39–63. Manchester University Press, 2016.

iAHO, and WHO. "Maternal Mortality: The Urgency of a Systemic and Multisectoral Approach in Mitigating Maternal Deaths in Africa," 2023.

Institute for Health Metrics and Evaluation. "Financing Global Health 2017: Funding Universal Health Coverage and the Unfinished HIV/AIDS Agenda." Institute for Health Metrics and Evaluation, 2018.

Institute for Health Metrics and Evaluation. "GBD Compare." Seattle, Washington, 2015.

Imray, Gerald. "Trump's Permanent USAID Cuts Slam Humanitarian Programs Worldwide: 'We Are Being Pushed off a Cliff.'" Associated Press News, February 27, 2025. https://apnews.com/article/trump-usaid-aid-cut-doge-musk-dbafoe89d72938caabee8251f7dfb4a7.

Inoue, Keiko, and Gili S. Drori. "The Global Institutionalization of Health as a Social Concern: Organizational and Discursive Trends." *International Sociology* 21, no. 2 (March 2006): 199–219. https://doi.org/10.1177/0268580906061376.

IPC. "Malawi IPC Chronic Food Insecurity Report," 2022.

Johnson-Hanks, Jennifer. "When the Future Decides: Uncertainty and Intentional Action in Contemporary Cameroon." *Current Anthropology* 46, no. 3 (June 2005): 363–85. https://doi.org/10.1086/428799.

Kaler, Amy. "AIDS-Talk in Everyday Life: The Presence of HIV/AIDS in Men's Informal Conversation in Southern Malawi." *Social Science & Medicine* 59, no. 2 (July 2004): 285–97. https://doi.org/10.1016/j.socscimed.2003.10.023.

Kaler, Amy, and Susan Cotts Watkins. "Disobedient Distributors: Street-Level Bureaucrats and Would-Be Patrons in Community-Based Family Planning Programs in Rural Kenya." *Studies in Family Planning* 32, no. 3 (September 2001): 254–69. https://doi.org/10.1111/j.1728-4465.2001.00254.x.

Kaler, Amy, Susan Cotts Watkins, and Nicole Angotti. "Making Meaning in the Time of AIDS: Longitudinal Narratives from the Malawi Journals Project." *African Journal of AIDS Research* 14, no. 4 (2015): 303–14. https://doi.org/10.2989/16085906.2015.1084342.

Kalinga, Owen, and John G. Pike. "A Pre-Colonial History of Malawi." *The Society of Malawi Journal* 18, no. 1 (1965): 22–54. https://www.jstor.org/stable/29779048.

Kalipeni, Ezekiel. "Structural Adjustment and the Health-Care Crisis in Malawi." *Proteus* 21, no. 1 (2004): 23–30.

Kalofonos, Ippolytos. "'All I Eat Is ARVs': The Paradox of AIDS Treatment Interventions in Central Mozambique." *Medical Anthropology Quarterly* 24, no. 3 (September 2010): 363–80. https://doi.org/10.1111/j.1548-1387.2010.01109.x.

Kalofonos, Ippolytos. *All I Eat Is Medicine: Going Hungry in Mozambique's AIDS Economy*. University of California Press, 2021.

Kamat, Sangeeta. "The Privatization of Public Interest: Theorizing NGO Discourse in a Neoliberal Era." *Review of International Political Economy* 11, no. 1 (2004): 155–76. https://doi.org/10.1080/0969229042000179794.

Kane, Sumit, Maryse Kok, Hermen Ormel, Lilian Otiso, Mohsin Sidat, Ireen Namakhoma, Sudirman Nasir, et al. "Limits and Opportunities to

Community Health Worker Empowerment: A Multi-Country Comparative Study." *Social Science & Medicine* 164 (September 2016): 27–34. https://doi.org/10.1016/j.socscimed.2016.07.019.

Karp, David A. "Taking Anti-Depressant Medications: Resistance, Trial Commitment, Conversion, Disenchantment." *Qualitative Sociology* 16 (December 1993): 337–59.

Kaspin, Deborah. "A Chewa Cosmology of the Body." *American Ethnologist* 23, no. 3 (August 1996): 561–78. https://doi.org/10.1525/ae.1996.23.3.02a00060.

Kellerman, Scott E., Saeed Ahmed, Theresa Feeley-Summerl, Jonathan Jay, Maria Kim, B. Ryan Phelps, Nandita Sugandhi, Erik Schouten, Mike Tolle, and Fatima Tsiouris. "Beyond Prevention of Mother-to-Child Transmission." *AIDS* 27 (November 2013): S225–33. https://doi.org/10.1097/qad.0000000000000107.

Kenny, Charles, and Justin Sandefur. "New Estimates of the USAID Cuts." Center for Global Development, March 20, 2025. https://www.cgdev.org/blog/new-estimates-usaid-cuts.

Kenworthy, Nora. *Mistreated: The Political Consequences of the Fight Against AIDS in Lesotho*. Vanderbilt University Press, 2017.

Kenworthy, Nora, Matthew Thomann, and Richard Parker. "From a Global Crisis to the 'End of AIDS': New Epidemics of Signification." *Global Public Health* 13, no. 8 (2018): 1–12. https://doi.org/10.1080/17441692.2017.1365373.

Keshavjee, Salmaan. *Blind Spot: How Neoliberalism Infiltrated Global Health*, vol. 30. University of California Press, 2014.

KFF. "U.S. Global Health Funding (in Millions), By Program Area, FY 2024." 2024. https://www.kff.org/global-health-policy/fact-sheet/breaking-down-the-u-s-global-health-budget-by-program-area/#Overview.

Kim, Maria H., Saeed Ahmed, W. Chris Buck, Geoffrey A. Preidis, Mina C. Hosseinipour, Avni Bhalakia, Debora Nanthuru, Peter N. Kazembe, Frank Chimbwandira, and Thomas P. Giordano. "The Tingathe Programme: A Pilot Intervention Using Community Health Workers to Create a Continuum of Care in the Prevention of Mother to Child Transmission of HIV (PMTCT) Cascade of Services in Malawi." *Journal of the International AIDS Society* 15, no. (Suppl 2) (July 2012): 17389. https://doi.org/10.7448/ias.15.4.17389.

Kim, Maria H., Alick C. Mazenga, Katie Simon, Xiaoying Yu, Saeed Ahmed, Pheobe Nyasulu, Pater Kazembe, Stanley Ngoma, and Elaine Abrams. "Burnout and Self-Reported Suboptimal Patient Care Amongst Health Care Workers Providing HIV Care in Malawi," *PLoS One* 13, no. 2 (February 21, 2018): e0192983. https://doi.org/10.1371/journal.pone.0192983.

Kim, Maria H., Alick C. Mazenga, Xiaoying Yu, Katie Simon, Phoebe Nyasulu, Peter N. Kazembe, Thokozani Kalua, Elaine Abrams, and Saeed Ahmed. "Factors Associated with Burnout Amongst Healthcare Workers Providing HIV Care in Malawi." *PLoS One* 14, no. 9 (September 24, 2019): e0222638 .https://doi.org/10.1371/journal.pone.0222638.

Kim, Maria H., Amy Zhou, Alick Mazenga, Saeed Ahmed, Christine Markham, Gerald Zomba, Katie Simon, Peter N. Kazembe, and Elaine J. Abrams. "Why Did I Stop? Barriers and Facilitators to Uptake and Adherence to ART in Option B+ HIV Care in Lilongwe, Malawi." *PLoS One* 11, no. 2 (February 22, 2016): e0149527. https://doi.org/10.1371/journal.pone.0149527.

King, Michael, and Elspeth King. *The Story of Medicine and Disease in Malawi: The 150 Years Since Livingstone*. Montfort Press, 1992.

Kleinman, Arthur. *The Illness Narratives: Suffering, Healing, and the Human Condition*. Basic Books, 1988.

Koch, Dirk-Jan, Axel Dreher, Peter Nunnenkamp, and Rainer Thiele. "Keeping a Low Profile: What Determines the Allocation of Aid by Non-Governmental Organizations?" *World Development* 37, no. 5 (May 2009): 902–18. https://doi.org/10.1016/j.worlddev.2008.09.004.

Kolko, Gabriel. "Ravaging the Poor: The International Monetary Fund Indicted by Its Own Data." *International Journal of Health Studies* 29, no. 1 (1999): 51–7. https://doi.org/10.2190/JG57-QQUD-MJ3G-291T.

Kritz, Fran. "Gavi, the Vaccine Alliance, Has Its Billion Dollar Grant Cut by Trump Administration." NPR, March 28, 2025. https://www.npr.org/sections/goats-and-soda/2025/03/28/g-s1-56881/vaccines-gavi-usaid-rubio.

Lakhani, Sarah Morando, and Stefan Timmermans. "Biopolitical Citizenship in the Immigration Adjudication Process." *Social Problems* 61, no. 3 (August 2014): 360–79. https://doi.org/10.1525/sp.2014.12286.

Lasker, Judith. *Hoping to Help: The Promises and Pitfalls of Global Health Volunteering*. Cornell University Press, 2016.

Leslie, Hannah H., Anna Gage, Humphreys Nsona, Lisa R. Hirschhorn, and Margaret E. Kruk. "Training and Supervision Did Not Meaningfully Improve Quality Of Care For Pregnant Women Or Sick Children In Sub-Saharan Africa." *Health Affairs* 35, no. 9 (September 2016): 1716–24. https://doi.org/10.1377/hlthaff.2016.0261.

van Lettow, Monique, Richard Bedell, Megan Landes, Lucy Gawa, Stephanie Gatto, Isabell Mayuni, Adrienne K. Chan, Lyson Tenthani, and Erik Schouten. "Uptake and Outcomes of a Prevention-of-Mother-to-Child Transmission (PMTCT) Program in Zomba District, Malawi." *BMC Public Health* 11, no. 1 (June 3, 2011): 426. https://doi.org/10.1186/1471-2458-11-426.

Levey, Ilana Ron, Nelson Gitonga, Meaghan Smith, Dawn Crosby, Jasmine Baleva, Emily Sanders, and Alison Wakefield. "Malawi Private Health Sector Assessment." Bethesda, MD: Strengthening Health Outcomes through the Private Sector Project, Abt Associates Inc., May 2011.

Li, Jonathan Z., Evgenia Aga, Ronald J. Bosch, Mark Pilkinton, Eugène Kroon, Lynsay MacLaren, Michael Keefer, et al. "Time to Viral Rebound After Interruption of Modern Antiretroviral Therapies." *Clinical Infectious Diseases* 74, no. 5 (March 2022): 865–70. https://doi.org/10.1093/cid/ciab541.

Libamba, Edwin, Simon Makombe, Anthony D. Harries, Richard Chimzizi, Felix M. Salaniponi, Eric J. Schouten, and Rex Mpazanje. "Scaling Up Antiretroviral Therapy in Africa: Learning from Tuberculosis Control Programmes; the Case of Malawi." *The International Journal of Tuberculosis and Lung Disease: The Official Journal of the International Union Against Tuberculosis and Lung Disease* 9, no. 10 (2005): 1062–71.

Livingston, Julie. *Improvising Medicine: An African Oncology Ward in an Emerging Cancer Epidemic.* Duke University Press, 2012.

Loembé, Marguerite Massinga, Akhona Tshangela, Stephanie J. Salyer, Jay K. Varma, Ahmed E. Ogwell Ouma, and John N. Nkengasong. "COVID-19 in Africa: The Spread and Response." *Nature Medicine* 26, no. 7 (June 11, 2020): 999–1003. https://doi.org/10.1038/s41591-020-0961-x.

Lordan, Grace, Kam Ki Tang, and Fabrizio Carmignani. "Has HIV/AIDS Displaced Other Health Funding Priorities? Evidence from a New Dataset of Development Aid for Health." *Social Science & Medicine* 73, no. 3 (August 2011): 351–5. https://doi.org/10.1016/j.socscimed.2011.05.045.

Luboga, Samuel Abimerech, Bert Stover, Travis W. Lim, Frederick Makumbi, Noah Kiwanuka, Flavia Lubega, Assay Ndizihiwe, et al. "Did PEPFAR Investments Result in Health System Strengthening? A Retrospective Longitudinal Study Measuring Non-HIV Health Service Utilization at the District Level." *Health Policy and Planning* 31, no. 7 (September 2016): 897–909. https://doi.org/10.1093/heapol/czw009.

Lutfey, Karen, and Jeremy Freese. "Toward Some Fundamentals of Fundamental Causality: Socioeconomic Status and Health in the Routine Clinic Visit for Diabetes." *American Journal of Sociology* 110, no. 5 (March2005): 1326–72. https://doi.org/10.1086/428914.

Lwanda, John. *Politics, Culture and Medicine in Malawi: Historical Continuities and Ruptures with Special Reference to HIV/AIDS*. Zomba, Malawi: Kachere, 2005.

MacKellar, Landis. "Priorities in Global Assistance for Health, AIDS, and Population." *Population and Development Review* 31, no. 2 (June 2005): 293–312. https://doi.org/10.1111/j.1728-4457.2005.00066.x.

Maes, Kenneth. "Experts' Tools, Altruists, and Job-Seekers: Visions of Community Health Workers in Ethiopia's Antiretroviral Centre of Excellence." *Critical African Studies* 8 (2016): 1–16. https://doi.org/10.1080/21681392.2016.1244959.

Maes, Kenneth. "Volunteerism or Labor Exploitation? Harnessing the Volunteer Spirit to Sustain AIDS Treatment Programs in Urban Ethiopia." *Human Organization* 71, no. 1 (February 23, 2012): 54–64. https://doi.org/10.17730/humo.71.1.axm39467485m22w4.

Maes, Kenneth, Svea Closser, Yihenew Tesfaye, and Roza Abesha. "Psychosocial Distress Among Unpaid Community Health Workers in Rural Ethiopia:

Comparing Leaders in Ethiopia's Women's Development Army to Their Peers." *Social Science & Medicine* 230 (June 2019): 138–46. https://doi.org/10.1016/j.socscimed.2019.04.005.

Maes, Kenneth, and Ippolytos Kalofonos. "Becoming and Remaining Community Health Workers: Perspectives from Ethiopia and Mozambique." *Social Science & Medicine* 87 (June 2013): 52–9. https://doi.org/10.1016/j.socscimed.2013.03.026.

Malawi Government, International Monetary Fund, and World Bank. "Malawi: Enhanced Structural Adjustment Facility Policy Framework Paper, 1998/99–2000/01." International Monetary Fund, December 3, 1998.

Malawi Government. *Malawi Growth and Development Strategy*, vol. 1. January 13, 2005. https://library.cepa.org.mw/wp-content/uploads/tainacan-items/201/5880/Malawi-Growth-and-Development-Strategy-Volume-One.pdf.

Malawi Government. *Non-Governmental Organizations Act, No. 3 of 2001.* http://ngora.mw/wp-content/uploads/2021/02/NGO-ACT-2001.pdf.

Manzi, M., R. Zachariah, R. Teck, L. Buhendwa, J. Kazima, E. Bakali, P. Firmenich, and P. Humblet. "High Acceptability of Voluntary Counselling and HIV-Testing but Unacceptable Loss to Follow up in a Prevention of Mother-to-Child HIV Transmission Programme in Rural Malawi: Scaling-Up Requires a Different Way of Acting." *Tropical Medicine and International Health* 10, no. 12 (December 2005): 1242–50. https://doi.org/10.1111/j.1365-3156.2005.01526.x.

Marchal, Bruno, Anna Cavalli, and Guy Kegels. "Global Health Actors Claim to Support Health System Strengthening—Is This Reality or Rhetoric?" *PLoS Medicine* 6, no. 4 (April 28, 2009): e1000059. https://doi.org/10.1371/journal.pmed.1000059.

Mattes, Dominik. "'We Are Just Supposed to Be Quiet': The Production of Adherence to Antiretroviral Treatment in Urban Tanzania." *Medical Anthropology* 30, no. 2 (March 2011): 158–82. https://doi.org/10.1111/j.1548-1387.2009.01034.x.

Mbembe, Achille. "Necropolitics." *Public Culture* 15, no. 1 (2003): 11–40.

McCoy, David, Sudeep Chand, and Devi Sridhar. "Global Health Funding: How Much, Where It Comes from and Where It Goes." *Health Policy and Planning* 24, no. 6 (November 2009): 407–17. https://doi.org/10.1093/heapol/czp026.

McCoy, David, Barbara McPake, and Victor Mwapasa. "The Double Burden of Human Resource and HIV Crises: A Case Study of Malawi." *Human Resources for Health* 6, no. 1 (2008): 16. https://doi.org/10.1186/1478-4491-6-16.

McCracken, John. *Politics and Christianity in Malawi, 1875–1940: The Impact of the Livingstonia Mission in the Northern Province*. African Books Collective, 2008.

McDonnell, Erin Metz. "Patchwork Leviathan: How Pockets of Bureaucratic Governance Flourish Within Institutionally Diverse Developing States."

American Sociological Review 82, no. 3 (June 2017): 476–510. https://doi.org/10.1177/0003122417705874.

McDonnell, Terence. *Best Laid Plans: Cultural Entropy and the Unraveling of AIDS Media Campaigns*. University of Chicago Press, 2016.

McDonnell, Terence. "Cultural Objects as Objects: Materiality, Urban Space, and the Interpretation of AIDS Campaigns in Accra, Ghana." *American Journal of Sociology* 115, no. 6 (May 2010): 1800–52. https://doi.org/10.1086/651577.

McKoy, Jillian. "Tracking Anticipated Deaths from USAID Funding Cuts." Boston University School of Public Health, March 21, 2025. https://www.bu.edu/sph/news/articles/2025/tracking-anticipated-deaths-from-usaid-funding-cuts.

Meinert, Lotte, Hanne O. Mogensen, and Jenipher Twebaze. "Tests for Life Chances: CD4 Miracles and Obstacles in Uganda." *Anthropology & Medicine* 16, no. 2 (2009): 195–209. https://doi.org/10.1080/13648470902940697.

Menon, Roshi. *Famine in Malawi: Causes and Consequences*. United Nations Development Program, 2007.

Messac, Luke. "Birthing a Nation: Political Legitimacy and Health Policy in Hastings Kamuzu Banda's Malawi, 1962–1980." *Journal of Southern African Studies* 46, no. 2 (2020): 209–28. https://doi.org/10.1080/03057070.2020.1689008.

Messac, Luke. "Moral Hazards and Moral Economies: The Combustible Politics of Healthcare User Fees in Malawian History." *South African Historical Journal* 66, no. 2 (2014): 371–89. https://doi.org/10.1080/02582473.2014.903292.

Messac, Luke. *No More to Spend: Neglect and the Construction of Scarcity in Malawi's History of Health Care*. Oxford University Press, 2020.

Meyer, John W., John Boli, George M. Thomas, and Francisco O. Ramirez. "World Society and the Nation-State." *American Journal of Sociology* 103, no. 1 (July 1997): 144–81. https://doi.org/10.1086/231174.

Meyer, John W., and Brian Rowan. "Institutionalized Organizations: Formal Structure as Myth and Ceremony." *American Journal of Sociology* 83, no. 2 (September 1977): 340–63. https://www.jstor.org/stable/2778293.

Mische, Ann. "Projects and Possibilities: Researching Futures in Action." *Sociological Forum* 24, no. 3 (September 2009): 694–704. https://doi.org/10.1111/j.1573-7861.2009.01127.x.

Mojola, Sanyu A., Nicole Angotti, Enid Schatz, and Brian Houle. "'A Nowadays Disease': HIV/AIDS and Social Change in a Rural South African Community." *American Journal of Sociology* 127, no. 3 (November 2021): 950–1000. https://doi.org/10.1086/718234.

Moran-Thomas, Amy. "A Salvage Ethnography of the Guinea Worm: Witchcraft, Oracles and Magic in a Disease Eradication Program." In *When People*

Come First: Critical Studies in Global Health, edited by João Biehl and Adriana Petryna, 207–40. Princeton University Press, 2013.

Morfit, N. Simon. "'AIDS Is Money': How Donor Preferences Reconfigure Local Realities." *World Development* 39 (January 2011): 64–76. https://doi.org/10.1016/j.worlddev.2010.09.003.

Morris, Brian. "Herbalism and Divination in Southern Malawi." *Social Science & Medicine* 23, no. 4 (1986): 367–77. https://doi.org/10.1016/0277-9536(86)90079-1.

Morris, Brian. "Medical Herbalism in Malawi." *Anthropology & Medicine* 18, no. 2 (2011): 245–55. https://doi.org/10.1080/13648470.2011.591200.

Moyer, Eileen. "The Anthropology of Life After AIDS: Epistemological Continuities in the Age of Antiretroviral Treatment." *Annual Review of Anthropology* 44, no. 1 (October 2015): 259–75. https://doi.org/10.1146/annurev-anthro-102214-014235.

Moyer, Eileen, Marian Burchardt, and Rijk van Dijk. "Editorial Introduction: Sexuality, Intimacy and Counselling: Perspectives from Africa." *Culture, Health & Sexuality* 15, no. S4 (2013): 431–39. https://doi.org/10.1080/13691058.2013.829977.

MSF (Médecins Sans Frontières). "Uncertainty Around PEPFAR Program Puts Millions at Risk." Médecins Sans Frontières, February 17, 2025. https://msf.org.au/article/statements-opinion/uncertainty-around-pepfar-program-puts-millions-risk.

MSH (Management Sciences for Health). "Evaluation of Malawi's Emergency Human Resources Programme." *Malawi Management Sciences for Health*, July 2, 2010, 1–86. http://www.who.int/workforcealliance/media/news/2010/Malawi_MSH_MSC_EHRP_Final.pdf.

Mtonya, Brian, Victor Mwapasa, John Kadzandira. *System-Wide Effects of the Global Fund in Malawi: Baseline Study Report*. The Partners for Health Reform plus Project. 2005. https://policycommons.net/artifacts/1721001/system-wide-effects-of-the-global-fund-in-malawi/view/.

Mueller, Dirk H., Douglas Lungu, Arnab Acharya, and Natasha Palmer. "Constraints to Implementing the Essential Health Package in Malawi." *PLoS One* 6, no. 6 (June 14, 2011): e20741. https://doi.org/10.1371/journal.pone.0020741.t005.

Mukherjee, Joia S., and Eddy Eustache. "Community Health Workers as a Cornerstone for Integrating HIV and Primary Healthcare." *AIDS Care* 19, no. sup1 (2007): 73–82. https://doi.org/10.1057/palgrave.jphp.3190013.

Munharo, Steven, Symon Nayupe, Patrick Mbulaje, Parth Patel, Confidence Banda, Kristine Joy Abordo Gacutno, Xu Lin, Isaac Thom Shawa, and Don Eliseo Lucero-Prisno. "Challenges of COVID-19 Testing in Low-Middle Income Countries (LMICs): The Case of Malawi." *Journal of Laboratory and Precision Medicine* 5 (October 2020): 32. https://doi.org/10.21037/jlpm-20-84.

Mussa, Richard. *Labour Market Transitions of Young Women and Men in Malawi: Results of the 2014 School-to-Work Transition Survey*. International Labour Office, 2016.

Mzungu, Watipaso. "Malawi Economic Crisis Deepens as U.S. Cuts $177 Million in Vital Aid, New Report Reveals." *Nyasa Times*, April 16, 2025.

Nachega, Jean B., Nadia A. Sam-Agudu, John W. Mellors, Alimuddin Zumla, and Lynne M. Mofenson. "Scaling Up Covid-19 Vaccination in Africa: Lessons from the HIV Pandemic." *The New England Journal of Medicine* 385, no. 3 (March 31, 2021): 196–8. https://doi.org/10.1056/NEJMp2103313.

Nading, Alex M. "'Love Isn't There in Your Stomach': A Moral Economy of Medical Citizenship Among Nicaraguan Community Health Workers." *Medical Anthropology Quarterly* 27, no. 1 (March 2013): 84–102. https://doi.org/10.1111/maq.12017.

Navon, Daniel. "'The Gene Didn't Get the Memo': Realigning Disciplines and Remaking Illness in Genomic Medicine." *Critical Inquiry* 46 (2020): 867–90. https://doi.org/10.1086/709227.

Nguyen, Vinh Kim. "Government-by-Exception: Enrolment and Experimentality in Mass HIV Treatment Programmes in Africa." *Social Theory & Health* 7, no. 3 (August 2009): 196–217. https://doi.org/10.1057/sth.2009.12.

Nguyen, Vinh Kim. *The Republic of Therapy: Triage and Sovereignty in West Africa's Time of AIDS*. Duke University Press, 2010.

Nguyen, Vinh Kim, Cyriaque Yapo Ako, Pascal Niamba, Aliou Sylla, and Issoufou Tiendre´be´ogo. "Adherence as Therapeutic Citizenship: Impact of the History of Access to Antiretroviral Drugs on Adherence to Treatment." *AIDS* 21 (October 2007): S31–5. https://doi.org/10.1097/01.aids.0000298100.48990.58.

Nilsson, Adriana. "Treating Market Failure Access Professionals in Global Health." In *Professional Networks in Global Governance*, edited by Leonard Seabrooke and Lasse Folke Henriksen, 165–81. Cambridge University Press, 2017.

Nixon, Rob. *Slow Violence and the Environmentalism of the Poor*. Harvard University Press, 2011.

Nolen, Stephanie. "U.S. to End Vaccine Funds for Poor Countries." *The New York Times*, March 26, 2025. https://www.nytimes.com/2025/03/26/health/usaid-cuts-gavi-bird-flu.html.

Novas, Carlos, and Nikolas Rose. "Genetic Risk and the Birth of the Somatic Individual." *Economy and Society* 29, no. 4 (2000): 485–513. https://doi.org/10.1080/03085140050174750.

Ntonya, George. "So, AIDS Is Money?" *The Nation*, March 14, 2007.

National Statistical Office. *2008 Population and Housing Census Main Report*. Zomba, Malawi, 2008.

National Statistical Office (NSO), and Macro International. *Malawi Knowledge, Attitudes and Practices in Health Survey 1996*. NSO and Macro International, 1997.

National Statistical Office. *Malawi Demographic and Health Survey: Preliminary Report*. National Statistical Office, 2004.

Okuonzi, Sam, and Joanna Macrae. "Whose Policy Is It Anyway? International and National Influences on Health Policy Development in Uganda." *Health Policy and Planning* 10, no. 2 (June 1995): 122–32. https://doi.org/10.1093/heapol/10.2.122.

Oni-Orisan, Adeola. "The Obligation to Count: The Politics of Monitoring Maternal Mortality in Nigeria." In *Metrics: What Counts in Global Health*, edited by Vincanne Adams, 82–101. Duke University Press, 2016.

Ooms, Gorik, Wim Van Damme, and Marlene Temmerman. "Medicines Without Doctors: Why the Global Fund Must Fund Salaries of Health Workers to Expand AIDS Treatment." *PLoS Medicine* 4, no. 4 (April 17, 2007): 605–8. https://doi.org/10.1371/journal.pmed.0040128.

Ooms, Gorik, Win Van Damme, Brook K. Baker, Paul Zeitz, and Ted Schrecker. "The 'Diagonal' Approach to Global Fund Financing: A Cure for the Broader Malaise of Health Systems?" *Globalization and Health* 4, no. 6 (2008): 1–7. https://doi.org/10.1186/1744-8603-4-6.

Packard, Randall M. *A History of Global Health: Interventions into the Lives of Other Peoples*. Johns Hopkins University Press, 2016.

Palmer, Debbie. "Tackling Malawi's Human Resources Crisis." *Reproductive Health Matters* 14, no. 27 (2006): 27–39. https://doi.org/10.1016/s0968-8080(06)27244-6.

Parker, Melissa, and Tim Allen. "De-Politicizing Parasites: Reflections on Attempts to Control the Control of Neglected Tropical Diseases." *Medical Anthropology* 33, no. 3 (2014): 223–39. https://doi.org/10.1080/01459740.2013.831414.

Parker, Richard. "Grassroots Activism, Civil Society Mobilization, and the Politics of the Global HIV/AIDS Epidemic." *The Brown Journal of World Affairs* 17, no. 2 (2011): 21–37. https://www.jstor.org/stable/24590789.

Parsons, Talcott. "Illness and the Role of the Physician: A Sociological Perspective." *American Journal of Orthopsychiatry* 21, no. 3 (1951): 452–60. https://doi.org/10.1111/j.1939-0025.1951.tb00003.x.

Pensulo, Charles. "'Bring Your Own Syringe': Malawi's Medical Supplies at Crisis Point." *The Guardian*, December 8, 2022.

Persson, Asha. "Non/Infectious Corporealities: Tensions in the Biomedical Era of 'HIV Normalisation.'" *Sociology of Health and Illness* 35, no. 7 (September 2013): 1065–79. https://doi.org/10.1111/1467-9566.12023.

Persson, Asha. "'The World Has Changed': Pharmaceutical Citizenship and the Reimagining of Serodiscordant Sexuality Among Couples with Mixed HIV Status in Australia." *Sociology of Health and Illness* 38, no. 3 (March 2016): 380–95. https://doi.org/10.1111/1467-9566.12347.

Petryna, Adriana. "Biological Citizenship: The Science and Politics of Chernobyl-Exposed Populations." *Osiris* 19, no. 2 (2004): 250–65. http://www.jstor.org/stable/3655243.

Petryna, Adriana. "Science and Citizenship Under Postsocialism." *Social Research* 70, no. 2 (2003): 551–78. https://www.jstor.org/stable/40971626.

Pfeiffer, James. "The Struggle for a Public Sector." In *When People Come First: Critical Studies in Global Health*, edited by João Biehl and Adriana Petryna, 166–81. Princeton University Press, 2013.

Pfeiffer, James, and Rachel Chapman. "Anthropological Perspectives on Structural Adjustment and Public Health." *Annual Review of Anthropology* 39, no. 1 (October 2010): 149–65. https://doi.org/10.1146/annurev.anthro.012809.105101.

Phiri, Kings M. "Pre-Colonial States of Central Malawi: Towards a Reconstruction of Their History." *The Society of Malawi Journal* 41, no. 1 (1988): 1–29. https://www.jstor.org/stable/29778587.

Pierret, Janine. "The Illness Experience: State of Knowledge and Perspectives for Research." *Sociology of Health and Illness* 25 (April 2003): 4–22. https://doi.org/10.1111/1467-9566.t01-1-00337.

Piot, Peter. "Why Aids Demands an Exceptional Response." Presented at the London School of Economics, 2005.

Ministry of Health and Population. "Malawi Health Facility Survey." Government of Malawi, 2003.

Poulin, Michelle, Kathryn Dovel, and Susan Cotts Watkins. "Men with Money and the 'Vulnerable Women' Client Category in an AIDS Epidemic." *World Development* 85 (September 2016): 16–30. https://doi.org/10.1016/j.worlddev.2016.04.008.

Pound, Pandora, Nicky Britten, Myfanwy Morgan, Lucy Yardley, Catherine Pope, Gavin Daker-White, and Rona Campbell. "Resisting Medicines: A Synthesis of Qualitative Studies of Medicine Taking." *Social Science & Medicine* 61, no. 1 (July 2005): 133–55. https://doi.org/10.1016/j.socscimed.2004.11.063.

Prince, Ruth J., and Phelgona Otieno. "In the Shadowlands of Global Health: Observations from Health Workers in Kenya." *Global Public Health* 9, no. 8 (2014): 927–45. https://doi.org/10.1080/17441692.2014.941897.

Psaros, Christina, Jocelyn E. Remmert, David R. Bangsberg, Steven A. Safren, and Jennifer A. Smit. "Adherence to HIV Care After Pregnancy Among Women in Sub-Saharan Africa: Falling Off the Cliff of the Treatment Cascade." *Current HIV/AIDS Reports* 12, no. 1 (January 27, 2015): 1–5. https://doi.org/10.1007/s11904-014-0252-6.

Rasschaert, Freya, Marjan Pirard, Mit P. Philips, Rifat Atun, Edwin Wouters, Yibeltal Assefa, Bart Criel, Erik J. Schouten, and Wim Van Damme. "Positive Spill-Over Effects of ART Scale Up on Wider Health Systems Development: Evidence from Ethiopia and Malawi." *Journal of the International AIDS Society* 14, no. S1 (July 2011): S3. https://doi.org/10.1186/1758-2652-14-s1-s3.

Ratevosian, Jirair. "PEPFAR Misses Reauthorization Deadline: What's Next for Global HIV Fight?" *Think Global Health*, March 26, 2025. https://www.thinkglobalhealth.org/article/pepfar-misses-reauthorization-deadline-whats-next

-global-hiv-fight#:~:text=As%20of%20March%2025%2C%202025,as %20political%20strife%20engulfed%20PEPFAR.

Ravishankar, Nirmala, Paul Gubbins, Rebecca J. Cooley, Katherine Leach-Kemon, Catherine M. Michaud, Dean T. Jameson, and Christopher J. L. Murray. "Financing of Global Health: Tracking Development Assistance for Health from 1990 to 2007." *The Lancet* 373, no. 9681 (June 20, 2009): 2113–24. https://doi.org/10.1016/S0140-6736(09)60881-3.

Richey, Lisa Ann. "Counselling Citizens and Producing Patronage: AIDS Treatment in South African and Ugandan Clinics." *Development and Change* 43, no. 4 (July 2012): 823–45. https://doi.org/10.1111/j.1467-7660.2012.01782.x.

Rodriguez, Julia. "Inoculating Against Barbarism? State Medicine and Immigrant Policy in Turn-of-the-Century Argentina." *Science in Context* 19, no. 03 (September 2006): 357–80. https://doi.org/10.1017/s0269889706000974.

Rosenthal, Anat. "'Doing the Best We Can': Providing Care in a Malawian Antiretroviral Clinic." *Medical Anthropology* 35, no. 2 (2016): 132–46. https://doi.org/10.1080/01459740.2015.1076409.

Rosenthal, Anat. *Health on Delivery: The Rollout of Antiretroviral Therapy in Malawi*. Routledge, 2017.

Rowden, R. *The Deadly Ideas of Neoliberalism: How the IMF Has Undermined Public Health and the Fight Against AIDS*. Zed Books, 2009.

van de Ruit, Catherine. "Unintended Consequences of Community Health Worker Programs in South Africa." *Qualitative Health Research* 29, no. 11 (2019): 1535–48. https://doi.org/10.1177/1049732319857059.

van de Ruit, Catherine, and Amy Zhou. "The Problem of Insecure Community Health Workers in the Global South." In *Global Agenda for Social Justice 2*, edited by Glenn W. Muschert, Kristen M. Budd, Heather Dillaway, David C. Lane, Manjusha Nair, and Jason A. Smith, 71–79. Bristol University Press, 2022.

Sandefur, Justin, and Charles Kenny. "USAID Cuts: New Estimates at the Country Level." Center for Global Development, March 26, 2025. https://www.cgdev.org/blog/usaid-cuts-new-estimates-country-level.

Savage, Rachel. "'Devastating': Malawi Left in Dire Straits by Trump's Decision to Freeze Aid." *The Guardian*, February 9, 2025. https://www.theguardian.com/world/2025/feb/09/malawi-left-in-dire-straits-by-trump-decision-to-freeze-aid.

Schouten, Erik J., Andreas Jahn, Anne Ben-Smith, Simon D. Makombe, Anthony D. Harries, Francis Aboagye-Nyame, and Frank Chimbwandira. "Antiretroviral Drug Supply Challenges in the Era of Scaling up ART in Malawi." *Journal of the International AIDS Society* 14, no. S1 (July 2011): S4. https://doi.org/10.1186/1758-2652-14-S1-S4.

Schouten, Erik J., Andreas Jahn, Dalitso Midiani, Simon D. Makombe, Austin Mnthambala, Zengani Chirwa, Anthony D. Harries, et al. "Prevention of

Mother-to-Child Transmission of HIV and the Health-Related Millennium Development Goals: Time for a Public Health Approach." *The Lancet* 378, no. 9787 (July 16, 2011): 282–4. https://doi.org/10.1016/s0140-6736(10)62303-3.

Scott, James C. *Seeing Like a State: How Certain Schemes to Improve the Human Condition Have Failed*. Yale University Press, 1998.

Seabrooke, Leonard, and Lasse Folke Henriksen. *Professional Networks in Transnational Governance*. Cambridge University Press, 2017.

Shiffman, Jeremy. "Donor Funding Priorities for Communicable Disease Control in the Developing World." *Health Policy and Planning* 21, no. 6 (November 2006): 411–20. https://doi.org/10.1093/heapol/czl028.

Shiffman, Jeremy. "Has Donor Prioritization of HIV/AIDS Displaced Aid for Other Health Issues?" *Health Policy and Planning* 23, no. 2 (March 2008): 95–100. https://doi.org/10.1093/heapol/czm045.

Shircore, John Owen. *Report on the Nyasaland Medical Service with Special Reference to a Grant Under the Colonial Development Fund*. Government Printer, 1930.

Sindima, Harvey. *Malawi's First Republic: An Economic and Political Analysis*. University Press of American, 2002.

Smith, Kirsten P., and Susan Cotts Watkins. "Perceptions of Risk and Strategies for Prevention: Responses to HIV/AIDS in Rural Malawi." *Social Science & Medicine* 60, no. 3 (February 2005): 649–60. https://doi.org/10.1016/j.socscimed.2004.06.009.

Sonenthal, Paul D., Jones Masiye, Noel Kasomekera, Regan H. Marsh, Emily B. Wroe, Kirstin W. Scott, Ruoran Li, et al. "COVID-19 Preparedness in Malawi: A National Facility-Based Critical Care Assessment." *The Lancet Global Health* 8, no. 7 (July 2020): e890–92. https://doi.org/10.1016/s2214-109x(20)30250-3.

Southwood, Ivon. *Non-Stop Inertia*. Zero Books, 2011.

Sparke, Matthew. "Austerity and the Embodiment of Neoliberalism as Ill-Health: Towards a Theory of Biological Sub-Citizenship." *Social Science & Medicine* 187 (August 2017): 287–95. https://doi.org/10.1016/j.socscimed.2016.12.027.

Storeng, Katerini T. "The GAVI Alliance and the 'Gates Approach' to Health System Strengthening." *Global Public Health* 9, no. 8 (2014): 865–79. https://doi.org/10.1080/17441692.2014.940362.

Storeng, Katerini T., and Dominique P. Béhague. "'Playing the Numbers Game': Evidence-Based Advocacy and the Technocratic Narrowing of the Safe Motherhood Initiative." *Medical Anthropology Quarterly* 28, no. 2 (June 2014): 260–79. https://doi.org/10.1111/maq.12072.

Street, Alice. "Affective Infrastructure: Hospital Landscapes of Hope and Failure." *Space and Culture* 15, no. 1 (February 2012): 44–56. https://doi.org/10.1177/1206331211426061.

Street, Alice. *Biomedicine in an Unstable Place: Infrastructure and Personhood in a Papua New Guinean Hospital*. Duke University Press, 2014.

Suh, Siri. *Dying to Count: Post-Abortion Care and Global Reproductive Health Politics in Senegal*. Rutgers University Press, 2021.

Sullivan, Noelle. "Mediating Abundance and Scarcity: Implementing an HIV/AIDS-Targeted Project Within a Government Hospital in Tanzania." *Medical Anthropology* 30, no. 2 (2011): 202–21. https://doi.org/10.1080/01459740.2011.552453.

Swidler, Ann, and Susan Cotts Watkins. *A Fraught Embrace: The Romance and Reality of AIDS Altruism in Africa*. Princeton University Press, 2017.

Swidler, Ann, and Susan Cotts Watkins. "'Teach a Man to Fish': The Sustainability Doctrine and Its Social Consequences." *World Development* 37, no. 7 (July 2009): 1182–96. https://doi.org/10.1016/j.worlddev.2008.11.002.

Swiss, Liam. "Security Sector Reform and Development Assistance: Explaining the Diffusion of Policy Priorities Among Donor Agencies." *Qualitative Sociology* 34 (2011): 371–93. https://doi.org/10.1007/s11133-011-9194-0.

Tavory, Iddo, and Nina Eliasoph. "Coordinating Futures: Toward a Theory of Anticipation." *American Journal of Sociology* 118, no. 4 (January 2013): 908–42. https://doi.org/10.1086/668646.

Tenthani, Lyson, Andreas D. Haas, Hannock Tweya, Andreas Jahn, Joep J. van Oosterhout, Frank Chimbwandira, Zengani Chirwa, et al. "Retention in Care Under Universal Antiretroviral Therapy for HIV-Infected Pregnant and Breastfeeding Women ('Option B+') in Malawi." *AIDS* 28, no. 4 (February 2014): 589–98. https://doi.org/10.1097/qad.0000000000000143.

Thornton, Robert J. *Unimagined Community: Sex, Networks, and AIDS in Uganda and South Africa*. University of California Press, 2008.

Ticktin, Miriam. "Where Ethics and Politics Meet." *American Ethnologist* 33, no. 1 (February 2006): 33–49. https://doi.org/10.1525/ae.2006.33.1.33.

Trinitapoli, Jenny, and Sara Yeatman. "Uncertainty and Fertility in a Generalized AIDS Epidemic." *American Sociological Review* 76, no. 6 (December 2011): 935–54. https://doi.org/10.1177/0003122411427672.

Trinitapoli, Jenny. *An Epidemic of Uncertainty: Navigating HIV and Young Adulthood in Malawi*. University of Chicago Press, 2023.

Trinitapoli, Jenny, and Alex Weinreb. *Religion and AIDS in Africa*. Oxford University Press, 2012.

Turshen, Meredith. *Privatizing Health Services in Africa*. Rutgers University Press, 1998.

UNAIDS. "AIDS Epidemic Update: December 2000." UNAIDS/WHO, 2000.

UNAIDS. "Country Factsheets: Malawi." 2023. https://www.unaids.org/en/regionscountries/countries/malawi.

UNAIDS. "Fact Sheet 2022." 2022. https://www.unaids.org/sites/default/files/media_asset/UNAIDS_FactSheet_en.pdf.

UNAIDS. "Global HIV & AIDS Statistics: Fact Sheet." 2025. https://www.unaids.org/en/resources/fact-sheet.

UNAIDS. "Groundbreaking Trial Results Confirm HIV Treatment Prevents Transmission of HIV." UNAIDS, 2011. https://www.unaids.org/en/resources/presscentre/pressreleaseandstatementarchive/2011/may/20110512pstrialresults.

UNAIDS. "HIV Financial Dashboard." July 2023. https://hivfinancial.unaids.org/hivfinancialdashboards.html#.

UNAIDS. "Start Free, Stay Free, AIDS Free." 2015. https://free.unaids.org.

UNAIDS. "World AIDS Day 2023." 2023.

University of North Carolina. "UNC Project Malawi: About Us." 2025. https://globalhealth.unc.edu/malawi/about-2/.

UNDP. "Human Development Insights." 2024. https://hdr.undp.org/data-center/country-insights#/ranks.

UNESCO. "Malawi: Education Country Brief." January 2024. https://www.iicba.unesco.org/en/malawi.

UNICEF. "Options B and B+: Key Considerations for Countries to Implement an Equity-Focused Approach." UNICEF, July 2012.

USAID. "Malawi: Nutrition Profile." 2018. https://2017-2020.usaid.gov/global-health/health-areas/nutrition/countries/malawi-nutrition-profile.

USAID and IMPACT. "Malawi and HIV/AIDS." USAID, 1999.

USAID Stop-Work. "USAID Stop-Work." 2025. https://www.usaidstopwork.com/.

Vaughan, Megan. *Curing Their Ills: Colonial Power and African Illness*. Polity Press, 1992.

Veenstra, Gerry, and Patrick John Burnett. "A Relational Approach to Health Practices: Towards Transcending the Agency-Structure Divide." *Sociology of Health and Illness* 36, no. 2 (February 2014): 187–98. https://doi.org/10.1111/1467-9566.12105.

Venn, Susan, and Sara Arber. "Understanding Older Peoples' Decisions About the Use of Sleeping Medication: Issues of Control and Autonomy." *Sociology of Health and Illness* 34, no. 8 (November 2012): 1215–29. https://doi.org/10.1111/j.1467-9566.2012.01468.x.

Vernooij, Eva, and Anita Hardon. "'What Mother Wouldn't Want to Save Her Baby?' HIV Testing and Counselling Practices in a Rural Ugandan Antenatal Clinic." *Culture, Health & Sexuality* 15, no. S4 (2013): 553–66. https://doi.org/10.1080/13691058.2012.758314.

Vijayakumar, Gowri. *At Risk: Indian Sexual Politics and The Global AIDS Crisis*. Stanford University Press, 2021.

Vijayakumar, Gowri. "'I'll Be Like Water': Gender, Class, and Flexible Aspirations at the Edge of India's Knowledge Economy." *Gender and Society* 27, no. 6 (December 2013): 777–98. https://doi.org/10.1177/0891243213499445.

Vijayakumar, Gowri. "Lessons from India's Sex Worker Activists on Surviving USAID Freeze." *Scroll.In*, February 23, 2025.

Watkins, Susan Cotts. "Navigating the AIDS Epidemic in Rural Malawi." *Population and Development Review* 30, no. 4 (December 15, 2004): 673–705. https://doi.org/10.1111/j.1728-4457.2004.00037.x.

Watkins, Susan Cotts, and Ann Swidler. "Hearsay Ethnography: Conversational Journals as a Method for Studying Culture in Action." *Poetics* 37, no. 2 (April 2009): 162–84. https://doi.org/10.1016/j.poetic.2009.03.002.

Wendland, Claire. *A Heart for the Work: Journeys Through an African Medical School*. University of Chicago Press, 2010.

Wendland, Claire. "Estimating Death: A Close Reading of Maternal Mortality Metrics in Malawi." In *Metrics: What Counts in Global Health*, edited by Vincanne Adams, 57–81. Duke University Press, 2016.

Wendland, Claire. *Partial Stories: Maternal Death from Six Angles*. University of Chicago Press, 2022.

Whitehead, F. E. *Annual Medical Report on the Health and Sanitary Conditions of the Nyasaland Protectorate for the Year Ended 31st December, 1925*. Medical and Sanitary Services, 1925.

Whitford, Josh. "Pragmatism and the Untenable Dualism of Means and Ends: Why Rational Choice Theory Does Not Deserve Paradigmatic Privilege." *Theory and Society* 31 (June 2002): 325–63. https://doi.org/10.1023/a:1016232404279.

WHO. *Antiretroviral Drugs for Treating Pregnant Women and Preventing HIV Infection in Infants*. WHO HIV/AIDS Programme, March 28, 2010.

WHO. "Declaration of Alma-Ata," September 12, 1978. https://cdn.who.int/media/docs/default-source/documents/almaata-declaration-en.pdf?sfvrsn=7b3c2167_2.

WHO. "Global Health Estimates: Leading Causes of Death." The Global Health Observatory, 2015. https://www.who.int/data/gho/data/themes/mortality-and-global-health-estimates/ghe-leading-causes-of-death.

WHO. "HIV/AIDS." 2023. https://www.afro.who.int/health-topics/hivaids.

WHO. "HIV/AIDS: Report by the Director-General." March 22, 2000. https://apps.who.int/gb/archive/pdf_files/WHA53/ea6.pdf.

WHO. "Implementation of Option B+ for Prevention of Mother-To-Child Transmission of HIV: The Malawi Experience." WHO Regional Office for Africa, 2014. https://apps.who.int/iris/bitstream/handle/10665/112849/9789290232520.pdf?sequence=1&isAllowed=y.

WHO. "Population, Malawi." 2025. https://data.who.int/countries/454.

WHO. *The Strategic Use of Antiretrovirals for Treatment and Prevention of HIV Infection: Report of a WHO Technical Consultation 14–16 November 2011, Geneva, Switzerland*. Geneva, 2011. https://apps.who.int/iris/bitstream/handle/10665/70912/9789241503808_eng.pdf?sequence=5&isAllowed=y.

WHO. "WHO Health Workforce Support and Safeguards List," April 4, 2024. https://www.who.int/news-room/questions-and-answers/item/who-health

-workforce-support-and-safeguards-list#:~:text=Countries%20included %20in%20the%20WHO,coverage%20index%20less%20than%2055.

WHO. "World Health Organization Data: Population, Malawi." 2015. https://data .who.int/countries/454.

WHO, UNAIDS, and UNICEF. "Towards Universal Access: Scaling Up Priority HIV/AIDS Interventions in the Health Sector." 2010.

Whyte, Susan Reynolds, Michael Whyte, Lotte Meinert, Jenipher Twebaze, Joao Biehl, and Adriana Petryna. "Therapeutic Clientship: Belonging in Uganda's Projectified Landscape of AIDS Care." In *When People Come First: Critical Studies in Global Health*, edited by João Biehl and Adriana Petryna, 140–65. Princeton University Press, 2013.

World Bank Group. "Antiretroviral Therapy Coverage (% of People Living with HIV)," 2022. https://data.worldbank.org/indicator/SH.HIV.ARTC.ZS.

World Bank Group. "Domestic General Government Health Expenditure (% of General Government Expenditure)." Accessed August 25, 2025. https://data bank.worldbank.org/Malawi/id/e94e950d.

World Bank Group. "Low-Birthweight Babies (% of Births)." 2015. https://data .worldbank.org/indicator/SH.STA.BRTW.ZS?end=2015&most_recent_value _desc=true&start=2000.

World Bank Group. "Maternal Mortality Ratio (Modeled Estimate, per 100,000 Live Births)." 2015. https://data.worldbank.org/indicator/SH.STA.MMRT ?end=2015&most_recent_value_desc=true&start=1985.

World Bank Group. "Mortality Rate, Infant (per 1,000 Live Births)." 2015. https://data.worldbank.org/indicator/SP.DYN.IMRT.IN?end=2015&most _recent_value_desc=true&start=1960.

World Bank Group. "Mortality Rate, Neonatal (per 1,000 Live Births)." 2015. https://data.worldbank.org/indicator/SH.DYN.NMRT?end=2015&most _recent_value_desc=true&start=1960.

World Bank Group. "Prevalence of HIV, Total (% of Population Ages 15–49)." 2022. https://data.worldbank.org/indicator/SH.DYN.AIDS.ZS?end=2021& most_recent_value_desc=true&start=2021&view=bar.

World Bank Group. "Population, Total: Malawi." 2024. https://data.worldbank .org/indicator/SP.POP.TOTL?locations=MW.

World Bank Group. "Poverty & Equity Brief: Africa Eastern & Southern; Malawi." April 2023.

Wyrod, Robert. *AIDS and Masculinity in the African City: Privilege, Inequality, and Modern Manhood*. University of California Press, 2016.

Yu, Dongbao, Yves Souteyrand, Mazuwa A Banda, Joan Kaufman, and Joseph H Perriëns. "Investment in HIV/AIDS Programs: Does It Help Strengthen Health Systems in Developing Countries?" *Globalization and Health* 4, no. 1 (2008): 8. https://doi.org/10.1186/1744-8603-4-8.

Zuber, Alexandra, Carey F. McCarthy, Andre R. Verani, Eleanor Msidi, and Carla Johnson. "A Survey of Nurse-Initiated and -Managed Antiretroviral

Therapy (NIMART) in Practice, Education, Policy, and Regulation in East, Central, and Southern Africa." *Journal of the Association of Nurses in AIDS Care* 25, no. 6 (November 2014): 520–31. https://doi.org/10.1016/j.jana.2014.02.003.

Zulu, Eliya Msiyaphazi, and Gloria Chepngeno. "Spousal Communication About the Risk of Contracting HIV/AIDS in Rural Malawi." *Demographic Research*, Special 1 (September 2003): 247–78. https://doi.org/10.4054/demres.2003.s1.8.

Index

Founded in 1893,
UNIVERSITY OF CALIFORNIA PRESS
publishes bold, progressive books and journals on topics in the arts, humanities, social sciences, and natural sciences—with a focus on social justice issues—that inspire thought and action among readers worldwide.

The UC PRESS FOUNDATION
raises funds to uphold the press's vital role as an independent, nonprofit publisher, and receives philanthropic support from a wide range of individuals and institutions—and from committed readers like you. To learn more, visit ucpress.edu/supportus.

www.ingramcontent.com/pod-product-compliance
Lightning Source LLC
Chambersburg PA
CBHW032345280326
41935CB00008B/460
* 9 7 8 0 5 2 0 4 0 9 1 9 4 *